NEITHER
UNIONIST NOR
NATIONALIST

Dedicated to the memory of my great-grandfather Private John Best, Royal Inniskilling Fusiliers (served 1898–1919).

NEITHER UNIONIST NOR NATIONALIST

The 10th (Irish) Division
in the Great War

STEPHEN SANDFORD

First published in 2015 by Irish Academic Press
8 Chapel Lane,
Sallins,
Co. Kildare,
Ireland

© 2015 Stephen Sandford

www.iap.ie

British Library Cataloguing in Publication Data
An entry can be found on request

978 07165 3260 6 (paper)
978 07165 3261 3 (cloth)
978 07165 3262 0 (PDF)

Library of Congress Cataloging-in-Publication Data
An entry can be found on request

Printed in Ireland by SPRINT-print Ltd.

Contents

Acknowledgements

No book is the work of the author alone; there are therefore many people I have to thank for their assistance in the completion of this work. First, and by far the most important, is Professor Keith Jeffery, whose knowledge of the period and assistance and advice provided during the research and writing of earlier drafts of the book has proved invaluable. In the course of my research, I have also received advice on various areas from Dr John Bourne, Dr Tim Bowman, Dr Edward Spiers, and Tom Burke of the Royal Dublin Fusiliers Association for which I am most grateful. I would also like to thank John and Celia Lee for their hospitality during an enjoyable afternoon discussing Sir Ian and Lady Hamilton. Particular thanks go to Professor Richard Grayson, not only for his advice, but also for providing data from his extensive database, on West Belfast men who joined the 10th (Irish) Division. In addition I would like to thank the staff from the following libraries and archives: Queen's University Library, the British Library, the National Library of Ireland, the National Library of Scotland, the National Archives Kew, the Public Records Office of Northern Ireland, the Imperial War Museum London, the National Army Museum London, the Australian War Memorial, Canberra, the Liddell Hart Centre for Military Archives at Kings College, London, the Liddle Collection, the Brotherton Library, University of Leeds and Belfast Central Newspaper Library.

Material from a number of archives have been reproduced with the kind permission of the following: F.W. Battersby, R.C. Broun, David Campbell, J.C. Dart and T.T.H. Verschoyle (Leeds University, Liddle Collection); Noel E. Drury and H.F.N. Jourdain (the Council of the National Army Museum); James A. Edmonds, Archibald A. Montgomery-Massingberd, Ian S. Hamilton (Liddell Hart Centre for Military Archives). Permission to quote from the papers of John Redmond and the Earl of Granard has been granted by the National Library of Ireland and those of Sir Douglas Haig by the National Library of Scotland. The British Library has granted permission to quote from letters from Sir Aylmer Hunter-Weston to his wife. Material from the papers of W.S. Spender, the Earl of Granard and the Farren Connell papers is quoted with permission of the Deputy Keeper of the Records, Public Records Office of Northern Ireland.

Permission to quote from private papers held by the Imperial War Museum has been granted as follows: J.H.M Staniforth (Rosamund Du Cane); Guy Dawnay (Rupert Dawnay); Ivone Kirkpatrick (Krysia Kirkpatrick); Reginald Cockburn (Rosemary Pearson).

As regards to the papers of Dr Orlo Williams, John McIlwaine, Christopher S. Hughes, Archibald Surfleet and John Crozier also held at the Imperial War Museum, every effort has been made to trace copyright holders and the author and museum would be grateful for any information which might help to trace those whose identities or addresses that are not currently known.

I also appreciate the help given in sourcing photographs, in particular Jonathan Maguire and Caroline Corvan of the Royal Irish Fusiliers Museum, Wendy Bowen, Hampshire County Council Arts and Museum Service, Rachael Holmes of the Royal Hampshire Regiment Museum, Jean Prendergast of the Royal Munster Fusiliers Association and Hugh Lamont and John Thompson for the use of family photographs.

A special word of thanks is due to the editor of *History Ireland* who printed my request for descendants of men who served in the division to contact me, and to all those who replied, in particular Leo Cooper, Daniel Treacy and Margaret Purcell, who also provided some interesting photographs of her father. Thanks are also due to Graham Croad for information and photographs of his grandfather, Frederick Croad. I also wish to thank Major Huw and Jill Rodge whose request for an impromptu talk on the 10th (Irish) Division during a visit to Suvla Bay kick-started my interest in the topic.

Last, but certainly not least, a special thanks to my parents, Thomas and Iris Sandford, for their patience with my lifelong interest in history and all things military.

List of Abbreviations

A&Q	Adjutant and Quartermaster General
AWM	Australian War Memorial
ANZAC	Australian and New Zealand Army Corps
BEF	British Expeditionary Force
BMJ	*British Medical Journal*
CEF	Canadian Expeditionary Force
CR	Connaught Rangers
CRE	Commander, Royal Engineers
CQMS	Company Quarter Master Sergeant
DSO	Distinguished Service Order
FP1	Field Punishment 1
FP2	Field Punishment 2
GHQ	General Headquarters
GOC	General Officer Commanding
GSO2	General Staff Officer, Grade 2
HMSO	His Majesty's Stationery Office
ISO	Imperial Service Obligation
IWM	Imperial War Museum
IRA	Irish Republican Army
JSAHR	*Journal of the Society for Army Historical Research*
Leins.	Leinster Regiment
LHCMA	Liddell Hart Centre for Military Archives
MGC	Machine Gun Corps
NAM	National Army Museum
NATS	Ministry of National Service
NCO	Non-Commissioned Officer
nd	Not dated
NLI	National Library of Ireland
NLS	National Library of Scotland

OTC	Officer Training Corps
PRONI	Public Records Office for Northern Ireland
RAMC	Royal Army Medical Corps
RDF	Royal Dublin Fusiliers
RE	Royal Engineers
RFA	Royal Field Artillery
RFC	Royal Flying Corps
RGA	Royal Garrison Artillery
RHA	Royal Horse Artillery
RI	Royal Irish Regiment
RIC	Royal Irish Constabulary
RIrR	Royal Irish Rifles
RMA	Military Academy, Woolwich
RMC	Royal Military College, Sandhurst
RMF	Royal Munster Fusiliers
RSM	Regimental Sergeant Major
RUC	Royal Ulster Constabulary
RUSI	Royal United Services Institute
SBR	Small Box Respirator
TF	Territorial Force
TMB	Trench Mortar Battery
TNA	The National Archives, Kew
UVF	Ulster Volunteer Force
Wilts	Wiltshire Regiment
WO	War Office
WO II	Warrant Officer, Grade 2
Y.M.C.A.	Young Men's Christian Association

List of Graphs

List of Tables

List of Maps and Plates

Map 1. Map of the Anzac-Suvla area, August 1915 (source: B. Cooper, *The Tenth Irish Division in Gallipoli*, London, 1918).

Map 2. Action at Kosturino, Serbia, 7 December 1915 (source: C. Falls, *Military Operations Macedonia, I*, London, 1933).

Foreword

The 10th (Irish) Division was the first of Ireland's three 'New Army' Kitchener divisions to be raised and deployed in battle. Less closely identified with nationalism or unionism than the two other 'New Army' divisions — the 16th (Irish) and the 36th (Ulster) respectively — it might be hazarded that those Irishmen who enlisted in the 10th Division were the keenest to do their bit in what soon became known as 'the Great War'. Cyril Falls, a fervent unionist and historian of the Ulster Division, recalled after the war that, while he and his father took commissions in the Ulster Division, his brother Leslie enlisted in the 10th Division 'simply because it was the first formed and, having hurried home from Canada, he did not wait to join us'. While these early recruits surely thought they would be sent to the Western Front, in fact they went to Gallipoli, and from there the division served in the Balkans and the Middle East. The 10th Division, therefore, is also distinguished by having the most exotic experience of the three Kitchener formations raised in Ireland. A number of excellent books have been written about the 36th (Ulster) Division, and Terence Denman's fine study of the 16th (Irish) Division, *Ireland's Unknown Soldiers* (first published by Irish Academic Press in 1992) was a notable and pioneering recovery of the service of nationalist Ireland's men in the First World War. These works are now joined by Stephen Sandford's volume which is the first full account of the 10th (Irish) Division, and, while it is researched to high scholarly standards, it also explores the vital, human story of the division. 'Lest we forget' is a common inscription on war memorials, and a regular reminder to anyone who contemplates the terrible experience of the Great War. Apart from the families involved and a few Irish military history buffs, the story of the 10th (Irish) Division was largely forgotten. One hundred years on, this need no longer be so, and Stephen Sandford's excellent book makes a very significant and timely contribution to the better understanding of Ireland's important part in the First World War.

Keith Jeffery
Queen's University Belfast

Introduction

'Ireland', wrote Bryan Cooper in the closing sentence of his book *The Tenth (Irish) Division in Gallipoli*, 'will not easily forget the deeds of the 10th Division'.[1] Yet, almost a century after it was raised, only a stained glass window in the Guildhall, Derry, exists in the land from which it took its title to mark its service. Until the late 1980s and early 1990s, except in the north, there was little interest in Ireland's involvement in the Great War and even there interest was skewed towards the 36th (Ulster) Division. The period since has seen a renewal of interest, particularly in light of the Northern Ireland peace process, resulting in the recognition of a shared history between communities, not only in Northern Ireland but across the whole island. Not only have recent years seen the establishment of groups interested in the disbanded Irish regiments, such as the Royal Dublin Fusiliers Association, it has also seen the renovation of the memorial gardens at Islandbridge in Dublin which had lain derelict for almost a generation. Rehabilitation of those Irishmen who fought in the British army reached a zenith in 1998 with the opening of the Island of Ireland Peace Park at Messines in Belgium by Queen Elizabeth II and Mary McAleese, the President of Ireland. But this monument, built to commemorate where the unionist 36th (Ulster) Division and the nationalist 16th (Irish) Division fought side by side against a common enemy on the Western Front, makes only a passing reference to those who fought on other fronts (at Gallipoli, in the Balkans and the Middle-East) with the 10th (Irish) Division.

Ireland's apparent amnesia towards the 10th (Irish) Division began early. Despite the enthusiastic send-off given to the division when it left Ireland in May 1915, and the shock felt by the casualty returns following Gallipoli, by the end of the war it had been eclipsed in the public mind by the events of Easter 1916 and the Somme.

When Peace Day celebrations marking the signing of the Treaty of Versailles were held in July 1919 throughout the British Isles, in parts of Ireland they were marked by a degree of ambivalence. In Belfast, however, a programme of parades, entertainment and sporting events was held for the men of the 16th (Irish) and 36th (Ulster) Divisions and their respective communities.[2] By comparison, the contribution made to the war effort by the 10th (Irish) Division passed almost unacknowledged. One (nationalist) newspaper observed the contrast between the reception given in Belfast to the 16th and 36th Divisions with that of 'the poor 10th, sad and heroic, having their little function at the Gresham Hotel, nobody noticing them – while all this fanfare from Belfast fills the air!'.[3] Apart from an oblique reference in the republican ballad, 'The Foggy Dew', written in 1919, which claims 'Twas better to die 'neath an Irish sky, Than at Suvla or Sedd el Bahr', the 10th (Irish) Division appears to have passed from Irish collective memory even to the extent of it being the only Irish division not to have had a divisional history published. And yet, while the men of the 16th (Irish) and 36th (Ulster) Divisions may have shared a common experience on the Western Front, in the main, they did so separately. In contrast, the men of the 10th (Irish) Division, unionist, nationalist, Protestant, Catholic and Dissenter, trained, lived, fought and often died side by side.

This book not only belatedly rectifies an important omission from Ireland's historiography of the First World War but also offers a new approach to the study of divisional history by adopting a holistic methodology, setting the division within the context in which it was raised and served, and assessing the representativeness of its experience by comparing and contrasting its development with the 13th (Western) Division, raised at the same time. It also offers a new approach to the exploration of unit identity which allows a more detailed level of analysis, not only of ethnicity but also of age, religion, employment and social background, than previously undertaken.

This book breaks new ground in the identification of individual soldiers by using regimental medal rolls, rather than depending on *Soldiers died in the Great War* as the basis of its analysis. Although it was not possible to identify all the original members of a battalion from regimental medal rolls, their use, cross-referenced with casualty lists, obituaries, rolls of honour and unit histories enabled the identification of 60-70 per cent of the original members of those divisional units which landed at Gallipoli in early August 1915. Cross-referencing this information with other sources, such as service, census and war graves records has enabled conclusions to be reached regarding the social and economic backgrounds of the rank and file. The superiority of this approach to the use of *Soldiers died in the Great War* (*SDGW*), even as a source of identifying deaths among original members of a battalion, is most effectively demonstrated by the data extracted from the medal roll regarding the 6th Royal Irish Rifles that records that 220 of the battalion's original rank and file died as result of active service, while *SDGW* lists only 183 members of the battalion, both originals and replacements, who died before 1921 when it was published.

Small scale studies, such as Edward Spiers' analysis of the 1st Battalion Black Watch, concluded that the pre-war British army was dependent on the peerage, gentry, military families, the clergy and the professions, with a small minority from business, commercial and industrial families, as the main sources of its officer corps.[4] Furthermore the majority of candidates for commissions in the regular army had been educated at a public school. While comments have been made in passing in some divisional, brigade and battalion histories to the backgrounds of officers in New Army divisions, there has, until now, been no systematic analysis undertaken at a divisional level.[5] In researching the 10th (Irish) Division, 97 per cent of the officers in the division's twelve Irish infantry battalions were identified while 68 per cent of the line officers of the 13th (Western) Division were identified for comparative purposes.

While the methodology adopted for the creation of the officers' data set is similar to that undertaken for the rank and file, greater emphasis was placed on the use of officers' service records which were more readily available than those of the other ranks, many of which were destroyed by enemy action during the Second World War. Nevertheless, it was impossible to examine all extant service records as those of officers who served after 1922 are still retained by the Ministry of Defence.

In the decade immediately prior to the Great War the majority of senior British officers, including Sir Ian Hamilton the future GOC of the Mediterranean Expeditionary Force, believed that the answer to the increased firepower of modern warfare was to achieve a moral ascendancy over the enemy. This ascendancy, a belief in one's corporate and individual superiority and ability to win, was thought to be, at the time, brought about by a combination of morale and discipline. Where this study differs from previous divisional histories is in its detailed examination of these phenomena and whether they had an impact on unit performance. It also compares, to a greater depth than previously undertaken, the disciplinary record of two divisions, one English, the other Irish, and both raised at the beginning of the war, to determine if the nature of offences committed and the penalties incurred was consistent across both divisions. The study also examines whether the exercising of military discipline was consistent across theatres by comparing court-martial levels and sentencing in the Irish divisions on the Western Front with the 10th (Irish) Division.

Finally, the study also examines how the division adapted to technical and tactical change during the course of the war and how much developments on the Western Front contributed to the changes in warfare, as experienced by the 10th Division, in other theatres.

While this book's main focus is on the original twelve Irish line battalions of the 10th (Irish) Division, this is not meant in any way to denigrate the achievements of other units of the division, in particular the 10th Hampshire Regiment, which served alongside them throughout the Gallipoli and Serbian campaigns until its transfer to the 27th Division in November 1916.

CHAPTER 1

A Country Divided

Ireland in 1914 was a country divided on a number of levels. The north-south split on religious and political lines was mirrored by similar economic and social divisions, for while Dublin was Ireland's civic and administrative capital, Belfast was its commercial and industrial powerhouse.

Belfast's growth, particularly in the final quarter of the nineteenth century had been phenomenal. From just 19,000 in 1800 its population of 349,180 had by 1901 outstripped Dublin's population of 290,638.[1] Built on the commercial success of shipbuilding, linen and related industries such as engineering and rope-making, Belfast had grown to meet the demands of an expanding workforce. The population of Dublin also grew over the period, largely due to natural increase and rural immigration after the Famine, but unlike Belfast, or indeed similar cities in Great Britain, Dublin's population growth was not linked with industrial development, for since the 1850s Dublin had been in a state of industrial decline.[2]

In the first decade of the twentieth century while representing around 10 per cent of the British population Ireland accounted for only 4.2 per cent of its industrial employment which was unevenly spread throughout the island.[3] In 1907 almost 50 per cent of Ireland's net industrial output by value came from just three industrial sectors: textiles, clothing and shipbuilding/engineering.[4] The concentration of the textile sector in the six north-eastern counties is evident from a 1912 production census which indicated that 87,427 (94%) of the total 92,570 persons employed in the sector were employed there.[5] Likewise the 1901 census showed that Ulster, and in particular Londonderry and its hinterland, employed some 75 per cent of those engaged in clothing manufacture in Ireland.[6] While shipbuilding facilities existed in a number of Irish ports, the industry was dominated by the two great Belfast companies of Harland & Wolff and Workman & Clark which produced all but 2,207 gross tons of the 120,867 gross tons of shipping built in Ireland in 1909.[7]

The importance of these three sectors was not just confined to Ireland but had an importance in the wider national and international context. The two Belfast shipyards were not only the largest industrial employers in Ireland but between 1901 and 1909 the output of Harland & Wolff and Workman & Clark was the second and fourth highest gross tonnage of any shipyard in the United Kingdom; indeed by 1914 Harland & Wolff's Belfast yard was the largest shipyard in the world.[8] Complementing the male-dominated workforce of the shipyards, the Belfast linen factories were large employers of women and included the York Street Flax Spinning Mill which was reputed to be the largest linen mill in the world, while Londonderry in 1912 was the centre of the shirt making industry.[9] The Belfast Ropework Company and the recently opened Gallagher's cigarette factory were also the largest factories of their type in the world, the former employing more than 3,000 people.

In contrast to the north-east's industrial growth, the social impact of Dublin's long term industrial decline is apparent from the 1911 census. By 1911 male manufacturing employment had fallen to just over 20%, for although the city had the world famous Guinness brewery, Power's distillery and Jacob's biscuit factory, they could not deliver the volume of employment provided by the shipyards and linen mills of Belfast.[10] Of these three, the Guinness brewery was the largest single industrial employer in the city, employing 2,505 manual workers in 1910 of which 2,083 were unskilled labour.[11] The census also recorded that of the city's population of 304,000 only 44% were listed as having any definite occupation, while the remaining 56%, which included 56,000 males, were classified in the "Indefinite and non-productive Class".[12] In all one-third of Dublin's working population were unskilled labourers and, unlike Belfast and Londonderry where the mills and factories provided ample employment, there was little scope for the employment of women outside of domestic service.

Dublin's high levels of underemployment depressed earning capacity; consequently the average weekly wage of an unskilled worker in pre-war Dublin was 18 shillings (90p), although wages as low as 15 or 16 shillings were recorded; a quarter less than that of London or Liverpool and lower than those in the industrialised north-east.[13] The low wages of unskilled labour, coupled with the even lower wages of female employment, when it was available, meant that the combined average income for a Dublin family was 1 pound 2 shillings and 6 pence (£1.12½) per week.[14] Given the casual nature of much of Dublin's unskilled employment, many families at times subsisted on much less than this. While the average earnings of an unskilled worker in Belfast was a shilling or two higher than that of Dublin the ability of female labour to supplement family income made a significant difference. Whereas domestic servants in Dublin might earn £10 to £12 a year, the average weekly wages for spinners in the Belfast line mills was 15 shillings per week.[15] By comparison skilled workers in Dublin earned between £1 16s and £2 per week with perhaps a couple of shillings more in Belfast in comparable industries.[16]

Low levels of household income resulted in widespread deprivation among Dublin's unskilled poor particularly in relation to housing. While Belfast had grown rapidly during the nineteenth century its rapid growth had not led to the same degree of squalor and rundown housing that existed in pre-war Dublin. In 1911 the population density per acre in Dublin was almost 50% higher than that of Belfast while the average occupancy per house was 8.2 persons in comparison to 5 persons in Belfast.[17] These figures however hide the true extent of housing deprivation in Dublin. By 1914 Dublin was a city of decaying grandeur with many of the former homes of the wealthy being let to the poor at a weekly rent of 2 to 3 shillings per room.[18] In 1913 the working class population of Dublin was 194,250 excluding domestic servants.[19] Of these 37,552 persons (19.3%) lived in houses which were 'on or fast approaching the border-line of being unfit for human habitation' while a further 22,701 (11.7%) were living in houses 'unfit for human habitation and incapable of being rendered fit for human habitation'.[20] In contrast the artisan's dwellings in Belfast were described as being 'self-contained houses of good size … constructed in a style which renders them exceptionally comfortable and thoroughly sanitary'.[21] In 1911, 22.9 per cent of those living in Dublin occupied a single tenement room compared with only 0.3 per cent of the population of Belfast.[22]

Low wages and the uncertain nature of the employment of many in Dublin's unskilled workforce meant that there was little interest by the private sector in the building of working class housing, and where such houses were provided the rents were usually beyond the means of those for whom they were intended.[23] Dublin's inability to provide new houses at an economic rent was largely due to the high cost of acquiring and clearing existing slum properties, whereas new house building in Belfast largely took place on the relatively cheap periphery of the city. This, together with regular wages, meant that skilled and semi-skilled men, and even unskilled labourers whose household income was supplemented by a working wife, were able to afford higher rents, making investment in housing by the private sector worthwhile, such that before 1914 about 99 per cent of house building in Belfast was undertaken by the private landlords.[24]

The state of Dublin's housing for its unskilled and unproductive classes had a direct impact on both their health and access to certain types of employment. The death rate in Dublin in the early twentieth century was on a par with that of Calcutta and figures contained in the 1911 Irish census revealed that nearly half the children in large families died in childhood. [25] Even if they survived to adulthood the prospects of those raised in the unhealthy conditions of the tenements affected their ability to obtain regular employment. In 1911 only 34.6 per cent of Guinness workers were Dublin-born, the majority being migrants from the surrounding counties of Leinster. Guinness's justification for their preference for migrant workers was that 'few town-bred men could satisfy requirements of the company regarding physique'. In 1907 the company rejected 51 per cent of applicants for labouring jobs on what were described as general grounds, while 16 per cent were rejected by the medical officer.[26]

Overarching the social, economic and industrial divisions in Ireland in the years immediately preceding the Great War was the issue of Home Rule. In April 1912 the Liberal government had introduced the third Home Rule Bill in the House of Commons and, without the Lords' veto (which had blocked previous attempts to grant Home Rule to Ireland), it was due to become law in 1914.[27] Resistance to Home Rule by Ulster unionists is often viewed purely in terms of religion and politics, but as the Ulster Covenant signed by 471,414 Ulstermen and women on 28 September 1914, stated they were 'convinced in our consciences that Home Rule would be disastrous to the material well-being of Ulster'. Such fears were not without foundation; in 1909/10 government expenditure in Ireland exceeded revenue by some 28 per cent.[28] This was partially as a result of the introduction of old age pensions on 1 January 1910 which for the last three months of the financial year cost the exchequer £553,876, 29 per cent of the total cost of all old age pensions paid in the United Kingdom.[29]

Ulster's armed resistance to Home Rule has largely overshadowed many of the other issues involved, especially how it was to be financed. In January 1911, the Prime Minister, H.H. Asquith, informed the cabinet that funding was a major problem given the bankrupt condition of Irish public sector finances.[30] With this in mind the unionists of the north-east feared that the burden of financing the deficit would fall on them, particularly as Belfast was already paying almost four times the annual customs duty as Dublin.[31] The thrust of the north-east's industry was directed towards exports and there were also fears that a Home Rule parliament would adopt protectionist measures to encourage the small scale industries that existed outside Ulster.[32]

In January 1913 Ulster unionists adopted the most extreme form of unconstitutional resistance to Home Rule by the formation of an armed citizen militia, the Ulster Volunteer Force (UVF) which by February 1914 was almost 90,000 strong.[33] Military resistance to Home Rule was not confined to the Protestants of Ulster. On 20 March 1914, believing that they were being asked to suppress opposition to Home Rule in Ulster, Brigadier-General Hubert Gough and sixty officers of the 3rd Cavalry Brigade indicated that they preferred to accept dismissal if ordered north.[34] The 'Curragh Mutiny', as this incident came to be known, (although described by the government as arising from 'an honest misunderstanding') nevertheless extracted a promise from a member of the government that 'they had no intention whatsoever of taking advantage of this right to crush political opposition to the policy or principles of the Home Rule Bill'.[35] On the night of 24/25 April 1914 the UVF landed 20,000 rifles and 2,000,000 rounds of small arms ammunition at a number of ports around Belfast Lough in an operation that largely took place without incident or casualties.[36]

A nationalist response to the formation of the Ulster Volunteer Force was slow to materialise and it was not until 11 November 1913 that eleven prominent nationalists met at a Dublin hotel to discuss the formation of the Irish Volunteers (IV).[37] The IV's reaction to the landing of guns in Ulster was to organise a similar venture but on a much smaller scale. On 26 July Erskine Childers, the author of the pioneering spy novel *The Riddle of the Sands* and a British civil servant, landed 900 Mauser M1871 11mm calibre single-shot rifles and 29,000 rounds of ammunition at Howth harbour where its cargo was unloaded by uniformed members of the Irish Volunteers and boys of Na Fianna Éireann.[38] Unlike the UVF operation, no attempt was made to avoid a confrontation with the authorities and as a consequence a contingent of the Dublin Metropolitan Police commanded by Assistant Commissioner William Harrell was sent to disarm the Volunteers. Reinforced by a company of the King's Own Scottish Borderers (KOSB), Harrell attempted to negotiate the peaceful seizure of the weapons but during the negotiations the Volunteers managed to spirit the arms away. Whilst returning to their barracks, however, the troops encountered a hostile, but unarmed protest. At Bachelor's Walk, Dublin, the Borderers were attacked by a crowd on whom the soldiers opened fire killing three people and wounding a further 38.[39] A further 600 rifles and 20,000 rounds of ammunition for the Irish Volunteers were landed at night without incident at Kilcoole, south of Dublin, on 1 August.[40]

Less than a week before the British declaration of war on Germany, a country divided on so many levels stood on the brink of civil war.

CHAPTER 2

Filling the Ranks

While there have been Irish regiments in the British regular army since the 1680s it was not until the creation of the 10th (Irish) Division in August 1914 that battalions of all eight Irish line regiments served in a single formation. In the intervening 230 years Ireland had been a rich source of manpower for the army, so much so that by the 1830s Irish soldiers represented 42% of its total strength. While this proportion had declined during the nineteenth century, nevertheless the percentage of recruits, in the years immediately before the Great War, was largely in line with its proportion of the total United Kingdom population.[1] This relative decline had mainly been brought about by a combination of improved economic conditions, emigration, and an anti-recruiting campaign by Sinn Féin, nonetheless, on the outbreak of war there were still some 21,000 Irishmen serving in the British army, who were joined by a further 30,000 on the mobilisation of reservists.

When war was declared on 4 August 1914 the strength of the British army was 691,118 men of all ranks, of which only 233,995 were regulars, the remainder being members of the Regular Reserve (145,347), Special Reserve (55,912) and the Territorial Force (255,864).[2] Unless they volunteered to do so members of the Territorial Force were not obliged to serve outside the United Kingdom, and despite its size, only 17,621 officers and men of the Territorial Force, including five complete units, had agreed to serve overseas in the event of war.[3] Of the regular army's 233,995 men, more than half were unavailable for immediate deployment in the event of a European war. With the exception of the Foot Guards and Household Cavalry, half of its 148 infantry battalions, 12 of its 28 cavalry regiments and 23 of the 59 brigades of the Royal Horse and Royal Field Artillery, in addition to support arms, such as the Royal Engineers, Royal Army Medical and Army Service Corps were stationed outside the United Kingdom when war was declared.[4] As the role of home service battalions was to keep their overseas battalion(s) up to strength, they were usually under-strength, and comprised mainly recent recruits and partially-trained young soldiers. Accordingly, these battalions were dependent on reservists to fill the ranks and bring them up to strength in the event of war. John Terraine estimates that at Mons reservists accounted for 50% of the total strength of British battalions, a fair estimation given that the 1st Battalion, Black Watch required 500 men to bring it up to its war establishment while the 2nd Leinster Regiment received 693 reservists before 'the Battalion was reported complete and ready to take the field'.[5]

Discounting those members of the Territorial Force who had not committed themselves to serve overseas, the number of men available for war service at the beginning of August 1914 to form the British Expeditionary Force (BEF) and garrison the Empire was 452,875, of which about 18,000 were 'boy soldiers'. Pre-war planning had envisaged an expeditionary force in the event of a European war of six infantry and one cavalry division which with support troops would amount to about 130,000 officers and men.[6] Its planned commitment to provide an expeditionary force in the event of war while still garrisoning the Empire stretched the army's resources. Indeed just weeks before, the extent of its ability to meet its commitments had been cast in doubt to such an extent by the situation in Ireland that Sir Charles Douglas, Chief of the Imperial General Staff (CIGS), informed the Army Council that 'if the whole of our Expeditionary Force were used in Ireland and to maintain order in Great Britain we should be quite incapable of meeting our obligations abroad'.[7] A political truce on the eve of the declaration of war, however, removed this obstacle but fear of possible invasion initially reduced the number of infantry divisions sent with the

BEF to four. By the time the BEF reached its planned strength of six divisions on 8-9 September all but two battalions of line infantry stationed in the United Kingdom on the declaration of war had joined the expeditionary force in France.[8]

Almost alone among Britain's political and military leaders, Field Marshal Lord Kitchener, now Secretary of State for War, realised that the war would not be 'over by Christmas' and called for 100,000 men to join the colours.[9] This was followed by a decision to create an army division in six of the army's eight regional commands, including Ireland, which with the exception of the 14th (Light) Division raised in the Southern command, would bear the name of the command in which they were raised.[10] The inclusion of the designation 'Irish' in the name of the 10th Division raised by the Irish command therefore had no political significance. These first six divisions became known collectively as K1 divisions to differentiate them from other New Army divisions raised later in the war.[11] Designed to mirror the organisation of the regular divisions of the BEF, they were organised on the standard model of three brigades, each of four infantry battalions, supported by artillery, engineers, signal companies, field ambulance units and a squadron of divisional cavalry. Initially the three infantry brigades of the 10th (Irish) Division were to be found from service battalions of all eight Irish line regiments, however, the 10th Hampshires were later attached to the division for training purposes.[12]

On 12 August, Lieutenant-General Sir B.T. Mahon, the future commander of the 10th (Irish) Division, crossed to Dublin to confer with the leaders of the Irish Volunteers.[13] Mahon was not impressed by the Irish Volunteers and told Kitchener that they were 'a collection of independent bodies of men, under no discipline, and under self-appointed so-called officers ... their usefulness is nil'.[14] Yet these were the very men to whom the army was looking for recruits.

Much was made in the Irish press at the time of the number of men joining the colours. On 26 August, the *Irish Times* reported that 'on Wednesday evening about 220 men of the three of the Tyrone Battalions of the Tyrone Regiment of the Ulster Volunteers – namely the 1st, 2nd and 4th, marched into Omagh depot and enlisted in Lord Kitchener's new army for the period of the war'. The report continued that 'since mobilisation of the Army and Special Reserves recruiting has been very brisk in Tyrone, and, apart from men enlisted for special corps or for the Special Reserve, about 500 men have joined at Omagh depot for Kitchener's new army. It has been decided to form two extra battalions of the Royal Inniskilling Fusiliers'.[15] In the absence of an agreement on the formation of an Ulster division these members of the Tyrone Regiment of the Ulster Volunteer Force, and 40 men from the Belfast Regiment who had enlisted in the Inniskillings on 17 August, had decided to enlist in the 10th (Irish) Division.[16] Whether they remained in the division or not is open to conjecture as Captain A. St. Q. Ricardo, the officer commanding the regimental depot, held back some recruits from the UVF for the Ulster Division when it formed. Nevertheless 'some of the men he [Ricardo] recruited were attached to the 5th and 6th Battalions, Royal Inniskilling Fusiliers, which went with the 10th (Irish) Division to Gallipoli … the remainder elected for the Ulster Division and were the nucleus of the 9th (S) Royal Inniskilling Fusiliers'.[17]

Newspapers tried to be upbeat in their reports of recruitment in Ireland. On 28 August 1914 the *Irish Times* reported:

> that recruiting for all the battalions to be comprised in the Irish division of Kitchener's new army is proceeding satisfactorily. … All over Ireland there is evidence that Irishmen are anxious that the fame of the Irish regiments should be maintained in the present war, as was done on previous occasions, when the valour of Irish soldiers turned the tide in many important battlefields.[18]

Compared with peace time recruitment, that of the first few weeks of the war might be considered encouraging. At the Depot in Great Brunswick Street (now Pearse street), Dublin for a two-week period at the beginning of August, 1,000 men were recruited for the army compared with the average pre-war weekly intake of 30, while between 23 August and 31 October the average daily recruitment rate at recruiting offices in Dublin was 69.[19] What on the surface appears to be a rush to the colours however hides a great disparity, not only between different parts of the country, but also across the period. Belfast, for example, recorded a daily average recruitment of 219 during this period; more than three times that of Dublin although its population was only some 27% higher. Figure 2.1 (Annex 1) illustrates the daily recruitment by province and shows that, even in Ulster, the recruitment rush was largely over by the end of September.[20] Despite attempts by the *Irish Times* to present a positive response to Kitchener's call to arms, recruitment to the new division was slow in comparison with other K1 divisions. By 29 August only 2,729 officers and men had joined the division, less than 32% of the average for the six New Army divisions then being formed; the strength of the other five divisions ranging from the 7,729 officers and men of the 12th (Eastern) Division to the 13,272 in the 13th (Western) Division.[21] As a proportion of recruits to this first New Army, those of the 10th (Irish) Division represented only some 5.24% of total enlistments, whilst the male population of Ireland accounted for almost 10% of that of the British Isles.[22]

As the momentum of those joining the colours grew in Great Britain, recruitment in Ireland fell even further behind. Returns for 5 September show that while the average strength of the six divisions had increased by 97% over the previous week that of the Irish Division had only increased by 84%.[23] Even within the division, recruitment was inconsistent. A minute sent to General Maxwell on the evening of Saturday 5 September stated that 'the only battalion which is full is the Royal Irish Rifles'.[24] Of the remaining 11 Irish battalions in the division, only the 5th Connaught Rangers exceeded half strength and the 6th Royal Irish Fusiliers had only 8 officers and 39 men.[25] Returns also show that even at this early stage recruitment in Ulster was proportionately higher than that for the other three provinces and that while the population of Ulster represented 36% of the total population, the three regiments with recruiting districts in the Province accounted for 45% of recruits to the division.[26] This was despite Ulster having proportionately fewer men between the ages of 18 and 35 than the average for the whole island.[27]

	29 Aug 1914		5 Sept 1914	
	Officers	**Other Ranks**	**Officers**	**Other Ranks**
5th Royal Irish Regiment	6	335	9	443
6th Royal Irish Rifles	12	656	14	905
5th Connaught Rangers	7	428	8	557
6th Leinster Regiment	8	270	9	334
6th Royal Munster Fusiliers 7th Royal Munster Fusiliers }	9	210	17	571
6th Royal Dublin Fusiliers	11	324	8	397
7th Royal Dublin Fusiliers	3	54	10	354
5th Royal Inniskilling Fusiliers	5	95	8	397
6th Royal Inniskilling Fusiliers	3	-	8	412
5th Royal Irish Fusiliers	8	283	11	496
6th Royal Irish Fusiliers	2	-	8	39

Table 2.2: Battalion strength of units of the 10th (Irish) Division[28]

By 5 September the infantry battalions of all six New Army divisions, with the exception of the 10th (Irish), were fully up to strength, indeed a single brigade (the 40th) of the 13th Division had almost three times as many men as the whole of the Irish Division.[29] Such was the concern over recruitment to the 10th (Irish) that views were expressed that the division would have to be reclassified from a K1 to a K2 division with the resultant reallocation of the resources earmarked for it.[30] Similar concerns were expressed concerning the 12th Division from the rural east of England where recruitment was also initially slow; Kitchener, however, appears to have been less concerned about the situation there believing that the delay was a result of the requirements of harvesting.[31] In this Kitchener proved correct as the strength of the 12th Division almost doubled in the week between 29 August and 5 September, reaching a level in excess of the complement required of an infantry division.[32]

In comparison with the 10th Division's struggle to fill its battalions, those of the 13th (Western) Division had, with the exception of suitable officers, reached their capacity by the beginning of September 1914 (see Table 2.3 below), the 8th battalion Cheshire Regiment having 4,042 men in its ranks while two other battalions in the division each had over 3,900 men.

	29 Aug 1914		5 Sept 1914	
	Officers	Other Ranks	Officers	Other Ranks
6th Royal Lancaster Regt.	15	1094	11	1042
8th Cheshire Regiment	15	1145	10	4042
8th Royal Welsh Fusiliers	12	999	13	2855
4th South Wales Borderers	11	1222	11	3939
7th Gloucestershire Regt.	13	672	12	3953
9th Worcestershire Regt.	19	1464	17	1075
6th East Lancashire Regt.	9	1162	10	1482
6th South Lancashire Regt.	9	835	8	1630
8th Welsh Regt.	7	1113	8	1882
6th Loyal North Lancashire Regt.	14	1276	11	2931
5th Wiltshire Regiment	7	886	10	1201
7th North Staffordshire Regt.	13	1125	12	1668
9th Warwickshire Regiment	8	1020	15	1018

Table 2.3: Battalion strength of units of the 13th (Western) Division.[33]

Although all battalions in the division had a full complement of rank and file by 5 September 1914 some battalions in largely rural counties, such as the 5th Wiltshire Regiment, struggled to fill their ranks with men from within their own recruiting district:

> In round numbers some 800 recruits have been enrolled by Captain Ennis, the recruiting officer, and been entered by Colour-Sergeant Harman and his orderly room staff in the regimental records [since the beginning of August 1914]. Of this 800 about 640 are in the new [5th] Battalion. It cannot be too strongly emphasised, however, that 1,000 men are required for this, and the officers are anxious, for the credit of the county, that there should be as many

Wiltshiremen as possible in that thousand. Last week the official information was that over 75 per cent were natives of the county but that the standard has not been kept up. Men have poured in from London and other large centres, and the percentage of Wiltshire men has rapidly gone down.[34]

Despite this the Adjutant-General's Office was able to report that nine of the thirteen battalions in the Western Division's recruiting area were in a position to fill a further battalion for Kitchener's Second New Army [K2], while describing the K1 battalions of the Royal Irish Regiment, Royal Irish and Munster Fusiliers as 'very weak'.[35] Within weeks, however, battalions of the 10th Division were being brought up to strength by drafts from England. Redmond would later claim that 'when recruiting for the 10th Division was going on fairly well in Ireland, for some unexplained reason, a number of English recruits were suddenly sent over to join its ranks. They were quite unnecessary, and protests against their incursion into the Division fell upon deaf ears'.[36]

| | 29 Aug 1914 | | | 5 Sept 1914 | | |
	Officers	Other Ranks	All Ranks	Officers	Other Ranks	All Ranks
9th Div.	122	8,316	8,438	132	13,826	13,958
10th Div.	74	2,655	2,729	110	4,905	5,015
11th Div.	78	10,881	10,959	93	20,578	20,671
12th Div.	131	7,598	7,729	157	15,072	15,229
13th Div.	145	13,127	13,272	138	27,517	27,655
14th Div.	105	8,800	8,905	125	20,080	20,205
Total Recruits	655	51,377	52,032	755	101,978	102,733

Table 2.4: Strength of each of the K1 divisions on 29 Aug. and 5 Sept. 1914.[37]

Cooper tried to pass off these drafts as being mostly men of Irish extraction living in England, while at the same time admitting that

'Lord Kitchener decided early in September to transfer a number of recruits for whom no room could be found in English regiments to fill up the ranks of the 10th Division'.[38] An examination of the locations from which drafts were drawn and an analysis of soldiers in the division, born or living outside Ireland on enlistment suggests that they were more likely to be men from the three K1 divisions with the greatest level of surplus manpower.[39] Certainly when Major Geoffrey Drage, 7th Royal Munster Fusiliers, was sent to collect a draft from Yorkshire, he made his selection on the basis of physique rather than Irish ancestry.[40] These men were from the 11th Division recruiting area, which as early as 5 September had over 20,000 recruits. Under the headline 'Over 5,000 Recruits enrolled at Devizes in a Month', the *Wiltshire Gazette* recorded that 1,100 men, all recruited for the Wiltshire Regiment were to be sent to Irish battalions of the 10th Division:

> Under present arrangements the men will go to-day.
> Ireland is the destination of all the 1,100 split up amongst
> Irish Regiments as follows:
> 380 to the 6th Leinsters at Fermoy
> 250 to the 6th Munsters at the Curragh
> 100 to the 6th Dublins at the Curragh
> 370 to the 7th Dublins at the Curragh[41]

That these men were being sent for reasons other than their Irish ancestry is supported by the *Gazette's* comment that 'Though they are being posted to Irish Regiments now, they will be given the opportunity, as the Irish units fill up, to transfer to the Wilts Regiment as vacancies occur to facilitate their absorption in the county battalions'.[42] The *Gazette* later observed, however, that while 'it is generally known that there was some dissatisfaction among the men sent to Irish regiments, especially the Wiltshiremen, as they had enlisted for the Wiltshire Regiment, but apparently they are becoming reconciled'.[43] Not everyone was happy with the arrangement however as two young Welshmen, seventeen-year-old Frederick Croad and his friend Elmer Anthony, decided to go absent without leave when the train taking them to their embarkation port for Ireland stopped at a junction near their home. Their absence however was short lived and within days they were returned to their unit, 6th Royal Munster Fusiliers. Frederick Croad would serve with the regiment at Gallipoli, Salonika and in France before being discharged at the end of the war.[44]

In 1925 Major C.W. Hughes who had tried to enlist in the 5th Wiltshires, expressed his opinion on why such transfers had taken place:

> I have often wondered if the War Office worked on any system in the drafting of men to the various County regiments, why a large number of the first recruits from Wiltshire should have been drafted to Irish regiments, it is hard to say unless it was to delude the public into thinking that the Irish had changed their attitude towards this Country and were anxious to help us.[45]

The transfer of 1,100 men from the Wiltshires to battalions of the 10th (Irish) Division had the dual benefit of not only helping to make good low levels of recruitment in parts of Ireland but also to relieve pressure on billeting facilities at the depot in Devizes. Hughes recorded the situation on 2 September 1914 when he tried to enlist that 'recruiting was for the moment stopped, the number of men reporting had so greatly exceeded the accommodation at the Barracks that some nights men had been sleeping under hedges without food and without money to buy food, some had therefore gone home, many others had been sent home while those within the depot were absorbed into units'.[46]

Cooper's assertion that about 70% of the other ranks were Irish or of Irish descent is broadly supported by analysis of the division's casualties at Gallipoli.[47] According to Nicholas Perry, 'two-thirds of the infantry were Irish, with one battalion (6th Royal Irish Rifles) over 80 per cent Irish and six of the other eleven over 50 per cent'.[48] Perry's analysis is based on casualties at Gallipoli, which includes reinforcements who were not necessarily original members of the division. A more detailed analysis of the origins of the other ranks who landed at Gallipoli is obtained by analysing all known deaths of original members of the battalions who subsequently died not only at Gallipoli but in other theatres, with other battalions or following commissioning and in a small number of cases those men who died after the end of the war as a result of active service. *Soldiers died in the Great War* (SDGW), the official record of other ranks who died during the war, lists the names of 90 and 110 other ranks respectively of the 6th Leinster Regiment and 7th Royal Dublin Fusiliers who died during the Gallipoli campaign. Further analysis,however,shows that at least 201 soldiers from the 6th Leinster Regiment who landed at Gallipoli and 189 from the 7th Royal Dublin Fusiliers died in the course of the war or as a result of wounds in the years immediately after. Analysis of these figures reveals that less than 50% of the men of the 6th Leinster Regiment and 60% of the men of the 7th Royal Dublin Fusiliers were born in Ireland. Using newspapers and census returns to identify the birthplace of other original members of the 6th Leinster Regiment suggests that approximately 43% of the regiment were born in Ireland which is approximately what would be expected given the numbers transferred from England.[49] Cooper's suggestion that many of the men who joined from England were of Irish descent is not borne out by the evidence as less than 2% of the men born outside Ireland had an Irish parent.[50]

Regimental histories and diaries kept by both officers and men show the extent of transfer of men from outside Ireland into the infantry battalions of the division. As early as 11 September 1914 the 5th Connaught Rangers received 350 recruits from Pontefract, Yorkshire, who had originally enlisted in the York and Lancaster Regiment 'but had been transferred to the Connaught Rangers by War Office Order'.[51] The 6th Leinsters also benefited from a sizeable draft from England and, according to the regimental historian, a draft of 600 'young Englishmen' was received from the Bristol area, which presumably includes the draft of 380 from the Wiltshire Regiment.[52]

Both battalions of the Royal Inniskilling Fusiliers received drafts from the Duke of Cornwall's Light Infantry (DCLI), which must have been as much as surprise to the Inniskillings as it was to the men of the DCLI. Private Frank Battersby from Birmingham reported to the Town Hall for onward transportation to the regimental depot at Bodmin on 7 September. Two days later, still in civilian clothes, he was sent to Newquay and then a week later returned to Bodmin and sent to the Fusiliers in Dublin.[53] Writing of his company, Second Lieutenant Terence Verschoyle, 5th Royal Inniskilling Fusiliers, stated that 'one third of its strength consisted of a draft of Londoners who had, as they thought, enlisted in the DCLI; and almost a half came from Glasgow or Paisley'.[54] Verschoyle explained the presence of these Scotsmen as 'due entirely to a most remarkable shipyard worker (Private James Scollan) who, born in the regiment's home county but grown up in Glasgow, decided to enlist in his county regiment and such was his wholly deserved popularity among his mates – to bring a hundred along with him'.[55]

The impact of the War Office's decision to supplement local recruitment to the division with surplus manpower from other regiments and military recruiting areas was felt almost immediately. Within a week all the infantry battalions of the division, with the exception of 6th Royal Irish Rifles and 7th Royal Munster Fusiliers, exceeded the 1,066 rank and file which constituted a full strength battalion. The officers were harder to find and it was not until early in 1915 that all the battalions reached their full complement of officers.[56]

The inability to fill the ranks of the 10th (Irish) Division with local recruits was not helped when on 29 August the Adjutant-General was asked to draft proposals for raising a further six New Army divisions.[57] In response to a memorandum enquiring of each of the six military commands what additional battalions could be provided, No 11 District (Belfast) replied – 'battalions Royal Irish Rifles', while No 12 District (Dublin) reported 'under present conditions and at present rate – none. If National [sic] Volunteers allowed by party to enlist then Connaught Rangers, Leinster Regiment and Royal Irish Regiment should be able to form an extra battalion'.[58] On 11 September 1914 a further six New Army divisions, collectively known as K2 divisions to distinguish them from the original six divisions, including the 16th (Irish) were created by the War Office.[59]

On 3 September 1914 the Ulster Unionist Council gave formal approval for men of the Ulster Volunteer Force (UVF) to enlist and the next day 800 men of the North Belfast Battalion marched as a body to enlist at Belfast's Old Town Hall. This response was repeated in the following days by other Belfast battalions and throughout Ulster. According to Simkins 'before the end of the month the Belfast district had recruited some 12,000 men and other districts of Ulster over 20,000 more'.[60] This claim, however, is neither supported by recruiting statistics nor by the UVF. Recruiting figures for the month of September 1914 show that 12,275 men enlisted in Belfast with a further 1,469 men enlisting in other parts of Ulster; recruitment reached its peak on 25 September when 1,169 men from the Province enlisted.[61] That 32,000 men from the UVF had not enlisted in a month is confirmed by Sir Herbert Richardson, its commanding officer, who claimed that approximately 30,000 men had been recruited in Ulster as a whole by the end of 1914.[62]

On 11 September the War Office authorised the creation of a second Irish division, the 16th (Irish) Division, and on 20 September John Redmond, in a speech at Woodenbridge, County Wicklow, committed the Irish Volunteers to serve 'wherever the firing line extends, in defence of right, freedom and religion in this war'.[63] As Keith Jeffery has observed, however, Redmond did not make this speech in support of enlistment in the British army until after the legislation giving Home Rule to Ireland had received Royal Assent and analysis shows that in the three predominately nationalist southern provinces in the four weeks following Redmond's speech recruitment fell by over 40% compared with the previous four weeks.[64] The effect on northern nationalists of these two events is more difficult to identify as it is largely hidden amongst the surge in recruits from the UVF. However, the *Irish Times* estimated that by the end of 1914 approximately 1,450 Irish Volunteers from Ulster had enlisted in the 16th (Irish) Division.[65]

From his analysis of recruitment, Beckett claims what he terms the 'first rush' can be almost precisely dated to the period of 25 August to 15 September 1914.[66] Figure 2.2 in Annex 1 shows total recruitment for the period 23 August to 31 October 1914 together with projected recruitment in Ireland based on its percentage of United Kingdom population and its actual recruitment for the period.[67] The graph supports Beckett's assertion regarding 'the first rush' to enlist but clearly shows that no similar rush took place in Ireland during the period; indeed not until 13 September when organised recruitment by the UVF commenced did Ireland achieve daily levels of recruitment equivalent to that of Great Britain.

The apparent ambivalence towards recruitment in Ireland was a result of a combination of demographic, economic, social and political factors. Antipathy towards the army was not a new phenomenon, indeed it had been reflected in the fall of the proportion of Irishmen serving in the army for a number of decades. Lord MacDonnell in a House of Lords debate on 8 January 1915, reminded his fellow peers that 'the contribution made by Ireland to the Imperial Army was in 1883 25%, in 1892 it was 15% and in 1893 it was 20%. In 1903 it had sunk to 13% and last year the contribution was 9%'.[68] This downward trend reflected a general decline in the Irish male population at a time when the male population of the rest of the United Kingdom was rising. Between 1861 and 1911 the male population of Ireland fell from 2,837,370 to 2,192,048, a reduction of almost 23% in 50 years, while in Great Britain over the same period the male population increased from 10,232,658 to 19,452,843, an increase of some 90%.[69] A major factor in the fall in the Irish population was emigration, 80,625 males emigrating between 1912 and 1914 alone.[70]

Of more significance to Ireland's response to calls for recruits in 1914 was the fall in the number of men of military age. Although Kitchener's initial appeal was for men between 19 and 30, the upper age limit was subsequently extended to 35 for new recruits from 27 August 1914.[71] During the period 1861 to 1911 the number of men of military age in Ireland decreased by almost 750,000, a reduction of 28%. These demographic changes had a significant impact on the number of men available for recruitment and points towards a male population with a declining proportion of men of military age (1861 – 33%; 1911 – 30%).

Socio-economic factors also impacted on the level of recruitment in Ireland. Although the number of men employed in agriculture had fallen by over 180,000 over the previous 50 years, Ireland was still predominantly an agricultural country with some 720,000 men employed in agriculture, forestry, horticulture and fishing. This represented almost 33% of the total male population and was therefore the major source of employment, particularly outside the industrial counties of the north-east. Indeed, while the number of men participating in agriculture in the years immediately prior to the war was significantly lower (25%) than it had been in 1861, the proportion of men so employed was actually higher, i.e. 32% compared to 33% in 1911, having declined from a peak of some 36% in 1890s.[72]

What is of more significance, however, is the number of men of military age employed in the sector. While agriculture in Ireland was generally an aging sector with 71% of employees being over military age in 1911 compared with 68% in 1871, it still employed over 208,000 men of military age, approximately 32% of all young men within the age range. By its nature, the agricultural sector is likely to have employed a relatively small proportion of those who would have been rejected for military service for medical reasons. As a result a significant number of the remaining 448,000 men of military age not employed in the agricultural sector would be rejected on medical grounds. This group would also have provided members of the Special Reserve and Extra Special Reserve battalions of the Irish regiments who would already have a prior military commitment in excess of 15,000 men, which would have excluded their recruitment to a Kitchener battalion such as those of the 10th Division.

There appears to be no evidence of economic factors having a negative effect on recruitment to the division in the period immediately following the commencement of hostilities. On the contrary, the evidence from newspapers, particularly in the industrialised north-east, indicates a downturn in economic conditions resulting in men being made redundant in a number of sectors, thus releasing men for enlistment. Within days of the declaration of war, newspapers were reporting on the effect the war was having on industry. The *Belfast Evening Telegraph* reported on 6 August the introduction of short time working in the linen industry amid fears regarding supplies of flax from Belgium and Russia, followed by a report the following week of a reduction in working hours at the Sirocco [engineering] Works.[73] The Belfast shipyards were not exempt from the impact of war when, following the departure of skilled workmen for England to hurry the completion of warships being built there, pay-offs were announced.[74] Between July and the end of October 1914 the workforce of Harland and Wolff alone fell from 24,425 to 18,412 with perhaps reductions of similar proportions in the smaller yard of Workman and Clarke.[75]This downturn in economic activity is more likely to have had a positive rather than a negative effect on recruitment to the division particularly as many employers such as Belfast City Corporation resolved that the dependents of employees who enlisted would continue to receive half their wages.[76] In the medium to long term, however, economic factors did have an impact on recruitment. John Dillon, a nationalist MP and recruiting official, complained in 1915 that the availability of well-paid jobs in England was making it difficult to obtain recruits for the army, particularly when a government agency was offering £2 10s a week for munitions workers in a reserved occupation compared with the basic shilling a day of an infantry private.[77] According to his biographer, Redmond calculated that by the end of 1915 about 40,000 Irishmen were employed in munitions work in Britain and Ireland.[78]

In a letter to Birrell on 17 September 1914, Redmond set out what he considered to be the economic impact on recruitment in Ireland:

> It must be remembered that the situation of a thickly populated manufacturing land and that of a thinly populated agricultural country is very different. In England or in manufacturing districts of Ulster the dislocation of commerce and industry favours recruiting … In agricultural districts, on the other hand, the case is reversed. There the work in the fields should be doubled. Already before the War more men were required for tillage. Any extensive recruiting in country districts at this time would have left a rich harvest rotting.[79]

Colin Cousins, in *Armagh and the Great War*, noted that as early as 15 August 1914 the *Lurgan Mail* was reporting the labour difficulties affecting many farmers:

> so great is the dearth of labourers about the Clougher Hill district that farmers are in a quandary how to save their flax crop – a situation which has its bearing on the staple industry of Lurgan now that the supply has been cut off from the continent. Offers of 2s 6d a day with

food, have failed to find any acceptances.[80]

The importance of the linen industry to the economy of rural Ulster was significant but by mid-August some 400 men employed in linen mills in Lurgan alone had already enlisted. Torn between economic self-interest and patriotism, the Flax Spinners' Association agreed that:

> So far as it is consistent with the continued operation of their work, and as far as possible to assure to the dependents of those enlisting the same means of livelihood as they would have had if breadwinners were at home, and to promise not to permanently fill any place vacated through enlistment before the end of the war.[81]

Political factors may also have had an effect on recruitment to the division. On 26 July 1914, only a week before Britain's declaration of war, the army was involved in an incident when the King's Own Scottish Borderers tried to prevent the landing of a cargo of weapons for the Irish Volunteers at Howth. At Bachelor's Walk, Dublin, the Borderers were stoned by a crowd on whom the soldiers opened fire killing 3 people and wounding a further 38. It was therefore against a background of anger following this incident that Kitchener made his appeal for men to join the ranks.

Progress of the Home Rule Bill also had an impact on recruiting of both unionists and nationalists. In *The Times* of 1 August, Sir Edward Carson had declared that a large body of the Ulster Volunteer Force were willing to provide their services for home defence, with many others willing to join the colours to fight wherever required. Initially John Redmond was more limited in the support forthcoming from the Irish Volunteers, telling the House of Commons on 3 August that the government 'may tomorrow withdraw every one of its troops from Ireland'.[82]

The number of enlistments in Ireland, as elsewhere, does not necessarily reflect the number of those who actually volunteered to serve. The *Irish Times* reported in mid-November 1914 on enlistments at the Grafton street recruiting office in Dublin since it had opened at the end of September – 'During the seven weeks 602 men offered themselves for enlistment. Of these 359 were passed as medically fit, 243 were rejected, 10 developed heart trouble after they had been passed the doctor, and 349 definitely joined the colours.'[83]

If so early in the war this is a fair reflection of the percentage of volunteers rejected on medical grounds, i.e., a 40% rejection rate, then the 10th (Irish) Division was always going to struggle to meet its quota, particularly after the authorisation of the 16th and 36th Divisions. Such high rejection rates appear not to be unusual because, as already noted, on 4 September 800 men of the North Belfast Regiment of the Ulster Volunteers marched as body to enlist at the Old Town Hall in Belfast and yet daily recruitment figures only record 408 men enlisting in Belfast on that date.

It may be thought that such levels of rejection were confined to working class urban areas but an *Irish Times* report of 22 October 1914 recorded that:

> Up to 5 o'clock yesterday evening there were 36 men enlisted at the Recruiting Offices, Great Brunswick street and at the special Recruiting Office, Grafton street, 8 were enlisted. The class of men who offered for enlistment this week were of a superior type, including a great many clerks and young business men. Quite a lot have had to be rejected in consequence of valvular affection of the heart, which the inspecting medical officers attribute to over exertion in sporting exercises.

Using the annual recruiting reports for the period 1903/04 to 1912/13, Patrick Callan has calculated that the average annual rejection rate for those seeking to enlist in the regular army at recruiting offices in Ireland was 21%, almost half the rate of rejection implied by the *Irish Times* article of 14 November 1914.[84] A close examination of the data, however, reveals that Callan made a number of fundamental errors in his calculations resulting in an understatement of the proportion rejected by some 20%. Thus in the ten years prior to the war over a quarter of volunteers (26%) were rejected for various reasons.[85] A closer examination, however, shows that the average rejection rate in Ireland was not significantly different from that of the rest of the United Kingdom and slightly better than the average for recruiting districts in England and Wales. Table 2.1 (Annex 2) shows the average rejection rates for the United Kingdom for the ten years prior to the commencement of the war.[86] This table shows that across all skill sectors, with the exception of agricultural labourers, the proportion of men inspected but rejected prior to enlistment was lower in Ireland than in England and Wales. Fitzpatrick's claim that 'the Irish were less likely than the British to be rejected as unfit', although holding true for England and Wales, is unsupported by the evidence which shows that overall rejection rates in Scotland were similar to those of Ireland and actually lower in the key recruiting category of unskilled labour.[87]

After the failure of British troops at Suvla, Bean, the official historian for Australia wrote – 'The truth is that after 100 years of breeding in slums, the British race is not the same, and can't be expected to be the same, as in the days of Waterloo. ... The only hope of these puny narrow-chested little men may, if they come out to Australia, or NZ or Canada, within two generations breed men again'.[88] In contrast Bean, in helping to build the Anzac legend, described Australian troops as coming 'of a race whose tradition was one of independence and enterprise, and, within that race itself, from a stock adventurous, and for the most part physically more strong, than the general run of men'.[89] This idealised description of Australian troops implies that high rates of rejection for physical unfitness were a phenomenon confined to the British army. The *Alpine Observer*, an Australian rural newspaper, however, reporting on the results of a recruitment drive in late 1915, observed that 'After a slow start, enlistments picked up but were plagued by high rejection rate. In Bright, half the men volunteering were rejected on medical grounds: at Wangaratta, of the fifty-four volunteers, thirty were refused'.[90] In building the Anzac legend, Bean failed to mention that of the some 375,000 who enlisted in the Australian army during the war, approximate 17.5% were not Australian by birth, including 59,394 born in the British Isles.[91]

Table 2.5 in Annex 2 shows the strength of each of the Irish battalions of the division on 19 September 1914.[92] What is interesting is not only how quickly the battalions have filled up since the returns of a fortnight previously but the remarkable number of rank and file recorded as trained, particularly in the Connaught Rangers, which now had more trained men than its total number of men just two weeks before. There is no single explanation of why trained men should suddenly appear in the ranks of the division, though there are a number of possibilities.

The first possible source is time-expired former soldiers without any reserve commitment to a regular battalion. These would be men in their thirties, or older, who had completed their initial seven year enlistment followed by a further seven year reserve commitment. According to Cooper, 'it was estimated that within a month of the declaration of war, every old soldier in Ireland who was under sixty years of age had enlisted again'.[93] Even with a degree of exaggeration, this can only partially explain the number of trained men in the division, as their number on 19 September 1914 (2,196) is the equivalent of 45% of the total strength of the division on 5 September. It is possible, however, that a proportion of the recruits transferred from non-Irish battalions by the War Office fell within this group, although it would be surprising if any battalion would willingly have let trained recruits transfer to another regiment. One such man, however, was Private William Roynon who had enlisted in the Wiltshire Regiment before being transferred to the 7th Royal Dublin Fusiliers. Roynon was 45 when he was killed at Gallipoli, having served previously in the Boer War.[94] One old soldier from an Irish regiment who returned to his old regiment was Sergeant Allen Guest of D company 7th Royal Dublin Fusiliers who would add a bar at Gallipoli to the Distinguished Conduct Medal he had won in the Boer War and ultimately be commissioned in the battalion having first risen to the rank of Regimental Sergeant Major. Guest had left the army as Colour Sergeant in June 1914 after completing a full 21 years with the colours and, although 37 years old at the time re-enlisted in September 1914.[95]

Lieutenant-Colonel Greer, commanding officer of the 6th Royal Irish Fusiliers, provides an account of how he personally recruited one old soldier at the barracks in Cork:

On entering the gate, I saw a barrack labourer wheeling a

barrow and thought I recognised him. Yes, it was 'Baxter' late Drum Major in the 2nd Bn. After some talk I asked him if he would like to do Sergt Major in 'my Bn'. His eyes popped out of his head as if he had seen the gates of Paradise open to him. I took him on the car, turned round and drove down to the recruitment office, where he was reenlisted. So there were now 2 of us, anyway in 'my Bn'.[96]

Although the upper age limit for recruits had been increased to 35 on 27 August 1914, many older men did not let their age deter them from rejoining the colours and were willing to go to considerable lengths to hide their age.[97] One such was L/Sgt George O'Brien, 5th Connaught Rangers and a Boer War veteran,who served under the name Henderson to hide the fact that he was 53 years of age when he enlisted. O'Brien accompanied his battalion to Gallipoli and was killed in the attack on Hill 60 in the Anzac sector on 21 August 1915.[98]

At the other end of the scale, the lower age limit of 19 was likewise ignored. Private Ivor Evans, 6th Leinster Regiment, enlisted in August 1914 at the age of 15. Although under age, he fought at Gallipoli, Salonika and participated in the retreat in Serbia. Private Evans was invalided home, suffering from dysentery, frostbite and malaria in 1916 but rejoined the regiment on the Western Front in October 1916. He was killed in action, aged 18, on 23 November 1917 serving with 2nd Leinsters.[99]

As all but the Royal Irish Rifles received substantial drafts of men originally recruited for English regiments, it is possible that some trained men were former members of the Territorial Force or its predecessor. Evidence suggests, however, that such men were more likely to have rejoined their old unit. The 5th Scottish Rifles (T.F.) records show that there was 'a considerable crowd of eligible recruits anxious to join us, but, under orders, we were prohibited from enlisting any but trained ex-members', while the Civil Service Rifles, a London Territorial Force battalion, had on mobilisation mustered 869 made up to its full establishment of 1,000 as 'old members flocked back', including a number who had served with the regiment in South Africa.[100] Between 4 and 7 August 1914 a total of 350 men attested to bring the London Rifle Brigade up to strength of which at least 54 were time-served members who re-enlisted when war was declared.[101] It is therefore unlikely that many trained men were obtained from this source.

A third possibility is that these men were reservists who were surplus to requirement or members of an Extra Reserve battalion who were transferred either voluntarily or otherwise to a Kitchener battalion. Although the circumstances of his transfer are unclear, Private Henry MacDonnell, 6th Royal Irish Rifles, was one such man described by his local newspaper as 'a reserve man … called up on the outbreak of war'. At the time of his enlistment Private MacDonnell was employed by Ballymena Urban District Council.[102] Evidence suggests that this was not a major source of trained men. Comparison between the number of men in the reserve battalions of the Irish regiments immediately before the 10th Division was brought up to strength by the transfer of recruits from English regiments and 19 September 1915 when the transfers took place shows that the number of trained men in the reserve battalions did not change significantly and so the large number of trained other ranks cannot be explained in this manner, indeed in some reserve battalions the number of trained soldiers actually increased over the period.

David Campbell, an officer in the 6th Royal Irish Rifles, suggests that many reservists may have joined battalions of the division before mid-September:

> My platoon looked a pretty tough lot. Most of them, as I learned later, were reservists and were accustomed to being called up annually for a month's training. Many were middle aged and beery looking, they were not easy to manage at first, they hated violent exercise and physical jerks or doubling round the barrack square were anathema to them. The regular exercise and ample food, however, soon began to tell before very long, they began to face their work cheerfully enough, and to take pride in their smartness.[103]

An examination of the 1914-15 Star medal roll for the 7th Royal

Dublin Fusiliers suggests a possible fourth source of trained men. The medal roll notes the means by which a soldier was discharged from the battalion and shows that two men left the army on the completion of their period of enlistment, one during the war and the other within weeks of its end. Of these, Lance Corporal Farrelly was discharged in February 1916 being time expired, while Sergeant Michael Flynn was discharged in January 1919 on the completion of his regular enlistment.[104] According to Farrelly's enlistment papers he enlisted in 1897 and joined a reserve battalion in 1910, from which he was transferred to the 7th Royal Dublin Fusiliers when the battalion was raised in 1914.[105] Although no enlistment papers are available for Flynn, his medal index card shows that he was awarded a long service and good conduct medal during the war indicating continuous service of twenty-one years.[106] It is possible therefore that the number of trained men in each battalion included, as early as mid-September 1914, a number of pre-war regular soldiers. It should of course not be forgotten that each regular battalion was required to leave three officers and fifteen NCOs at the depot before joining the BEF.[107]

In recent years writers, including Richard van Emden, have examined the experiences of some of those who enlisted in the army while underage, but little has emerged on the true extent of underage enlistment either in the early days of the war or for that matter the extent of enlistment amongst men above the upper age limit.[108] Patrick Callan, using a sample of 561 records from the Commonwealth War Graves Commission, profiled the age structure of those who died while serving in Irish line regiments during the war drawing the conclusion that over 50% of the men were under 25, with 70% being under 30.[109] As Callan admits, this analysis using age at death bears no direct relevance to the ages of those men in the sample or others when they enlisted. However, with the release of the 1901 and 1911 census in Great Britain and Ireland it is now possible to undertake a more in-depth analysis.

Figure 2.3 (Annex 1) shows the distribution of recruits by age group of four battalions of the 10th (Irish) and one of the 13th (Western) divisions [110]This clearly shows that as a whole the men serving in Irish regiments tended to be older than their counterparts in the 13th (Western) Division and that there was a greater propensity for underage enlistment in the latter; 26% of enlistments compared with an average 15% in the 10th (Irish) Division. The reverse appears to be the case for overage enlistments where the proportion of men enlisting over the age of 35 was 14% compared with only 5% in the Wiltshire Regiment. Despite these extremes, and variation between battalions, almost the same overall proportion of recruits fell within the official age parameters for both divisions, although on average only 55% of men in Irish battalions were under 25 on enlistment compared with 75% in the Wiltshires, while 86% and 95% respectively were below the upper age for enlistment.

A possible reason for men enlisting in Irish battalions of the 10th (Irish) Division being older than those enlisting in the 13th (Western) Division is that the men from England who were sent to bring a number of Irish battalions up to strength tended to be older. However, an analysis of age by place of birth shows this not to be the case. Of the men in Irish battalions born in Ireland only 50% were under the age of 25 on enlistment and 82% under 35, thus suggesting the practice of transferring older men did not exist in this context. It is interesting to note that the battalion that most closely resembles the pattern of enlistment of the Wiltshires is that of the Royal Irish Rifles which largely drew its recruits from Belfast and the adjoining counties of Antrim and Down. Although distinctly different in population their recruiting areas both had a single dominant industrial centre supported by a largely rural hinterland.[111] This appears to have produced certain similarities in recruitment patterns between the 6th Royal Irish Rifles and the 5th Wiltshire Regiment, namely high levels of underage enlistment, at 24% and 26% respectively; 90% or more of men enlisting under the upper age limit and a lower level of enlistment by men over 35 than other Irish battalions.[112] This suggests that the wider variation in the age of recruits to other battalions of the 10th Division is due to demographic reasons such as the nature of employment available or an older potential recruitment pool caused by emigration and the resultant decline in the birthrate. This is particularly noticeable in the 5th Connaught Rangers where only 30% of Irish born recruits were under 25 when they enlisted and another 37% were over the age limit for joining the army. Indeed two member of the battalion, Lance Sergeant George O'Brien and Private James Quinn, were 53 and 55 respectively, when war was declared.[113] Both were killed on 21 August 1915 during the attack on Hill 60 at Gallipoli. As surprising as it may be, these two men were probably not the oldest serving in the ranks of the division. Drury records the celebration in March 1916 of the 43 years' service in the regiment (Royal Dublin Fusiliers) of their regimental cook, Sergeant Hughes.[114]

David Fitzpatrick's exploration of what influenced an Irishman's willingness to join the British army concluded that it was less to do with economic, religious or political factors than the attitudes and behaviour of the social sphere with which they interacted, such as family, friends, neighbours, fellow-members of organisations and fraternities.[115] While this may be true for recruitment as a whole, evidence regarding its validity to the 10th (Irish) Division is inconclusive. With a number of notable exceptions, there is little evidence to support Fitzpatrick's view of why men enlisted in the division. The decision by 220 members of the Tyrone battalions of the U.V.F. to enlist has already been noted, but by far the largest enlistment of men from a similar social background was that of the 'Pals', raised by the Irish Rugby Football Union from likeminded sportsmen, who served together as 'D' company of the 7th Royal Dublin Fusiliers. Their names are recorded in the suitably named book *The pals at Suvla*, which gives extensive, if not always accurate, details of their largely common social background, while the roll of honour of Clontarf Cricket and Football Clubs records the names of at least ten members who joined 7th Royal Dublin Fusiliers and accompanied the battalion to Gallipoli.[116]

Evidence of collective sacrifice on a smaller scale, such as family, friends and neighbours for example, is less easy to obtain. What evidence does exist is mainly found amongst the officers where a number of brothers, school friends and fellow members of the IV and UVF served together. Fitzpatrick's concept of collective sacrifice might usefully be extended to cover past affinities as a reason for enlistment. This is evidenced not only by the number of army pensioners who re-enlisted but also by the extent that some recruits would go to rejoin former comrades. One such man was Edward St.

George Tottenham Irvine, who enlisted as Private 495, St George T. Irvine, 5th Connaught Rangers. According to the *Irish Times* which reported on a petition of divorce submitted by his wife, the Hon. Flora Fitzmaurice Irvine, only daughter of Lord Muskerry, Irvine 'was a gentleman of considerable means, and at one time was an officer in the same battalion in which he was now serving as a private'.[117] Irvine, despite his social status and previous military experience, appears to have been content to have served out his enlistment in the ranks and later transferred to the RAF.

Richard Grayson's analysis of recruitment in west Belfast displays evidence that collective sacrifice was possible even in a community divided on political/religious lines. Although his book enables only a few cases of those who joined the 10th (Irish) Division to be discussed, his main focus being on the majority of men from the area who served either as regulars or with the other Irish divisions on the Western Front, Grayson's unpublished data contains at least 230 men from the area who enlisted in battalions of the 10th (Irish) Division.[118] While men from both communities in west Belfast were some of the first to answer Kitchener's call for volunteers, it is noticeable that, where religion is known, Catholics only represented 20% of enlistments from the area into the local battalion, the 6th Royal Irish Rifles, yet represented almost 45% of enlistments from the area into the 6th Royal Irish Fusiliers, suggesting that issues other than economic factors influenced their choice of regiment.

The collective nature of recruitment to Irish battalions was not, however, confined solely to Irishmen. The obituary of Walter Stanley Currie Griffith, a trainee solicitor who worked among the poor of east London, records how 'he, with a party of recruits from the Maurice Hostel [an Anglican establishment in Hoxton, London], volunteered and joined the 6th Leinster Regt'. There is no evidence to suggest that any of this group had any connection with Ireland but rather, as the obituary suggests, 'there could not be finer proof of the influence he had gained and the confidence he had inspired than the way in which 30 members of the Hostel followed him to the front'.[119]

Although the War Office had filled the ranks of the division with drafts from England by mid-September there is evidence that volunteers from England continued to join the division during training as late as December 1914. John David Purcell, an apprentice painter and decorator, and seven or eight friends from the Colne Catholic Club enlisted together at the beginning of December and were posted to the 5th Royal Irish Fusiliers. It is unclear whether this group volunteered specifically to join an Irish regiment or because of their Irish/Catholic background. Although none of the group was born in Ireland, at least four had a parent or grandparent born in Ireland.

Against the rather sparse evidence for collective sacrifice being a major contributory factor in recruitment to the 10th Division there is substantial evidence to support economic factors. According to Edward Spiers the social composition of pre-war recruits had changed little from that of their Victorian predecessors, the largest single group in the annual intake being drawn from unskilled members of the population.[120] Although table 2.6 shows annual recruitment by employment group, net of medical rejections, for the period 1903/04 - 1912/13 a report on the health of the army for 1909 estimates that 'well over 90 per cent'of those who had been inspected were out of work.[121] The table also indicates that the percentage of unskilled recruits enlisting in Ireland prior to 1914 was some 29% higher than the proportion of recruits enlisting in the rest of the United Kingdom, while proportionally those from a skilled background represented less than half that of those enlisting in Scotland. While Fitzpatrick states that 'between 1905 and 1913, half the recruits accepted in Ireland *thought of themselves* [my italics] as unskilled urban workers', the army differentiated between unskilled labour (30%) and other occupations (22%), which included fishermen, clerks, boatmen and tradesmen's assistants.[122]

	Ireland		Scotland		E&W		Total	
	Recruits	%	Recruits	%	Recruits	%	Recruits	%
Agricultural Labourers	8,059	27	3227	11	30601	11	41,887	12
Other unskilled workers	8,883	30	9916	34	96898	35	115,697	34
Total Unskilled	16,942	57	13,143	44	127,499	45	157,584	46
Skilled Labourer	4,440	15	9980	34	65161	23	79,581	23
Other occupations	6,548	22	5563	19	71004	25	83,115	24
Professionals, Students etc.	340	1	154	1	2476	1	2,970	1
Boys under 17	1,275	4	721	2	14198	5	16,194	5
	29,545		29,561		280,338		339,444	

Table 2.6: Recruits by employment group 1903/04 - 1912/13.[123]

As approximately 5% of total pre-war enlistments were boys under the age of 17 and, while recognising that many New Army recruits were underage, the official lower age limit for recruits when K1 battalions were being established was 19 years of age. The table above includes many recruits ineligible for overseas service. Table 2.7 therefore shows the proportion of recruits, excluding boy soldiers, by employment group for the period 1903/04-1912/13 and allows comparisons with those recruited into New Army battalions to be made.

	Ireland		Scotland		E&W		Total	
	Recruits	%	Recruits	%	Recruits	%	Recruits	%
Agricultural Labourers	8,059	29	3227	11	30601	11	41,887	13
Other unskilled workers	8,883	31	9916	34	96898	36	115,697	36
Total Unskilled	**16,942**	**60**	**13,143**	**46**	**127,499**	**48**	**157,584**	**49**
Skilled Labourer	4,440	16	9980	35	65161	24	79,581	25
Other occupations	6,548	23	5563	19	71004	27	83,115	26
Professionals, Students etc.	340	1	154	1	2476	1	2,970	1
	28,270		28,840		266,140		323,250	

Table 2.7: Recruits, excluding boy soldiers, by employment group 1903/04 - 1912/13.[124]

It has been claimed that that the Great War introduced greater diversity in the ranks of the army. In the opinion of John Bourne, Kitchener's army was 'an army of men who would never normally have contemplated a military 'career': the self-styled social and physical elites of provincial commerce ... working-class intellectuals ... skilled craftsmen with a keen sense of privilege and self-worth, tough miners proud of their strength and earning power, tee-total Methodists ... [and] city clerks'.[125] According to Peter Simkins the rapid expansion of the army had thrown together 'men of all social classes and occupational backgrounds. Stockbrokers, engineers, lawyers, and teachers and students now rubbed shoulders in the ranks with miners, fishermen, clerks, shop assistants and farm labourers'.[126] Germains, however, claims that 'although men of education were not entirely lacking, the men of the First New Army [of which the 10th and 13th Divisions were part], generally speaking, were of the same class as the average run of Regular recruit'.[127] To establish which of these contrasting views reflects recruitment to the 10th (Irish) Division, the occupations of new recruits was tested against the profile for regular army recruits in Table 2.7 and, in recognition that many battalions received large drafts from English regiments, employment data was analysed on the basis of a recruit's place of birth to remove any distortion these drafts may have caused.

	Pre-War Recruits	6 RIrR	5 CR	6 Leins	5 RI	7 RDF
	%	%	%	%	%	%
Agricultural Labourers	29	1	12	20	0	1
Other unskilled workers	31	61	49	50	11	5
Total Unskilled	**60**	**62**	**61**	**70**	**11**	**6**
Skilled Labourer	16	23	12	10	44	5
Other occupations	23	13	15	20	33	64
Professionals, Students etc.	1	1	12	0	11	25

Table 2.8: Irish-born recruits by employment group and battalion.[128]

The above table largely confirms Germains' assessment that New Army units remained largely dependent on unskilled labour for the bulk of its recruits. The analysis of pre-war recruits from Ireland shows that some 60% were unskilled labourers and an analysis of five Irish battalions shows that in three of these units the percentage of recruits from unskilled labour groups was in excess of the pre-war average. The other two battalions, the 5th Royal Irish and 7th Royal Dublin Fusiliers, however, show very low levels of unskilled labour amongst their Irish-born recruits. In the case of the former this may be due to the small number of Irish-born recruits (9) for which an occupation could be identified, while the employment group of the 7th Royal Dublin Fusiliers, is heavily skewed by the middle-class nature of the 'pals' company of that battalion. It is also of note that the percentage of men from the skilled labour group in the 6th Royal Irish Rifles, whose recruitment covered Belfast and counties Antrim and Down, was almost 50% higher than the pre-war average for this group, which may reflect the impact of redundancies and short-time working introduced in Ireland's industrial heartland at the beginning of the war.

While the proportion of unskilled recruits to the 7th Royal Dublin Fusiliers is undoubtedly skewed by the number of middle-class professions among the ranks of the 'pals company', literary evidence suggests that in other companies significant numbers of unemployed or unskilled recruits who had joined for economic rather than patriotic reasons existed. Hervey de Montmorency, an officer in the battalion recalled in later life that:

> we had many Welsh miners in our battalion, as recruiting amongst the Irish hung fire and it was impossible to fill our ranks with Irishman. There were many changes in the executive posts; but finally I settled down in command of a company of 'toughs': men enlisted on the Dublin quays, many of whom were Larkinites enticed to join the colours by the prospect of good food and pay, which were welcome to them after months of semi-starvation during the great strike of 1913 and 1914.[129]

An examination of the occupation of non-Irish born recruits as shown in Table 2.9 further strengthens Germains' view of the composition of New Army battalions. The majority of recruits to 10th (Irish) Division battalions of non-Irish birth were from England and Wales where 48% of pre-war recruits were from unskilled backgrounds. Analysis shows that with the exception of the 7th Royal Dublin Fusiliers, for reasons already noted, the other Irish battalions sampled contained drafts either more dependent on unskilled labour for recruits than the pre-war army or to an extent that was significantly less in the case of the 6th Leinsters. Any suggestion that English regiments may have sent a disproportionate number of unskilled recruits to Irish units while retaining the more skilled/professional/educated recruits for their selves is ruled out by the evidence of 5th Wiltshires of the 13th (Western) Division. This battalion which provided some 1,100 of its surplus recruits to Irish battalions, found almost 60% of its recruits from the unskilled labour group compared with the 48%

average for pre-war recruits from England and Wales. The battalion's increased percentage of unskilled recruits is almost certainly a result of the number of volunteers enlisting from the agricultural sector being more than double that of pre-war levels which reflects the predominately rural nature of the county. Taken together the evidence suggests that the source of First New Army recruits such as those of the 10th and 13th Divisions who enlisted prior to the recruiting boom of early September 1914 was largely no different from that of pre-war regulars and therefore they were more likely to have enlisted for economic rather than any other reason.

	Pre-War Recruits	6 RIrR	5 CR	6 Leins	5 RI	7 RDF	5 Wilts
	%	%	%	%	%	%	%
Agricultural Labourers	11	0	4	20	14	5	25
Other unskilled workers	36	57	51	23	38	10	34
Total Unskilled	**48**	**57**	**55**	**43**	**52**	**16**	**59**
Skilled Labourer	24	21	40	15	30	5	14
Other occupations	27	21	2	40	16	64	25
Professionals, Students etc.	1	0	4	2	2	16	1

Table 2.9: Non-Irish-born recruits by employment group and battalion.[130]

Although the religion of recruits was not an issue for most of the United Kingdom, in Ireland it was a subject that appeared to excite the press, politicians and both unionist and republican paramilitary factions. Following Redmond's Woodenbridge, speech T.P. O'Connor MP, scornful of Carson's claims concerning the U.V.F., wrote to Lloyd George that 'there will be now, as always, five catholic recruits for one Orange'.[131] Although Fitzpatrick suggests that 'Catholics were only slightly less likely than Protestants to enlist' and that 'despite Ulster's pre-eminence in the intensity of recruitment, only about 43 per cent of all Irish recruits were Protestants', analysis by Patrick Callan indicates that the ratio of enlistment of Protestants to Catholics in Ireland was 9:11 while the ratio in the population was 1:3 (see Table 2:10 below).[132]

	Catholic		Protestant	
	% of Population	% of Recruits	% of population	% of Recruits
Leinster	85	89	14	11
Munster	94	93	6	7
Ulster	44	27	53	73
Connaught	96	92	4	8
Ireland	74	55	25	45

Table 2.10: Recruiting response as proportion of religious group to 15 January 1918.[133]

Michael MacDonagh in his *The Irish at the Front* published in 1916 described the 10th (Irish) Division as 'voluntarily raised in Ireland and composed of 20,000 young men of fine character and high purpose, representative particularly of the Nationalist and Catholic sections of the community'.[134] Analysis shows that this is not the case. Ignoring recruits from other parts of the United Kingdom and elsewhere for which data on religious affiliation is largely unavailable, Table 2.11 below shows the relevant split by religion of five battalions of the 10th Division.

	7RDF	6 RIrR	5 RI	5 CR	6 Leinsters
	%	%	%	%	%
Irish Protestant	70	70	25	11	15
Irish Catholic	30	30	75	89	85

Table 2.11: Irish recruits as a proportion of religious group.[135]

The peculiar results obtained in Table 2.11 in respect of the nature of the sample for the Royal Irish and Royal Dublin Fusiliers has already been explained but in the case of the other three battalions the proportion of Protestants recruits is within +/- 4% of the percentage given in Table 2.10 and therefore may only represent a greater willingness by Protestants, particularly from southern counties, to enlist early in the war.

In response to claims in the English press that the division was 90% nationalist, the Right Rev Dr Crozier, Anglican chaplain to the division, wrote to the *Irish Independent* that 'in each of the three Brigades of which the Division is composed he had fully 2,000 men at each service at Basingstoke. There were about 7,500 Churchmen [Anglicans] in the Division (including 440 in the Leinster Regiment and 240 in the Connaught Rangers), and over and above these, there are at least 1,000 Presbyterians and Methodists'.[136] Any notion of the 10th (Irish) Division as a Catholic nationalist division ended after Gallipoli. A census of the religious persuasion of members of the division's three infantry brigades in November 1915 shows that less than 36% were Catholic and in none of the brigades did Catholics form a majority.[137]

CHAPTER 3

Officers and Gentlemen

The formation of the 10th (Irish) Division and the five other K1 New Army divisions created a need for over 3,000 new officers, the infantry alone needing over 2,000, at a time when trained officers were needed to replace casualties with the BEF. Given the size of the pre-war army these officers could not be obtained from existing resources and so units of the 10th Division were required to compete for the limited resources of potential officers available. In his study of the division at Gallipoli, Bryan Cooper, the division's unofficial historian claimed that, with the exception of the officers of the Hampshire Regiment, some 90% of the division's infantry officers were Irish.[1] This chapter tests the validity of this claim and by comparing the division with the 13th (Western) Division, another K1 division, and a sample of officers serving in pre-war Irish regiments, seeks to establish if the original officers of the division were significantly different from those of other New Army formations or their pre-war counterparts.

On the eve of the First World War the officer strength of the British regular army was approximately 12,738 with a further 2,557 attached to the Special Reserve and 3,202 in the Reserve of Officers. Of a further 9,563 officers of the Territorial Force, only 1,090 had agreed to serve overseas in the event of war.[2] While on the surface this may appear sufficient for an army that was 10,932 men (6%) under its peacetime establishment, it was totally inadequate for one that was to expand by over a million men in the first four months of the war.[3] At full strength an infantry battalion required 30 officers, although in peacetime – except for units stationed in India – this was rarely achieved. An infantry battalion was commanded by a Lieutenant-Colonel with a Major as second in command who, together with the machine gun officer, adjutant, quartermaster and a medical officer attached to the battalion from the Royal Army Medical Corps (RAMC), made up the battalion headquarters. A further six officers were attached to each of the battalion's four rifle companies, one of whom would double as battalion transport officer. It was usual practice for a battalion on active service to leave one of its officers at the regimental depot to bring out its 'first line' reinforcements to replace casualties. An infantry battalion would therefore usually go to the front with 29 regimental officers and a medical officer.[4]

Such was the need for additional officers caused by the army's rapid expansion that Kitchener issued an instruction on 6 September 1914 to 'Get from Post Offices names and addresses of every officer to whom letters are arriving addressed Colonel, Major, Captain and Lieutenant and, if he has not already sent in his name, write a letter to each inviting him to do so in such a manner that he can hardly refuse'. Despite his enthusiasm, Kitchener was soon persuaded that this was an impractical suggestion that would tie up the resources of the Post Offices at a time it was needed for other things and that 'an advertisement in the public press would be less cumbrous than the Post Office procedure'.[5]

Prior to the Great War there were four methods of obtaining a commission in the regular army. The most common method being, as now, graduation from one of the two officer training establishments, either the Royal Military College (RMC), Sandhurst, for officers of the infantry, cavalry and Army Service Corps, and the Royal Military Academy (RMA), Woolwich, for artillery and engineers. In 1913 Sandhurst accounted for 67% of new officers being commissioned into the relevant branch of service while the more technical nature of the skills required by artillery and engineer officers meant that 99% of new officers commissioned for these units were trained at Woolwich. Although by 1914 graduation from the RMC and RMA was the most common means of obtaining a commission, only about

55% of regular officers for the infantry and cavalry over the previous 40 years had been commissioned through this route and many such officers continued to serve during the war.[6]

Before 1908 the second most common method of obtaining a commission in the regular army was through service in the militia. This was a traditional route for those who, for whatever reason, were unable to gain admission to either Sandhurst or Woolwich, entrance to which was by competitive examination. This route was not viewed as a limiting factor in an officer's future advancement as both Field Marshal Sir John French, the commander of the British Expeditionary Force in 1914-15, and Lieutenant-General Sir Bryan Mahon, divisional commander of the 10th (Irish) Division at Gallipoli, obtained their regular commission in this manner. Although originally commissioned into the Royal Navy, which he did not find to his liking, French resigned his commission and joined a militia regiment through which an officer could obtain a regular commission provided he was nominated by his commanding officer and passed an examination. By this means French avoided attendance at Sandhurst and after two years in the Suffolk Artillery Militia was gazetted as an officer in the 8th (Queen's Royal Irish) Hussars in February 1874.[7] In the following decade Mahon would be commissioned into the same regiment from a militia battalion of the Connaught Rangers.[8] In 1908 the Haldane reforms replaced the militia with Special Reserve and Territorial Force battalions, usually attached to existing regular army regiments; the main exception to this being the London Regiment, a regiment consisting entirely of Territorial Force battalions. These provided, for those with military training in the Special Reserve, Territorial Force or the Officer Training Corps, the opportunity to obtain a commission without graduating at Sandhurst or Woolwich. In 1913 this source provided 15% of all new officers commissioned.

The creation of the Officer Training Corps provided a third route to a regular commission. This was the direct commissioning of an officer who had been a member of the Senior Division of the Officer Training Corps into a regiment. This allowed university graduates who had satisfactory service with a University Officer Training Corps to obtain a commission after spending a satisfactory probationary period with their preferred regiment. This method of obtaining a commission accounted for 15% of all new officers to the infantry and cavalry in 1913.

The final route to a commission was the least common, commissioning from the ranks. This accounted for only about 2% of commissions, the most usual form of which was the commissioning of a long-serving NCO/Warrant Officer to the rank of Honorary Lieutenant and Quartermaster. However, in some circumstances where exceptional bravery or ability was recognised, a soldier could be commissioned from the ranks, without restriction of their responsibilities to administrative duties. The most famous example of an officer commissioned from the ranks is that of Field Marshal Sir William Robertson, universally known in the British army as 'Wullie'. Born in 1860, Robertson enlisted as a trooper in the 16th Lancers in 1877, rising to the rank of Troop Sergeant-Major before being commissioned as a 2nd Lieutenant in the 3rd Dragoon Guards in 1888. Through ability and hard work, Robertson rose through the commissioned ranks more quickly than many of his contemporaries who came from more privileged backgrounds such as Rawlinson and Gough.[9] He became a Major-General in 1910 and was appointed Chief of the Imperial General Staff in December 1915 and finally Field Marshal in 1920.[10]

Ignoring those commissioned from the ranks, Keith Simpson claims that pre-war regular officers were a class characterised by its social and financial exclusiveness, exemplified by the majority of candidates for commissions in the regular army being educated at a public school.[11] This, Simpson argued, not only demonstrated the social exclusiveness of the officer class but also the financial obstacles that membership of this select club placed on the families of aspiring officers because of the cost of their education alone. Consequently, although officers commissioned from the ranks were not unknown, the bulk of British officers before 1914 were from a relatively narrow social background. Spiers suggests that in 1914 the source of British officers had changed little since the end of the Victorian era and that the army was still dependent on its traditional source of supply, the peerage, gentry, military families, the clergy and the professions, with a small minority from business, commercial and industrial families.[12] Although those from this latter group may have been wealthier than many of their social superiors, there was still a tendency for officers from these backgrounds to be regarded as being 'in trade'. Otley, in his study of the origins of senior officers of the British army, restricted the classification of business, commerce or industrial class to only those officers from an entrepreneurial, director or managerial background rather than those of the true artisan or small business category.[13]

Analysis of the officers of Irish line regiments killed in action, or as a result of wounds received, up to the end of 1914 shows that in most respects this group conformed to the assessments of Simpson and Spiers.[14] Table 3.1 below shows that officers from a military/naval background form the majority of this group of which, all but one (the father of Lieutenant H.R. Vaughan, who was a retired Colour Sergeant of the Durham Light Infantry) was either a serving or former officer; not unsurprisingly Lieutenant Vaughan was also promoted from the ranks. Of the other officers with a military/naval background, two were the sons of Major-Generals while the fathers of a further 25 were either serving or former officers with the rank of Major, or its naval equivalent, or above.

The second major social grouping of pre-war officers is those with a father in the senior professions of the law, medicine and the church (20%) while those from the ranks of the junior professions include Lieutenant J.G.B. Thomas, 2nd Royal Inniskilling Fusiliers, whose father was Walter Thomas, the playwright and author of *Charlie's Aunt*. Of the officers whose social background fall within the category of 'other', three or 50% gave their father's occupation as gentleman while 2nd Lieutenant Arthur Winspear's father is recorded as being a railway guard.

Peer	2%
Gentry	-
Military	53%
Clergy	10%
Medicine	8%
Law	2%
Other Professions	5%
Business, Commerce & Industry	10%
Other	10%

Table 3.1: Background of officers of Irish Line Regiments killed to 31 Dec 1914.[15]

From the biographies of the 88 officers, the school/schools attended by 75% have been identified.[16] As expected, the majority, almost 58%, attended a public school.[17] Of the remainder, 13% attended a school in Ireland, 6% in Scotland and the rest attended a non-public school in England or elsewhere. Among this latter group are a number of officers who attended English Catholic boarding schools, such as Stonyhurst and Downside, which although not then considered public schools, displayed all their characteristics.

As already noted, 55% of serving infantry and cavalry officers in 1914 were Sandhurst graduates but analysis of this sample of officers from Irish line regiments shows a somewhat different pattern. In this sample only 44% of the officers were commissioned by this route and not surprisingly a higher than expected proportion from the militia and Special Reserve, and none from the Territorial Force, the establishment of which was not extended to Ireland. Most surprising is the proportion of officers commissioned from the ranks, which is approximately double the average for the army as a whole, none of whom filled the post of Quartermaster. Table 3.2 below shows the method of obtaining a commission for officers in the sample.

	%
RMC, Sandhurst/RMA, Woolwich	44
From the Militia	29
From the Special Reserve	23
From the Ranks	4

Table 3.2: Method of obtaining a commission by regular officers of Irish line regiments killed Aug – Dec 1914.[18]

Cooper states that 90% of the 10th Division's officers were Irish but an analysis of pre-war regular officers suggests that if this were the case, then it was wholly exceptional.[19] Analysis of the 72 officers in Irish line regiments killed in action between the beginning of the war and the end of 1914 for whom information is available indicates that only 31% were either born or had addresses in Ireland, compared with 47% from the rest of the United Kingdom. However, as a further 18% were born in India, 3% in Malta and 1% in China where their fathers were serving in either the army or Royal Navy, some of these may still be of Irish extraction.[20] The most likely reason why so many non-Irish officers were serving in Irish regiments is provided by Simpson who identifies a hierarchy of regiments in terms of social acceptability and cost. Irish regiments of the line were viewed well down the pecking order with Welsh regiments and those from the north of England and the Midlands.[21] One step up from those units such as the Army Service Corps and Army Ordnance Corps, still considered by many in the army as 'trades', Irish line regiments provided a means by which a young officer without independent means could pursue a military career without the expense incurred in more fashionable regiments.

Having established a profile of a pre-war officer serving in an Irish line regiment as someone more likely to have been commissioned from the militia or Special Reserve than to have attended Sandhurst/ Woolwich, from a military family, educated at a public school and born outside Ireland, it is possible to compare this with the officers of the 10th (Irish) Division at Gallipoli.

In common with all Service battalions, those of the 10th (Irish) and 13th (Western) Divisions had to compete for the small number of trained officers available and not immediately required for the BEF or already committed to other battalions. The first source of trained officers was within the regiment itself. For the English and Welsh regiments of the 13th Division this meant the regimental cadre of regular officers at the depot, officers of the regiment's Special Reserve battalions, and those officers of the regiment's Territorial Force battalions that had made an Imperial Service commitment to serve overseas in the event of war. Although Irish regiments of the 10th Division had no Territorial Force battalions, the eight Irish line regiments had, in addition to their Special Reserve battalions, twelve Extra Reserve battalions with at least one battalion attached to each regiment.

In addition to the cadre of regular officers at the regimental depot, each battalion was required to leave behind three officers before going overseas. Those officers left behind tended to be officers of the regiment who had before the war been detached to overseas units such as the West African Frontier Force and were home on leave when war was declared. Many of these officers brought with them valuable experience of overseas soldiering, having been in action in a number of minor campaigns usually suppressing native unrest in Africa.

A third group of experienced officers were those British officers of the Indian Army on furlough in the United Kingdom at the declaration of war. According to Gordon Corrigan some 500 such officers, approximately 25% of the British officer corps of the Indian army, were on leave in the United Kingdom when war was declared.[22] Although about half these officers subsequently returned to their own units, the remainder were redeployed to other duties by the War Office, in particular New Army units.[23] Cooper states that practically every battalion in the 10th Division had at least one Indian Army officer and bears witness to the professionalism and influence these officers had on their new battalions.[24] Many of these officers were veterans of service on the North-West Frontier as well as campaigns in other theatres and some, such as Major Jephson, late of the 5th Bengal Light Infantry, after whom Jephson's Post on Kiretch Tepe ridge is named, would be immortalised not just in the division but wherever Gallipoli and Suvla are discussed. Cooper acknowledges the immeasurable debt that the division owed to these officers of the Indian Army and the immensity of the loss that was sustained when they were killed.[25] Arguably, however, the true impact of their loss was more apparent in the Indian battalions from which they were appropriated because although an Indian battalion had the same number of officers as its British equivalent, only twelve, including the medical officer, were British and all Indian officers were subordinate to even the most junior British officer.[26] The loss of so many British officers of the Indian Army to New Army units was therefore to have a considerable impact on the fighting capacity of Indian regiments, particularly on the Western Front, when it became impossible to replace British officer casualties with sufficiently experienced replacements.[27]

The final source of existing officers was from the Reserve of Officers.[28] Cooper notes the difficulties that many of these officers, often in their late forties or early fifties, and who in many cases had not served since the Boer War, had readjusting to military life, often junior in rank to those they had previously commanded. Although recognising that many were unequal to the strain of their task, he gives credit to those who were to 'stick it out' for the help they gave to their less experienced junior colleagues.[29] Sir Ivone Kirkpatrick, then a subaltern in the 5th Royal Inniskilling Fusiliers, describes one such officer, his company commander, as 'a hard master, but an admirable soldier, who took his work more seriously than he cared to show'.[30] Indeed Noel Drury, an officer in the 6th Royal Dublin Fusiliers, considered that they 'were very lucky to have such a big proportion of officers who were either regular soldiers or who had soldiered before'.[31] Of course as the senior Service battalion of the Royal Dublin Fusiliers, the 6th would have had first choice of the officers available, a problem which did not exist within the 13th Division as no regiment supplied more than one battalion to the division.

A less charitable view of an officer from the Reserve of Officers, and which illustrates how out of touch many of these officers were, is given by Lieutenant Verschoyle, a subaltern in the same company as Kirkpatrick, who wrote of 'one extremely dug-out major to whom the new drill was wholly novel and read his commands from a drill book held under his nose'.[32] Private Battersby, also of the 6th Royal Inniskilling Fusiliers, describes another of the 'dug-outs' who had helped train the battalion, on its leaving for England – 'at the gates of the barracks was Colonel Kirkpatrick on horseback with all his medals on, his white hair shining in the sun, standing at the salute and as we passed him the order came, 'Eyes Right!' and we could see the tears in the old man's eyes'.[33]

Not all the officers obtained from the Reserve of Officers were 'dug-outs' out of touch with developments in military practice. Of the four battalion commanders obtained from this source, all had retired within the previous four years and one, Lieutenant-Colonel Downing, 7th Royal Dublin Fusiliers, had only relinquished command of the regiment's first battalion in 1913. Three had also brought with them much needed combat experience albeit from the Boer War.[34]

The 13th Division was equally reliant on officers from the Reserve of Officers as it provided a number of its battalion commanders, including 56-year-old Lieutenant-Colonel Cole-Hamilton, 6th East Lancashire Regiment, who had participated in the unsuccessful campaign to relieve Gordon in 1882. The division's two other commanding officers drawn from this source Lieutenant-Colonels H.G. Levinge and M.H. Nunn, were both almost 50 and had retired in 1905 and 1906 respectively. Of 11 former officers who joined the division in 1914 at least eight were in their late 40s or early 50s while another, Captain J.W. Mather, had not served since 1899 and had enlisted as a private with the Canadian Expeditionary Force (CEF) at the beginning of the war.

The creation of the Service battalions also resulted in the promotion of a senior NCO from their respective regular battalions to the rank of Honorary Lieutenant and Quartermaster. The Quartermaster was responsible for the housing, provisioning, and stores of a battalion and ensuring that it was properly supplied with all necessities in the field, including food, water and ammunition. Due to their long service and knowledge of the system, this was a post generally given to Warrant Officers or senior NCOs, with a sufficient level of education and a good conduct record. The Quartermaster was a non-combat role and perhaps because of its association with shop keeping, and thus trade, it was not considered a suitable position for a gentleman, hence the honorary nature of their commission.

The 10th (Irish) Division also had a source of ready-trained officers unavailable to other K1 units of the New Army – the Royal Irish Constabulary (RIC). Much like its successor the Royal Ulster Constabulary, the RIC was a paramilitary police force trained, drilled and equipped along military lines. From this source the division obtained eight to ten District Inspectors who, despite joining the colours with the rank of Captain, according to Cooper demonstrated their patriotism by taking a cut in pay of £100 per annum.[35]

Having exhausted these sources of trained officers, battalions turned to volunteers seeking a commission, in particular those with previous military experience, members of the Officer Training Corps or those who could demonstrate leadership potential. Despite a reference in the diary of a subaltern in the 6th Royal Irish Rifles concerning a photograph of the officers of his battalion that showed 21 officers of whom 14 were regulars, it was from this group of young, and in some cases not so young, volunteers that the majority of officers that landed with the battalions of the 10th and 13th Divisions at Gallipoli were found.[36]

Data obtained from the personal files of regimental officers of the Irish battalions of the 10th Division shows that although the background of officers remained largely the same as that of their pre-war counterparts the distribution had changed with a significantly reduced dependence on the sons of military families. The data also shows that the proportion of officers whose fathers worked in the professions rose by 65% while those with a background in the entrepreneurial classes of business, commerce and industry, which once would have been looked down upon as being in trade, doubled. What is perhaps more surprising is that a small number of commissions were granted to those outside the normal 'officer class' who had not been promoted from the ranks of the regular army. This represented to some extent the relaxation of the social constraints placed on aspiring but impecunious young men wishing to become army officers before the war when some sort of private income or at least parental subsidy was required, on top of regimental pay, to meet the social requirements that went with the rank. This group included officers such as Second Lieutenant Leon Gaffney whose father was a railway porter and Second Lieutenant William Porter whose father was a city rate collector. David Campbell, an officer in the Irish Rifles, noted a drawback with this:

> There was one snag, one fly in the ointment. When I joined the battalion, the pay of a Second Lieutenant was 6/8 a day and messing cost 10/- a day minimum. To those of us who had no income, apart from our pay, this placed us in a somewhat embarrassing position. It was not too long however, until the position was rectified by raising our pay to 10/- and cutting the messing to 7/6.[37]

	%
Peer	1
Gentry	2
Military	21
Clergy	11
Medicine	9
Law	10
Other Professions	11
Business, Commerce & Industry	18
Other	17
	100

Table 3.3: Background of the officers of Irish battalions of 10th (Irish) Division serving at Gallipoli.[38]

Within each of the categories, however, there is a substantial difference in the backgrounds of many of the officers. The fathers of all the officers from a military background had been officers themselves, unlike their pre-war counterparts. Of the officers of the Irish battalions within the 10th Division from a military background, some 15% had fathers who had been generals while half the remainder had a father who was or had been a major, a proportion that could in fact be higher if many officers had not described their father's profession simply as army officer. Of those officers from a military background, over half were already serving at the beginning of the war and therefore only about 10% of new officers came from a military background.

Even within those categories that would normally be regarded as 'trade' i.e. commerce, business and industry, the emphasis was still very much on the middle class and entrepreneurial element of this group excluding actual artisans, skilled workmen or those from the more general working class. This trade group includes, G. P. Costello of the tobacco manufacturing family, the owner of Avonmore Flour Mills, a ship owner and the managing director of the Limerick Clothing Company Ltd. The majority, however, are described as various types of merchant.

A third of the group categorised as 'other' is made up of retired officers of the Royal Irish Constabulary, none of whom were below the rank of District Inspector, the equivalent of a captain in the army, while another third includes those who describe their background as 'gentleman' or 'gentleman of independent means' indicating that they derive their income from some source other than work. The balance of this group is largely made up of clerks and landowners/ farmers.

In the case of at least one officer, however, his social status might be better defined in respect of his mother rather than his father. Lieutenant J.E.G. O'Byrne, 6th Royal Munster Fusiliers (whose father was a barrister) was a Count of the Holy Roman Empire by virtue of his mother being the daughter of the Austrian, Baron von Heubner. Although born and educated in Ireland, O'Byrne had been commissioned into the battalion from a Canadian militia unit in which he had been serving before the war.[39]

The social status of Lieutenant I.A. Millar, 6th Royal Irish Rifles, is certainly unclear with reference to either his father or his mother. Although born in Aberdeen, his address at the time of his death is given as Forestall Hall, Appledore, Kent and while having attended Queen Elizabeth's School, Cranbrook and been a member of its OTC, he is described in Letters of Administration following his death as 'a Bachelor and a Bastard'.[40]

While the proportion of officers in the 10th (Irish) Division from a military background had fallen from the 54% serving in pre-war

Irish regiments to about 21%, officers from a military background formed an even smaller proportion of those serving in the 13th Division, which may be a reflection of the number of New Army Divisions being raised in England and Wales or the relatively low pecking order of the division's English county and Welsh regiments. Evidence suggests that for some officers at least, a battalion of the 13th Division may not have been their preferred choice. Of the 275 officers identified as embarking with the division for Gallipoli, three at least had very strong connections with Ireland, including Second Lieutenant R.A. Rutherford, a former member of Queen's University Belfast OTC who had requested a commission in the Ulster Division.[41] Another was Lieutenant R.N. Bellairs who was a member of the Ulster Volunteer Force, while the third was Lieutenant R.G. Livens also a former member of Queen's OTC who had originally enlisted as a private in the 14th Royal Irish Rifles (Young Citizens Volunteers), a battalion of the 36th (Ulster) Division.[42]

Whatever the reason for the lower percentage of officers from military/naval backgrounds, the 13th Division appears to have been more reliant on officers from professional backgrounds, who accounted for more than half the division's officers, than the 10th (Irish) Division. However, while the percentage of officers in the 13th Division drawn from backgrounds categorised as 'other' remained largely in line with the pre-war proportion found in Irish regiments, the proportion in the 10th Division rose by some 70%.

Table 3.4 below shows the distribution of family backgrounds of officers who served in the infantry battalions of the 13th (Western) Division at Gallipoli.

	%
Peer	0
Gentry	1
Military	15
Clergy	27
Medicine	6
Law	11
Other Professions	8
Business, Commerce & Industry	21
Other	11
	100

Table 3.4: Background of the officers of the 13th (Western) Division serving at Gallipoli.[43]

Arguably the most brilliant soldier to begin their military career as an officer in a New Army division was the son of a commercial traveller serving among the original officers of the 13th (Western) Division at Gallipoli, Lieutenant William J. Slim of the 9th Warwickshire Regiment.[44]

Simpson argues that the pre-war officer class was characterised by the preponderance of officers educated at public schools.[45] Analysis of the available records of officers of the 10th Division indicates that the demand for officers at the beginning of the war brought about a reduction in the number of officers that had attended a public school. Table 3.5 below clearly shows that more reliance was being placed on officers from non-public school backgrounds and particularly noticeable is the increased number of officers educated at schools in Ireland, which has more than tripled compared with the sample of pre-war officers killed whilst serving in a regular Irish battalion.

Even among the officers educated in Ireland, almost 60% were educated in the more prestigious schools, including those with boarding facilities such as Belvedere, Blackrock, Clongowes Wood and Wesley Colleges, the Portora Royal and the Royal School, Dungannon. Of the remainder all but one attended a grammar school, the exception being Lieutenant J.E. Elliot of the 6th Royal Irish Rifles who attended St. Jude's National School, Belfast.[46]

	%
Public School	42
Irish School[47]	45
Other	13

Table 3.5: Type of school attended by officers of 10th (Irish) Division who served at Gallipoli.[48]

The above table shows that 42% of officers in the division had attended a public school. This however hides the true impact of wartime recruitment on the availability of public school educated officers. Of the officers that attended a public school over a third were commissioned before the war and, if these were excluded, the proportion of officers who were public school educated would fall to about 33%. If the analysis of the schools attended by officers is confined to those commissioned since the outbreak of war, then the proportion educated in Ireland increases to 54%. What is significant is that the proportion of pre-war officers in the Irish battalions of the division who attended a public school (78%) is more than a third higher than the proportion in pre-war Irish line battalions.

What makes the educational backgrounds of the officers of the two divisions significantly different is the proportion of officers attending public schools. The percentage of all officers in the Irish battalions of the 10th (Division) who attended a public school was some 42% compared with the 54% in pre-war Irish battalions. However, the percentage of all officers in the 13th Division who attended a public school was some 82%, almost double the proportion in the Irish Division. Analysis of the schools attended by the officers of the 13th Division shows little difference in the percentage of officers commissioned pre-war (87%) and those obtaining their first commission in New Army battalions (81%). However, if those Irish schools with boarding facilities are regarded as the equivalent of a public school then the percentage of all officers in the 10th (Division) who had attended a public school increases to some 61%.

Unsurprisingly, where the officers of the division obtained their initial military training changed considerably from that of the pre-war regular battalions. Cooper states – 'each battalion had a Regular or retired Regular Commanding Officer, a Regular Adjutant, and the four company commanders had as a rule had some military experience'. To these can be added a Quartermaster commissioned from the ranks of a regular battalion of the regiment. For the rest the battalions were mainly dependent on candidates who had received some basic military training with an Officer Training Corps. Disturbingly Cooper states that the majority of subalterns when they joined 'were quite ignorant of military matters, and had to pick up their knowledge while they were teaching the men'. Not until the end of 1914 were classes for young officers organised at Trinity College, Dublin, although it was only a minority of officers who received any training through this route, 'the bulk of them had no training other than that which they received in their battalions'.[49]

Of the officers who accompanied the Irish battalions of the 10th Division to Gallipoli, the method of obtaining their commission has been identified for 228 while 180 have been for the 13th Division. Table 3.6 shows that the distribution of the sources of commissions within the two divisions differs widely, although the majority of officers being commissioned either directly, or from an OTC, is common to both. In both divisions over one third, and in the 10th Division the majority, of officers received their commission as a result of current or past membership of an Officer Training Corps. David Campbell, a subaltern with the 6th Royal Irish Rifles at Gallipoli, recalled, how tenuous this membership was in some cases:

> In order to clear the books, those who went into the army had to be discharged from the O.T.C. When it came to my discharge, it was found I had not attended any parades. Now the O.T.C. gets a bonus for every cadet who attends a specified number of parades and passes an efficiency test. As I had done neither, I had to be graded as 'inefficient' and to pay the amount of the bonus, £5.[50]

	10 Div.	13 Div.
	%	%
RMC, Sandhurst/RMA, Woolwich	12	5
Militia/Special Reserve/Colonial Forces	17	11
Commissioned from the Ranks	6	10
Serving or Past member of an OTC	44	36
Direct commission	21	38

Table 3.6: Source of the commission of officers of the 10th (Irish) and 13th (Western) Divisions who served at Gallipoli.[51]

Two main factors account for the relatively low percentage of officers in both divisions that were Sandhurst or Woolwich trained compared with the sample of officers in pre-war Irish battalions, these are:

1. The relatively small number of pre-war regular officers in each of the battalions; and
2. The fact that many of these pre-war officers held senior rank in their respective battalions and thus were commissioned before attendance at Sandhurst and Woolwich became the most prevalent method of obtaining a commission.

That the 10th (Irish) Division had more than double the number of Sandhurst or Woolwich graduates than the 13th Division is probably explained by the larger number of serving/former Indian Army officers (twelve) that have been identified as serving amongst its officers compared with five in the latter division.

In the years before the Great War it was also normal practice for a battalion's Quartermaster to have been commissioned from the ranks of experienced Warrant Officers or senior NCOs. The creation of twelve new Irish battalions therefore resulted in the promotion of an equivalent number of Quartermasters from the ranks. Excluding officers who had enlisted as privates after the declaration of war, it has been possible to identify fourteen officers commissioned from the ranks, including the twelve appointed to the rank of Quartermaster on the creation of the new Irish battalions of the division. The average time spent in the ranks of this group of officers is just over 20 years.

Of the twelve officers appointed to the rank of Quartermaster, two - Daly (6th Leinsters) and Clements (5th Royal Irish) - were no longer serving at the beginning of the war and both were in receipt of army pensions, having each served more than 23 years with the colours.[52] On the outbreak of war both applied for commissions as a Quartermaster, although at the time Daly was approaching 50 and had been discharged from the army in 1903 while Clements was already 50 but had not taken his discharge until 1910. Of the remaining ten Quartermasters appointed to the division's Irish battalions, all were either Warrant Officers or serving in the ranks at the time of their promotion and ranged in age from 37 to 44 years of age, although the majority were over 40. Despite an average of over 20 years with the colours each, only three of this group of twelve had seen action, two in South Africa and the third, Clements, in the Hazara campaign on the North-West Frontier in 1888.

The two officers commissioned from the ranks who were not appointed as Quartermasters were Captain L.K.V. Brown and Lieutenant J. Barnwell. Of these two, Barnwell was promoted from the ranks in early 1915 while Brown had been promoted in 1910 and was serving as a Lieutenant in the Royal Irish Regiment when war was declared and had already served with BEF before being transferred to the 5th Royal Irish. From his age on being first commissioned and the fact that he had only spent 2 years 92 days in the ranks, he has all the characteristics of a 'gentleman ranker', not in terms of the Kiplingesque definition of a soldier from the upper class serving in the ranks because of some form of disgrace, but rather in terms of having insufficient funds or ability to gain a commission by more common routes. Barnwell, on the other hand, had spent almost 13 years in the ranks, including 37 days as a Warrant Officer Second Class and it is likely that this is the first instance in the division of what would become an increasingly common phenomenon during the war, of promoting officers from the ranks to fill combatant posts. According to Otley, 41% of officers commissioned during the period 1914–18, excluding Quartermasters and Riding Masters, were commissioned from the ranks.[53]

Besides the commissioning of former or serving members of an

OTC, the most common method of obtaining a commission in both divisions was by direct commissioning into a battalion. This method accounted for about 21% of the division's regimental officers in the Irish battalions and 38% in the English and Welsh battalions of the 13th Division. This group however was not totally devoid of military experience and indeed some had considerably more than those officers commissioned from an OTC. Table 3.7 shows the military experience of 48 officers of the 10th Division who received a direct commission:

Served in the Second Boer War	2
Formerly served in the Militia/Special Reserve/Territorial Force	5
Formerly served in a Colonial Force	3
Serving District Inspectors, Royal Irish Constabulary[54]	8
Member of the Ulster Volunteer Force	2
Member of the Irish National Volunteers	3
Ranks of a New Army Battalion	7
French Foreign Legion	1
None	17

Table 3.7: Former military experience of officers directly commissioned into battalions of the 10th (Irish) Division.[55]

The largest single group of directly commissioned officers was drawn from the District Inspectors of the Royal Irish Constabulary (R.I.C.), who brought with them not only an experience of command but also a practical knowledge of drill and musketry.

Directly commissioned officers were not against using influence to obtain their commission. From their War Office files it is apparent that at least six officers with no formal military experience used their influence to obtain a commission. Of these one was recommended by the Lord Lieutenant of Ireland, one by the brother of the officer commanding the battalion to which he had applied, one was the grandson of a Major General, one was the stepson of the commanding officer of his battalion, one used a family friendship with Colonel (later Lieutenant-General) Kiggell at the War Office, and one was recommended by the officer commanding the regimental depot. In the last case, the basis of the support was that – 'This gentleman came in with 100 Ulster Volunteers to enlist. He has commanded a company of the Ulster Volunteers for nearly 2 years'.[56]

It was not just those without military experience who sought to obtain a commission through the use of influence. John Cecil McCutcheon, who had been educated at Methodist College and Queen's University Belfast, obtained his military experience in the ranks of the Shanghai and Hong Kong Volunteer Corps, having previously served in the university's OTC. McCutcheon application for a commission was supported by a letter from His Majesty's Minister Plenipotentiary to the Republic of China.[57]

In light of this discussion, John Redmond's statement in his introduction to Cooper's account of the 10th Division at Gallipoli that 'they were a Division of the new Army entirely made up of men who had no previous military experience, and had never heard a shot fired' is patently untrue, at least in terms of the officers of the Division.[58] Putting aside the divisional and brigade staffs, who were all regular officers, at least 233 of the 348 regimental officers that accompanied the Irish battalions of the division to Gallipoli had some degree of military training, although admittedly 39% had obtained it in an OTC. In addition, almost 17% of regimental officers had actual combat experience, which because of the 2nd Boer War (1899–1902) was not confined to regular officers alone. Of the 348 regimental officers, 39 had served during the South African War, with a further eleven obtaining combat experience in other theatres of operation, mostly with the West African Frontier Force or on the North-West Frontier.

Not all combat experience had been received with British Forces. Lieutenant H.G. Montagu, an Australian serving with the 7th Royal Munster Fusiliers, had obtained his in the Turkish army.[59] Originally commissioned into the 5th (S.R.) Royal Fusiliers in 1911, Montagu left the battalion without permission to serve in the Turkish army in North Africa during the Turco-Italian war, where he was decorated, and subsequently attached to Pancaldi Military College, Constantinople. As a result of what was in fact desertion, Montagu was dismissed from the army, but due to the need for experienced officers at the beginning of the war he was reinstated. Although

Mahon recommended his dismissal for dishonouring cheques before leaving England, Montagu accompanied his battalion to Gallipoli where the unprecedented step was taken of recalling him from active service to face allegations concerning his time in Turkey, in particular, his trial for murdering a Jewish friend who was 'more than suspected of unnatural offences', visiting places of ill-repute and drug taking. Having been wounded he was sent home from Gallipoli in order that the allegation could be more fully investigated. While there is no evidence of the outcome of any investigation, Montagu's disreputable behaviour continued. A doctor of the Royal Army Medical Corps reported that 'in view of conduct of this officer in hospital continuing to be unsatisfactory, I should be glad if a decision regarding resignation of Commission might be expedited'.[60] The doctor further stated that Montagu was addicted to morphine. Montagu resigned his commission on 2 September 1916 and now being eligible for conscription, enlisted as Private H.G. Montagu in the 2/4th Oxfordshire and Buckinghamshire Light Infantry and proceeded with his battalion to France on 2 November 1916 where according to official records he was killed on 25 November.[61] His service record shows, however, that the story does not end there. In July 1919, a family friend, who had been at Montagu's wedding in October 1913, alleged to have seen him in Bournemouth with a Belgian woman but although an investigation was undertaken by military police there is no evident to suggest that the alleged sighting was ever proved.[62]

The most significant area in which the officers of both divisions differed from those of the pre-war Irish regiments is that for the majority soldiering was not their profession. Whereas the officers of the British Expeditionary Force were, in the main, either serving regular soldiers or time expired regulars recalled to the colours from the reserves, the majority of officers of the two New Army divisions were civilians with civilian occupations. Table 3.8 shows the distribution of occupations of the officers of the 10th (Irish) and 13th (Western) Divisions based on a population of 209 and 192 respectively. It is apparent from the table that the 10th Division was less dependent than the 13th on students as its main source of officers, drawing a higher proportion of officers from the professional, managerial and entrepreneurial classes and what would now be termed the public sector, the civil service, the police and education. Among the senior academics that joined the divisions was Ernest Lawrence Julian, the 34-year-old Reid Professor of Law at Trinity College Dublin and nephew of Lieutenant-General Parsons, the commanding officer of the 16th (Irish) Division. Another was Captain Clement Richard Attlee of the 6th South Lancashire Regiment, a university tutor and future Prime Minister of the United Kingdom.

	10th Div.	13th Div.
	%	%
Military (retired and serving including members of the Indian Army)	29	26
Barristers/Solicitors etc.	8	3
Accountants		1
Bank employees	2	2
Business and Manufacturing (Manager/Owner/Director)	5	2
Civil and Marine Engineers etc.	5	3
Civil Servants	4	
Clerks	4	3
Farmers/Tea Planters/Ranchers etc.	4	4
Police Officers	4	
Students	26	45
Teachers and University Lecturers	2	5
Misc.	7	6

Table 3.8: Occupations of officers of the 10th (Irish) and 13th (Western) Divisions at Gallipoli.[63]

Perhaps the most contentious characteristic of the division's officer corps is its 'Irishness'. Cooper estimated that 'in the Infantry of the Division 90% of the officers … were either Irish of Irish extraction'.[64] The difficulty presented in analysing this statement is the definition of what constitutes 'Irish or Irish extraction'. Of the regimental officers in the division, (excluding those of the 10th Hampshires) it has been possible to identify the place of birth of approximately one third, of which 67% were born in Ireland with the remainder largely being born in Great Britain or other parts of the British Empire.

For the purposes of defining the 'Irishness' of those not born on the island of Ireland – and in the absence of evidence of the birthplace of either parents or grandparents – records of family residence or education in Ireland (other than at a university) were used instead. Consequently, examination of those officers identified as being born outside Ireland revealed that 20% had either been educated or had a family residence there. When this is taken into account, the percentage of officers from the sample that could be either termed Irish or of Irish extraction rises to 74%, still significantly less than the 90% estimated by Cooper.[65]

One particular aspect which is of interest within the Irish context is that of religion. Analysis of 107 officers whose religion can be determined shows an approximate 1:3 ratio of Roman Catholics to Protestants.[66] However, if the analysis is confined to birth or education in Ireland, the ratio is reduced to nearer 1:2. Although the importance of religion may be viewed only as an Irish phenomenon (officers unlike enlisted men were not asked their religion), it is interesting to note that Lieutenant Colin Leigh Meyer, 6th Kings Own, a Jew, served under the alias of Mere.[67] However, an officer might adopt an alias for reasons other than religion as was the case with Captain Carl Herman Clare de Fallott, 6th Loyal North Lancashire Regiment, who had been born von Fallott in Silesia, Germany, before emigrating as a child to Japan and then Canada.[68]

To summarise, the officers of both the 10th and 13th Divisions were less likely to be from a military background than their pre-war counterparts and more likely to originate from a professional or entrepreneurial background in business, commerce or industry. Officers in the 10th (Irish) Division were less likely to have attended a public school than their counterparts in either a pre-war Irish regiment or the 13th Division, whose officers were twice as likely to have attended a public school as a 10th Division officer. Analysis also shows that while both divisions processed a significantly lower proportion of Sandhurst/Woolwich trained officers than pre-war battalions, the 13th Division (74%) was more dependent on past or serving members of OTCs and direct commissions as a source of officers than the 10th (Irish) Division (65%); the latter being able to obtain almost double the percentage of officers trained at Sandhurst, Woolwich or from reserve units. The evidence also suggests that as 45% of the officers of the 13th (Western) Division gave their profession on applying for a commission as 'student' compared with only 26% in the 10th (Irish) Division, the majority of men of the latter division were of more mature years and already involved in the professions, business, commerce and industry.

Of John Redmond's assertion that the 10th (Irish) Division was 'entirely made up of men who had no previous military experience and had never heard a shot fired', the evidence suggests that in terms of the officers of the division this was untrue. Approximately two-thirds of the division's officers had received some form of military training prior to the commencement of hostilities of which some 17% had combat experience. Likewise Cooper's claim that 90% of the division's officers were either born in Ireland or of Irish descent is not supported by the evidence although a significantly higher proportion are of Irish birth or descent than their pre-war counterparts in Irish regiments. In terms of religion, the original officers of the 10th (Irish) Division were, even before the relative proportion of Catholics to Protestants in Ireland is taken into account, overwhelmingly Protestant. This may be because of the officers of the division who were born in Ireland Protestants were almost four times more likely to have OTC experience or attended a Public School than their Catholic counterparts; indeed, all the Catholics born in Ireland commissioned into battalions of the division who had OTC experience had attended a school outside Ireland.

CHAPTER 4

Preparing for Battle

On its formation the 10th Division was organised into three infantry brigades each of four battalions, to which was later added a divisional pioneer battalion. Originally the three brigades of the division, numbered 29 to 31, were formed from the senior service battalions of the eight Irish line infantry regiments. Initially, the 29th Brigade was formed from regiments from all four provinces of Ireland, while the 30th and 31st brigades comprised service battalions from fusilier regiments recruiting in the south of Ireland and Ulster respectively. In June 1915 the 5th Royal Irish Regiment became the divisional pioneer battalion and was replaced in the 29th Brigade by the 10th Hampshire Regiment. Divisional pioneer battalions were created as a response to the need for increased labour arising from the static nature of trench warfare.[1] Designed to be equipped and trained as conventional infantry, pioneer battalions received addition training and equipment to enable them to provide 'organised and intelligent labour' for engineering operations.[2]

Due to its turbulent history, Ireland, and in particular the southern counties, had at the beginning of the war not only the depots of the Irish line regiments but also proportionately more military accommodation than the rest of the United Kingdom including the headquarters of the Irish Command at the Curragh, the largest army camp in the United Kingdom after Aldershot. Dublin alone had the Richmond, Portobello, Wellington, Marlborough, Royal and Beggars

Bush Barracks. As a consequence, the men of the new division could all be housed in military accommodation rather than billeted with local civilians or under canvas as many of their counterparts in other new army divisions were. Nevertheless, not even Ireland possessed sufficient facilities to accommodate a complete division at a single location and as a result elements of the division were scattered across a wide area. The raising of the 16th (Irish) Division in October 1914 led to many battalions of the 10th Division moving accommodation more than once. During a six-month period the 5th Connaught Rangers moved three times before eventually moving with the rest of the division in April 1915 to complete its training at Basingstoke in Hampshire, while the men of the 6th Leinster Regiment experienced a similar number of moves during the same period.[3]

The same Army Order that had authorised the raising of the first six New Army divisions also provided a six-month syllabus for their training.[4] The syllabus provided a timetable for recruit training to be completed within three months, followed by five weeks of company training on the completion of which battalion and brigade training would take place. The training programme, however, did not specify the nature of any company, battalion or brigade training and only allowed for a week's divisional training at the end of the period.

Infantry training under the syllabus was forty-eight hours per week spread over six days, excluding breaks for meals, and after the first week's training this was to be supplemented by lectures on a range of subjects from 7 p.m. to 8 p.m. each evening. These lectures were to include such subjects as discipline, sanitation, health, history of the war, the organisation of the British Expeditionary Force (BEF) and the characteristics of enemy and allied armies.

Delivery of the programme within the prescribed timeframe, however, was heavily dependent on the availability of resources, especially training facilities, equipment, and manpower. The availability of both officers and men in the division had fallen behind that of other K1 divisions, with the initial exception of the 12th Division whose recruiting area in rural England gave rise to slow recruitment until after harvesting was completed. Even when the returns of 19 September 1914 show that practically all of the battalions of the division were up to strength, men were being diverted to form cadres for new battalions being raised to form the 16th (Irish) Division. According to Jourdain, commanding officer of the 5th Connaught Rangers, on 21 September 1914, 260 NCOs and men were transferred to the newly formed 6th battalion.[5] Similar transfers of men were also experienced by other battalions. The regimental historian of the Leinster Regiment stated that 'at the beginning of October 1914, when 6th battalion left the Old Barracks, Fermoy, for the Curragh, 67 non-commissioned officers and men were left behind and sent to the New Barracks, Fermoy, to form the nucleus of 7th battalion'.[6] For many battalions, particularly the 6th Royal Irish Fusiliers who on 5 September had only 8 officers and 39 other ranks, training could not commence to any real degree until they were brought up to full strength in mid-September and even then, this was hindered by the availability of trained officers and NCOs to provide instruction.

Although battalions joining the BEF were required to leave fifteen NCOs and other ranks at the depot to help train new recruits, this proved totally insufficient to provide training for reinforcements and New Army divisions. As a result, retired officers and men were recruited to make up deficiencies, not always successfully. Lieutenant Verschoyle, 5th Royal Inniskilling Fusiliers, records of his early experiences with his battalion that 'much drill was carried out on the barrack square (one extremely dug-out major to whom the new platoon drill was wholly novel and read his commands from a drill book held under his nose)'.[7] Retired NCOs such as Daniel McKeown of Forfar Street, Belfast, reenlisted in their former regiments and supplemented the meagre training cadre provided by those serving NCOs retained at the depot. McKeown, who had retired from the Royal Irish Fusiliers in 1910, after 21 years' service, enlisted in September 1914 in the 5th Royal Irish Fusiliers, as a private but was immediately reinstated to his former rank of sergeant. Aged 45 McKeown accompanied the battalion to Gallipoli with the rank of acting Company Quartermaster Sergeant.[8]

Former soldiers returning from civilian life also provided specialist training. Drury, 6th Royal Irish Rifles, recalled in his diary, 'I found Company Sergeant Major Murphy a very smart NCO and a very good athlete. He had been lately in charge of gym and sports at some school near London. I had many bouts at bayonet fighting with him and also with the gloves in the Gym'.[9] Such NCOs/instructors as could not be found from reservist, regular battalions or 'dug-outs' had to be found from the recruits themselves. While the 6th Royal Irish Rifles were fortunate enough to have CSM Murphy as a physical training instructor, other battalions were not so fortunate. Private Battersby, 6th Royal Inniskilling Fusiliers, remembered how:

> We had no PT instructors and as a result anyone who knew anything about PT were asked to report to the only PT instructor in the battalion. Two men from London were among those who went forward for the test, their names Rinaldi and Marshal, both were in our barrack room, both passed, both had lance stripes.[10]

Selection by test was not the only way of obtaining promotion as self-selection appears to have worked equally as well:

> Rinaldi and Marshal almost ran to Quartermaster Stubbs for their stripes and in the barracks crowed to Downing about how good they were. Downing a clerk from London was mad; he … left the room and quarter of an half later was back with a lance stripe on his arm; he had been to Quartermaster Stubbs, told him he was as good, even better than Rinaldi and Marshal, so Stubbs said if he felt like that, take a stripe from out of the box, I'll have you in orders tonight.[11]

Some recruits received promotion as a result of their civilian trade. Private Evans, of the same platoon as Rinaldi and Marshal, was a tailor by trade and was put in the tailor's shop and, as the battalion was issued with parts of old uniforms, altered them to fit their new owners. After they had been promoted to corporals Evans confided to Battersby:

> You watch their faces tomorrow, the Colonel was in the shop today and said he was pleased with the alterations

I had made to his uniform and he called me sergeant,
I told him I was only a private. 'Nonsense,' he said
'Master Tailor is always a sergeant; I'll have you in
orders tonight.'[12]

Promotion in other units could be even more unorthodox, indeed
unmilitary. In the 7th Royal Dublin Fusiliers the men of "D"
company were not only allowed to elect their own NCOs but also
their officers.[13]

In most cases uniforms and equipment took longer to provide,
despite Colonel Jourdain's claim that because there was less
pressure on existing stores in Ireland the 5th Connaught Rangers
received service dress within a few days of their formation in
August 1914.[14] This was not the universal experience of battalions
of the division. Private Battersby's description of receiving pieces
of uniform by stages is more typical of the experience of other New
Army battalions. Simpson in his account of the raising of the new
armies recorded that:

> In the period before the woollen industry was capable of
> clothing the crowds of volunteers in khaki, recruits either
> had to remain in civilian garb or accept a substitute. ...
> The use of obsolete scarlet uniforms assisted marginally
> but the principal stop-gap was 'Kitchener Blue', which
> Kipling was moved to denounce as 'indescribable...
> blue slops', devoid even of brass buttons.[15]

In his diary Battersby records how he reported to join the Duke of
Cornwall's Light Infantry on 7 September 1914 but found himself
with many of his fellow recruits two weeks later in Dublin as members
of the 6th Royal Inniskilling Fusiliers, 'still dressed in civilian clothes
and a more bedraggled mob could never be seen anywhere else, we
were wet and covered in slow drying salt'.[16] This condition was not
immediately improved by joining their new battalion although as
time passed they were issued with parts of old uniforms until:

a month later or thereabouts we were all issued with blue fatigue uniforms which took the place of our non-descript mixture of khaki and civilian clothes, [Private] Fell for instance, a tall thin round shouldered man wore a straw hat that was green with age, so some uniformity became necessary.

It was not until after Christmas, however, that the battalion received new uniforms, cap badges, numerals and so on.[17] Battersby's unit may just have been unfortunate in its allocation of uniforms as both the 7th Royal Dublin Fusiliers and the 6th Leinster Regiment record receiving their uniforms in late September and early October respectively, although the regimental historian of the latter lamented that only one suit was issued and 'that a soaking in the morning meant the remainder of the day with no dry change'.[18]

Captain (later Major) Godfrey Drage noted the enthusiasm of the men of the 7th Royal Munster Fusiliers who, in common with most Kitchener volunteers, were anxious to get at the enemy:

Most of the men had enlisted thinking they were going to be given a rifle, a bag of cartridges and sent off to Belgium to take pot-shots at the Kaiser. Instead they found themselves doing close order drill on the parade ground, varied by route marches to harden their feet, and they didn't like it.[19]

Captain David Campbell, 6th Royal Irish Rifles recalled that:

We worked pretty hard in those early days. It was a case of physical jerks every morning from 7 to 8, parades 8.30 to 12.30 and 2 to 5, lectures in the evenings, route marches, sham battles, night operations ... there was no respite.[20]

It was not only the other ranks that required to be trained. According to Brigadier F.F. Hill, commander of the 31st Brigade:

Nearly all the officers except the actual staffs had no previous military experience beyond that obtained at OTCs and of the Captains a few were posted from the Indian Army, others from Reserve of Officers and the Special Reserve. Many had not been employed for years. The NCOs were all from the retired ranks and Army Reserve and of these there were few; others had to be trained with the men.[21]

Some officers such as David Campbell were complete novices to military drill and when this was discovered one of the instructors took him to a remote corner of the camp to take him through the rudiments of drill without the need to cause him any embarrassment.[22] Despite his own lack of experience, Campbell was placed in charge of a platoon, which he was expected to lead:

> At 7 a.m. on my first morning, I found myself standing in front of a platoon of about seventy men. To say I was a bit scared is to put it mildly. As a matter of fact I was scared stiff. That first parade consisted of company drill and doubling around the barrack square and as I got warmed up, I lost my nervousness. I learned the words of command quickly enough and before very long I could handle my men with the confidence of an old hand.[23]

It was not just their men that the newly-appointed officer had to impress as they also had to win the trust of their fellow officers and their superiors:

> We newly appointed, temporary officers took our work very seriously. We were keen to win our spurs, as it were, keen to prove ourselves and win the confidence of our seniors. And by all accounts, we made marvellous progress. When we were not attending lectures, many of us would spend our off hours in our rooms, where the Manual of Infantry Training and the Manual of Field Service Regulations, became our constant companions.[24]

Not all young officers took such a professional approach to their new profession. Second Lieutenant G.F. MacNie, 6th Royal Dublin Fusiliers, in January 1915 was tried and acquitted by General Court Martial for drunkenness, prior to which Mahon had recommended his dismissal from the service. MacNie was killed in action on 4 Sept 1916, having never received any promotion.[25]

Although most barracks in Ireland provided the division with good accommodation, the training facilities of some, however, were less adequate due to their size or location. While the Curragh possessed all the training facilities necessary to provide the full range of training, it was not so at other barracks. As a consequence many units had to relocate on a number of occasions to obtain access to such facilities.[26] Hill wrote of the facilities provided for his brigade that:

> My Brigade formed and trained in Dublin and Basingstoke. No training facilities at either place. Except for the Barrack Square and Phoenix Park we had to beg, borrow and steal. The Rifle Range was constructed across Dollymount Golf Course ... We only had 200 latest pattern rifles per battalion. And were not fully armed until April 1915 nor fully equipped until June 1915 after two other sets had been supplied.[27]

In the meantime, the infantry had to make do with whatever weapons and equipment was available. In the absence of the standard infantry rifle, Mark III Short Magazine Lee Enfield, different marks pre-dating the Mark III's introduction in 1907, were provided, while Battersby noted that his battalion initially were issued with pre-Boer War Lee-Metford rifles.[28]

By the end of 1914 officers and men moved on from the basics of recruit and company training to the intricacies of battalion and higher formation training designed to reflect the change from open warfare to the trench warfare of the Western Front.

> It gradually became clear that the experience of South Africa and Manchuria had not fully enlightened us as to the power of modern heavy artillery and high explosives

and that many established tactical methods would have to be varied. We learnt to dig trenches behind the crest of a hill instead of on top of it; to seek for cover from observation rather than a good field of fire; to dread damp trenches more than hostile bullets.[29]

These changes were reflected in the training of the division. Hanna recorded that 'for training in attack and defence from trenches they [the 7th Royal Dublin Fusiliers] were taken to a set of model trenches which had been made by the engineers about two miles from the barracks, and here they had frequent practice which must have been of great service to them in the following year at Suvla Bay'.[30] Throughout February training concentrated on brigade field days, route marches, and night operations, which led to the introduction of combined operations with other arms from the division and the involvement of two reserve regiments of cavalry stationed at the Curragh.[31] Brigade field days did not impress Major Drage, however:

> Presently we were doing field days and a pretty mess was made of them. The men in the ranks weren't so bad but the NCOs were useless and we couldn't start to train them until the subalterns had learnt a little of their job and there weren't enough experienced officers to train the subalterns. However the Brigade Major [Captain E.C. Alexander] knew his stuff alright and knew how to stick to essentials in his instructions and bit by bit things began to improve.[32]

Other officers such as Noel Drury, an officer of the same brigade but from a different regiment, give a contrasting view of these field days, and their usefulness, although he appears to agree with Drage on the competence of the Brigade Major:

> Brigade field days were great fun as the men and junior officers had not much to do, these being excursions being intended more for staff training. Our Brigade Major Alexander was a very stern, harsh sort of man but

knew his work from end to end and I always enjoyed
his lectures very much and I learned a lot about outpost
duties, flank and rere [sic] guards, etc.[33]

Verschoyle of the 5th Royal Inniskilling Fusiliers appears to concur
with Drury as to the usefulness of brigade field days at this stage
of their training, 'since like ourselves, the staff were learning their
job, brigade exercises often involved over much sitting about, rather
than fighting. Of one such occasion I note in my diary: "personally
lunched and tea'd in the house [of a friend]; spent most of the time
drinking sloe-gin"'.[34]

Following recruit training many of the best men from each
battalion were selected for additional training as specialists to
serve with regimental transport, the machine gun section, and as
signallers. Cooper implies that this took place around mid-April
1915 but as this was only two weeks before the division's move to
England to complete their training it is unlikely. More likely the
selection of specialists to undertake these roles commenced at the
beginning of December 1914, which is when the 7th Royal Dublin
Fusiliers' machine gun section was formed.[35] In a letter to his father
and dated 27 March 1915 Lieutenant James Pollock, 6th Royal Irish
Rifles, regretted 'the reason I could not get home this week end was
the training of the [machine] gun sections'.[36] Certainly Noel Drury,
battalion signals officer for the 6th Royal Dublin Fusiliers, had time
to include a two-week signals course with the other battalion signals
officers before leaving for England. In his diary he states that 'a few
weeks before [the move to England], it had been decided that there
was no need after all to keep the signal officers away from their
platoons, so I was sent back to C. Coy'.[37] The implication of this is
that specialist sections were being formed and training commenced
before mid-April.

Following a review by Sir Bryan Mahon, the division left
for England at the beginning of May 1915 and final training at
Basingstoke, Hampshire. According to Drury the training in England
at first consisted of route marches intended to accustom the men to
the hot damp climate and rough roads of the area but soon progressed

to manoeuvres against other New Army divisions.[38] Ominously, in the light of subsequent events at Gallipoli, Drury recorded another route march when 'we marched there in four hours, starting at 5.30 a.m. to avoid the hot sun'.[39]

The brigade level training in Ireland was replaced by divisional training in the area surrounding Basingstoke. According to Campbell, the division left camp every Tuesday on

> a route march of 15 or 20 miles and then bivouacked for the night in the shelter of a hedge or bank if one was available. Reveille at dawn and breakfast cooked in the open, we spent the day doing an attack or some other stunt and camping again where the battle ended. On the third day we marched home again to our tents, having covered 50 or 60 miles in the three days. This sort of programme was carried out week after week. ... The exercises were for the purpose of training the Divisional staffs but we poor foot-sloggers suffered all the hardships.[40]

Cooper agrees with Campbell's assessment of the usefulness of this type of training to the men:

> These operations were of great value to the staff, and also to the transport, who learned from them how difficulties which appeared insignificant on paper became of paramount importance in practice. The individual officer or man, on the other hand, gained little military experience, since as a rule the whole time was occupied by long hot dusty marches between the choking overhanging hedges of a stony Hampshire lane.[41]

Although the division had completed the prescribed training programme in Ireland, an inspection by the staff of the Aldershot Training Centre found its training deficient in a number of areas, including the skills involved in bombing.[42] Bombing training was undertaken on Lord Curzon's estate at Hackwood Park, but as no proper grenades were available, home-made bombs were made out of jam and milk tins filled with nails. According to Drury, it was a wonder they were not blown up by these makeshift bombs. Similar views were expressed by Drage:

> I stood down in a trench and threw it as far as I could and most of the contents came whistling back and hit the bank behind my head. If I couldn't toss the infernal machine a safe distance I knew that no one else in my company could, and so I called the practice off.[43]

Prior to embarkation on active service, the division weeded out over a thousand men who were considered too old or infirm to stand the strain of active service and these men were transferred to reserve battalions of their regiment.[44] There appears to be some confusion as to when this weeding out took place. Cooper implies that it took place prior to the division's move to England, but it is more likely to have taken place in mid-June when Jourdain records the arrival of a draft of seventy-two from the 7th Royal Inniskilling Fusiliers to bring his battalion, the 5th Connaught Rangers, up to strength.[45] On 12 June the 6th Royal Irish Rifles received 120 men to bring it up to war strength, 'the new draft are all Irish Fusiliers from the 16 Division'.[46] It was also about this time that John Redmond, the leader of the Irish Parliamentary Party in the House of Commons, became aware of the source of these drafts to the division, the under-strength battalions of the 49th Brigade of the 16th (Irish) Division and immediately protested to Augustine Birrell, Chief Secretary for Ireland. In response to his protest Redmond received a letter from the War Office stating that:

> Only 1,200 men are needed, and if Ireland finds itself unable to fill up their vacancies – which seems incredible in view of the large number of men of recruitable age in Ireland – steps will be taken to bring up the depleted battalions to strength.[47]

According to Gwynn, every man in the four battalions of the 49th Brigade had, in fact, volunteered for the 10th Division when it was known to be preparing for immediate service abroad as an impression had been growing for several months in the 16th Division that it might be permanently retained in Ireland as a unit for supplying reserves.[48] In fact the 16th Division did not proceed overseas until December 1915 and was not joined by the 49th Brigade until February 1916.

On 28 May the whole division with the exception of the 31st Brigade was inspected by King George V at Hackwood Park, Hampshire. This was followed on 1 June by an inspection by Field Marshal Lord Kitchener who had been unable to accompany the King at the earlier inspection. In the last week of June the division received orders to prepare for active service in the Dardanelles.[49] As a result of these orders, the divisional cavalry squadron from the South Irish Horse and the division's heavy artillery battery were transferred to other divisions destined for France, presumably because the terrain at Gallipoli was unsuitable for their deployment. For similar reasons divisional and regimental transport, together with officers' chargers, were ordered to remain at Basingstoke. Apparently, however, junior officers were not privy to their destination as Pollock informed his father that 'by the time you get this we will be on the sea, which part of the sea I don't know, all we know is that we leave here at 9pm to night for somewhere or other, place unknown'.[50]

Due to the size of the division, brigades and even battalions were split for transportation purposes across a number of ships, which departed in the second week of July from a number of ports on the south coast of England. Sergeant John Hargrave of the division's 32nd Field Ambulance records, perhaps in the light of subsequent events, in the second of his books on his Gallipoli experiences that:

> As our troopship [the White Star's S.S. *Canada*] sidled away from the quay, the fife band of the Irish Fusiliers shrilled 'The wearin' o' the Green', thinly, wildly, sadly, with such a high, windy whistling that when they puffed the last wry-necked squeal of ear-piercing melancholy … before a month was out there was no fife band. It had perished to a man at Suvla Bay.[51]

CHAPTER 5

Gallipoli and After

On 29 October 1914 ships of the Turkish navy raided the Russian ports of Sevastopol and Odessa so entering the war on the side of the Central Powers, causing the United Kingdom and France to follow Russia's lead and declare war on Turkey on 5 November. Even before this, however, on 3 November the Royal Navy had opened fire on the outer fortifications of the Dardanelles, although no attempt was made to force the straits at this time. Fears that the Turks would seize the strategically important Suez Canal led to the build-up of British forces in Egypt including newly raised units from Australia and New Zealand en route for England.

In January 1915 Vice Admiral Sackville Carden, commanding a squadron in the eastern Mediterranean, submitted a plan to force the Dardanelles which involved the destruction of the straits' defences and the clearance of minefields before pushing through to Constantinople.[1] Carden's plan envisaged a naval operation, without any support from the army, and as there was no likelihood of troops being available for several months, permission was given for a naval bombardment of the fortifications at the mouth of the Dardanelles commencing on 15 February. Nevertheless, general opinion in the Admiralty appeared to be that the navy would be unable to force the Dardanelles without the support of the army.[2] On 10 March Kitchener announced that he intended to send the 29th Division to join the British and French forces gathering in the eastern

Mediterranean and two days later he appointed General Sir Ian Hamilton, his former chief of staff during the Boer War, as General Officer Commanding what was now designated the Mediterranean Expeditionary Force (MEF).

Any hopes that the Dardanelles might be forced by the navy alone, however, were ended on 18 March when the fleet suffered a major setback while attempting to silence the forts at the Narrows and the batteries protecting the Kephez minefields. During this operation three battleships of the Anglo-French fleet were sunk and three more so badly damaged as to need major repairs. Having viewed the latter stages of the naval action, Hamilton was forced to admit that the Dardanelles could not be forced without the aid of the army and not in the subsidiary role anticipated, but rather as a 'deliberate and progressive military operation carried out at full strength so as to open a passage for the Navy'.[3] As a consequence, on 25 April 1915 the allies launched a combined attack on the Turkish coast with British forces landing on the Gallipoli peninsula while the French undertook a diversionary landing on the Asiatic side of the Narrows at Kum Kale. At dawn the British 29th Division supported by detachments of the Anson Battalion of the Royal Naval Division, attempted to land, with varying success, on five beaches at Cape Helles, while the 1st Australian Division was landed at Ari Burnu (Anzac Cove) over a mile from their intended landing place, on the west shore of the peninsula. By the end of the day, with the exception of the French diversionary attack at Kum Kale, none of the allied landings had achieved their objectives. During the next three months the line at Helles advanced no more than two miles from the landing beaches while the front held by the Australian and New Zealand Army Corps (ANZAC) was confined to a radius of little more than 1,000 yards of Anzac Cove.

It was within the context of this prevailing stalemate that, after nine months training for trench warfare on the Western Front, the 10th (Irish) Division together with two other Kitchener divisions, the 11th (Northern) and 13th (Western), was sent to reinforce Sir Ian Hamilton's Mediterranean Expeditionary Force (MEF) at Gallipoli. The new IX Corps, under the command of Sir Frederick Stopford, a 61-year-old lieutenant-general with no previous senior command experience, was vital to Hamilton's plan for an August offensive. With the additional manpower provided by the new corps Hamilton planned an offensive on three fronts –

1. A holding action at Helles to pin down as many Turks as possible;
2. The capture and retention of Suvla Bay as an advanced base; and
3. A breakout from the Anzac sector to push the Turks off Koja Chemen Tepe and open a way to Maidos on the east coast of the peninsula and inside the Narrows.[4]

Of the three objectives, the breakout from Anzac was deemed the most important and although the 13th Division and 10th Division's 29th Brigade were landed at Anzac to support this advance, the main role of Stopford's IX Corps was the capture and retention of a base at Suvla. In the original orders from GHQ, Stopford stated that the Corps' first task was the capture of the two horns of the bay, Chocolate and W Hills, to be captured before daylight to prevent the artillery emplacements sited there being used against the troops in action on Hill 305, and obtain a foothold along Tekke Tepe ridge. It was hoped that as reinforcements arrived on 7 August they would push up the eastern spur of Hill 305 to assist Birdwood's attack from Anzac.[5] Clarification of Stopford's orders from GHQ on 29 July stated that 'your primary objective will be to secure Suvla Bay as a base for all forces operating in the northern zone', a priority reflected in the operational orders drafted by Stopford for approval by Hamilton.[6] Under Stopford's plan, Major-General Hammersley's 11th Division, was to land at three beaches during the night of 6/7 August. 'A' beach, where the division's 34th Brigade was to land, was inside Suvla Bay itself, while the landing sites of the 32nd and 33rd Brigades, were 'C' beach immediately south of Nibrunesi Point (the southern extremity of the bay) and 'B' beach further south. Following the landing, the division was intended to move 'as rapidly as possible on the enemy positions at Yilghin Burnu and Ismail Oglu Tepe and at the same time to secure the high ground at Karakol

Dagh'.[7] While the landings at 'B' and 'C' were initially unopposed, by the time the first of the 10th Division's units (the 31st Brigade under Brigadier-General F.F. Hill) arrived at dawn on 7 August, 11th Division had failed to achieve any of its objectives.[8]

At 'A' beach, the 34th Brigade had been unable to land at all because while approaching the beach the leading lighters carrying two of its four battalions ran aground some 100 yards from the beach in five feet of water, and the men in the lighters came under sustained fire from the shore.[9] Although the brigade was eventually landed south of the Cut, a narrow channel connecting the Salt Lake with the sea, it was decided to abandon any further landings on 'A' beach. As a consequence Stopford's plan to land two brigades of the 10th Division to capture Kiretch Tepe Sirt which overlooked Suvla Bay was also abandoned.[10]

At dawn on 7 August, Brigadier-General Hill and six battalions from two brigades of the division arrived from Mitylene at Suvla Bay 'with no orders or instructions of any kind'.[11] Having sought orders from Stopford, Hill was placed under the command of Major-General Hammersley (11th Division) and began disembarking his force at 'C' beach. By this time, however, Mahon had arrived and an alternative to 'A' beach, at Ghazi Baba, had been found from which to attack along the Kiretch Tepe Sirt, although by now Mahon had only two battalions of the Royal Munster Fusiliers and the divisional pioneer battalion to achieve an objective originally assigned to two brigades.

At 06.30 Hill landed 200 yards south of Nibrunesi Point and began to disembark his troops. Contacting Hammersley at his divisional headquarters, he was ordered to 'move out via north side of Salt Lake and deliver an attack on Yilghin Burnu (Chocolate Hills), Heights 53 and 50, my right [flank] to rest on the Salt Lake'.[12] This attack was to be undertaken in conjunction with Sitwell's 32nd and Haggard's 34th Brigade, which were to operate on Hill's left flank towards Ismail Oglu Tepe.[13] Haggard and Sitwell refused to co-operate, however, the latter on the grounds that the orders he had received differed from those of Hill and 'that his battns had already suffered very heavily during the night; in short, he could not undertake another operation'.[14] Not until late afternoon, and confirmation of his change of orders by one of Hammersley's staff officers, was Sitwell finally persuaded to support Hill's three advancing battalions which by now had rounded the northern edge of the lake and were coming under enemy fire on their exposed left flank.[15] Following a short naval bombardment at 5.15 p.m. the Irish, now supported by battalions of the Lincolnshire and Border Regiments, renewed their attack and, as night set in, Chocolate and Green Hills were in the hands of the attackers.[16]

While Hill was attacking Chocolate Hill south of the Salt Lake, a viable alternative to 'A' beach had been found and Mahon with the equivalent of a brigade had landed and was advancing up Kiretch Tepe Sirt to the north of the lake. The 6th Royal Munster Fusiliers passed through the 11th Manchester Regiment belonging to the 11th Division on the ridge at about 2.00 p.m. but were 'stopped by some well-sited and perfectly concealed Turkish trenches and – at about four hundred yards range – we [7th Royal Munster Fusiliers] were held up too'.[17] Although GHQ believed the ridge was only held by three companies of the *Gallipoli Gendarmerie* (approximately 350 men), the Manchester Regiment had lost 15 officers and between 250 and 300 men by the time it was relieved by the 5th Inniskillings at about 10 p.m.[18] Herbert Goodland, a Staff Captain attached to the 30th Brigade, however, questioned whether the brigade was actually facing the irregular troops they were told to expect: after examining the bodies of two Turkish soldiers on the beach, he formed the opinion from their uniforms and equipment that 'they were men of a regular Turkish Regiment, but what they were doing at that spot, when only Gendarmerie and armed peasants were supposed to be defending that section, I do not know'.[19]

Despite a description in the Royal Munster Fusiliers' regimental history of the an attack on Kiretch Tepe Sirt on 8 August, that day all across the Suvla front was a day of inactivity, which Aspinall-Oglander later described as 'a wasted day at Suvla'.[20] On 9 August Mahon renewed his attack on Kiretch Tepe Sirt. At 8.00 p.m. on 8 August Brigadier-General L.L. Nicol, of the 30th Brigade, 'received an order from the IX Corps that I was to continue the advance along the Ridge the following day' followed at mid-night by a further order 'that the reinforcements would be 2 battalions and one mountain battery (no mention of their titles) and that Gen. Mahon would arrive at my headquarters at 6 a.m. 9th to make final plans'.[21]

At 7.30 a.m. a general advance commenced along the ridge with the 7th Munster Fusiliers on the right, their line being extended onto the plain by the 5th Dorsets, the 6th Munster Fusiliers in the centre and the 5th Inniskilling Fusiliers on the left flank on the northern slopes of the ridge nearest the sea. The attack was supported by naval gunfire from the destroyers *HMS Foxhound* and *HMS Beagle*. Due, however, to the flat trajectory of naval guns their support was of little assistance to those units on the right of the line. Initially the attack progressed satisfactorily but, due to the nature of the terrain and stiffening resistance, cohesion between and within battalions began to be lost.

On the right flank the 7th Munster Fusiliers found that the broken nature of the ground had allowed parties of Turkish troops to occupy positions in their rear from which they were able to fire at the advancing British line.[22] The 7th Munsters' advance was further disrupted by the arrival of the 5th Dorset Regiment crossing the battalion's right flank and 'firing heavily across us, if not over us'.[23] This had the effect of pushing a second battalion into an already limited frontage thus disrupting further the cohesion of that battalion and pushing it away from its original objective as it tried to redress its line. Drage recalled 'it bad been hard enough to keep in touch as it was and a change in direction made matters hopeless. From that point on the four companies fought on their own.'[24]

In the centre and on the left flank, the 6th Munster and the 5th Inniskilling Fusiliers were, with the support of naval gunfire, able to make better progress. Led by Major J.N. Jephson, late of the 5th Bengal Light Infantry, the 6th Munsters carried a small post (subsequently known as Jephson's post) near the south-western end of the high crest where they preceded to dig-in. About 4 p.m. the attack had fizzled out and the 6th Munsters and 5th Inniskillings entrenched a new line, having gained about 800 yards. Because of the heavy fighting they had been involved in, the 5th Dorsets and the 7th Munsters (the latter having fought all day without water in their water bottles) were withdrawn to the old front line.[25]

While the troops under Nicol's command were attacking along

Kiretch Tepe Sirt, two of the battalions under Brigadier-General Hill were involved in an attack on the high ground behind Anafarta Saga. To assist the attack by the 11th Division and part of the newly landed 53rd (Welsh) Division (T.F.), Hill placed the 6th Royal Irish Fusiliers and the 6th Royal Dublin Fusiliers, two battalions which had suffered the least casualties in the attack on Chocolate Hill, under the command of Brigadier-General Maxwell of the 33rd Brigade. Initially, these battalions were to remain in reserve near Chocolate Hill while their machine gun detachments, escorted by a company of the Dublin Fusiliers, was to advance and give support to the right flank of the attack. Maxwell's orders were, however, predicated on a belief that British forces still held Scimitar Hill which due to a mix-up in orders had been evacuated during the night. As a consequence, soon after 5.00 a.m. Maxwell received an urgent request for reinforcements from the 6th Lincolnshire Regiment, to which he responded by sending three companies of the 6th Dublin Fusiliers, later followed by the 6th Irish Fusiliers to Scimitar Hill.[26]

The Dublin Fusiliers took over part of the line from the Lincolnshire Regiment about 6.00 a.m. but found themselves under fire not only from their front but also from behind by Turkish snipers in the brush through which they had just passed. Even battalion headquarters came under fire from the Turks as did the battalion's advance dressing station where the wounded were being treated. At 09.00, in the absence of orders from Maxwell, Lieutenant-Colonel Cox, 6th Dublin Fusiliers, ordered his reserve company up the hill to assist the 6th Border Regiment. His whole battalion now committed to the attack, Cox moved his battalion headquarters nearer the front line. By this time the Dublin Fusiliers had replaced the Lincolnshire Regiment in the attack as some members of that regiment had broken under pressure.[27]

Most of the line facing Scimitar Hill was now being held by the two Irish battalions but soon after 11 a.m. reinforcements arrived in the form of two companies of the 2/4th Queen's Royal West Surrey Regiment, a second-line Territorial Force battalion of the 53rd Division. Having still received no orders from Maxwell, Cox joined his men in the front line where he found groups of stragglers from the Lincolns and Border Regiment taking cover or attempting to make their way out of the line. About noon a heavy bombardment began with shells falling on the crest of the hill which caused the West Surreys to bolt, leaving 'B' company, 6th Royal Dublin Fusiliers, with only a handful of men to cover this section of the trench. At 1 p.m., having failed to get more reinforcements to cover his left flank which looked like it was about to give way, and with no chance of any further advance, Cox took the decision to withdraw to an old Turkish trench 300 yards from the crest of the hill, where the line was re-established with the 6th Royal Irish Fusiliers on their right flank and the Queen's Royal West Surreys on their left. During the day's action the 6th Royal Dublin Fusiliers suffered 11 officer and 259 other rank casualties in the three companies engaged.[28]

Meanwhile the troops on Kiretch Tepe suffered greatly from lack of hand grenades, none of which were available on the ridge between the time of their landing and 16 August.[29] However, in response to a threat from artillery being moved to where it could enfilade Jephson's Post, on 11 August the 6th Royal Munster Fusiliers carried out a dawn raid using grenades improvised from jam tins.The raid was a success, although 'at close quarters the Turks caused many casualties by their bombs', and the Munsters drove the enemy out of their position while inflicting considerable casualties.[30]

Following the abortive attack on Scimitar Hill, the English battalions attached to Nicol's brigade were replaced by Hill's troops from Chocolate Hill in preparation for a major assault to clear the Turkish positions on Kiretch Tepe ridge, thus bringing the 30th and 31st Brigades under Mahon's command for the first time. At 08.40 on 15 August Mahon's two brigades received orders to prepare for an attack at 13.00 which would be supported by battalions from other divisions and naval gunfire.

The divisional plan of attack was for Nicol's 30th Brigade to advance on the left wing covering the northern slope, the seaward side, and part of the southern slope where it would join the left flank of the two battalions of the Inniskilling Fusiliers of Hill's 31st Brigade which were to advance along the southern foothills and across the plain to a spur known as Kidney Hill,their right flank being protected by the men of the 162nd Brigade of the 54th Division.[31] The two battalions of the Royal Irish Fusiliers and the 7th Royal Dublin

Fusiliers were to provide the divisional reserve.

Before this plan of attack could be put into operation, Mahon received a telegram from Hamilton's headquarters informing him that Stopford had been replaced by de Lisle as corps commander with the temporary rank of Lieutenant-General, and expressing the hope that 'you will waive your seniority and continue to command the 10th Division at any rate during present phase of operations'.[32] Mahon declined to do so and Hill assumed temporary command of the division.[33]

Following an artillery bombardment of less than half an hour the 30th and 31st Brigades commenced their advance along the ridge. On the seaward side of the ridge the 6th Munsters and the 6th Dublin Fusiliers, assisted by shell fire from *HMS Grampus*, made steady progress clearing the Turks from most of the northern slopes of the ridge by 12 p.m. On the inland slope of the ridge the 5th and 6th Inniskilling Fusiliers, supported only by a mountain battery, found that not only was their advance opposed in greater numbers but the nature of the terrain also broke up and slowed their formation. Despite a determined effort, the 31st Brigade was unable to capture Kidney Hill or the southern side of Kiretch Tepe Sirt and was ordered to withdraw.

On the seaward side of the ridge the 6th Munsters and the 6th Dublin Fusiliers, reinforced by the 7th Dublin Fusiliers, dug in, but due to the inability of those units on the landward slopes to maintain their advance, they found their right flank exposed to enfilading fire. Throughout the night of 15/16 August units on the ridge were subjected to grenade and sniper attack to which, having no grenades of their own, they had no effective response. As a consequence, the men on the ridge resorted to throwing back Turkish grenades before they exploded, and even to throwing stones at the enemy. D Company, 7th Dublin Fusiliers, even attempted to drive off the Turkish bombers by an unsuccessful bayonet charge which resulted in the death of two of the battalion's most senior officers.

Following consultation with his battalion commanders, Nicol came to the conclusion that the ridge could not be held without fresh reinforcements and ammunition, in particular bombs, which were not forthcoming. With Hill's approval therefore about 7 p.m.

the order was given for a withdrawal to the line held by the division on the morning of 15 August.[34] Although the British would occupy the Suvla sector until 19/20 December 1915, they were unable to advance the line on Kiretch Tepe Sirt beyond that held by the 10th (Irish) Division.

On the night of 5/6th August, the day before the Suvla landings the 10th Division's 29th Brigade, without any of its support units, was landed at Anzac cove under the command of Brigadier-General R.J. Cooper, a former commanding officer of the Irish Guards. According to Bryan Cooper (5th Connaught Rangers), it was not until a conference of commanding officers at Brigade Headquarters at 4.30 p.m. on 6 August that it was realised that the brigade was on its own and the whereabouts of the rest of the division unknown.[35]

Even though the brigade landed with its own commander and brigade staff, its battalions were dispersed as required across the Anzac sector. On 7 August the 6th Leinsters were detached and allotted as a general reserve to the 1st Australian Division, and while two companies supported Australian units at Courtney's and Quinn's Posts, the remaining two companies and battalion headquarters remained at the end of Shrapnel Gully until the morning of 9 August when the battalion was ordered to report to the headquarters of the New Zealand Infantry Brigade at Rhododendron Ridge, part of the Chunuk Bair range. At 7.30 p.m. while bivouacked below an area of the ridge known as the Apex, the battalion came under heavy shrapnel fire during which 2nd Lieutenant W.S.C. Griffith and eleven other ranks were killed, and a further thirty-five men wounded.[36] According to the official history, at 4.45 a.m. on 10 August dense waves of Turkish infantry swept over the crest of Chunuk Bair practically wiping out the battalion in the front line and scattering another battalion in the valley below which had been taken by surprise.

> Five minutes later the Turks had captured the Pinnacle [the top of Rhododendron Ridge] but at that point their advance was stopped by annihilating fire from machine guns at the Apex. The Leinsters were rushed into line to hold the Apex position, and this they succeeded in doing for the rest of the day.[37]

Both the Australian official history and the Leinsters' war diary give the time of the Turkish assault at about 6 a.m.; no mention is made of any earlier attack.[38] Although Cooper gives no time for the Turkish attack, he provides the additional information that when it commenced two companies of the Leinsters were already in the trenches on the Apex having relieved some New Zealanders the previous evening. Accordingly when the attack came they were reinforced by the other two companies who had been called to action by 'a New Zealander, who ran down the hill shouting, "Fix your bayonets, boys, they're coming!" whereupon the Leinsters seized their weapons and charged up the hill'.[39]

While the Leinsters were operating with the Australians and New Zealanders, the 5th Connaught Rangers were given the unpleasant task of burying the dead from the Australian attack at Lone Pine in Victoria Gully, while the brigade's other two battalions, the 10th Hampshire Regiment and the 6th Royal Irish Rifles, spent the night of 7/8 August in Rest Gully. In the early afternoon of 8 August these battalions, together with brigade headquarters, received orders to 'Make good Hill Q [Chunuk Bair the highest point on the peninsula] at dawn. Farm is already in our hands'.[40] At about 3 p.m. the brigade began an advance up the Chailak Dere, a dried river bed, where it was subjected to heavy shelling. Halting to await nightfall, the brigade resumed its advance at 9 p.m. but after about two hours the route was found to be impractical, the valley being blocked by wounded soldiers coming down the hill, and it was ordered to retrace its steps crossing to the Aghyl Dere.

At 4 a.m. on 9 August the brigade reached a point 250 yards below the Sari Bair ridge where it began to dig in until at 0800 two companies of the Hampshires attempted to climb to the summit of Chunuk Bair along the side of Rhododendron Ridge. About 100 yards from the summit, they were stopped by enemy small arms and shell fire and dug in for the rest of the day. Meanwhile the Irish Rifles and the rest of the Hampshires advanced to the edge of a flat area known as the Farm where together with brigade headquarters it joined men from the Wiltshire Regiment, Maoris and Ghurkhas.

On 10 August the British line at the Farm extended from two companies of the Hampshires on the slope of Rhododendron Ridge to the battalion's other two companies on the left of the line, with the Royal Irish Rifles in the centre flanked by one and a half companies of the 5th Wiltshires on its right and one and a half companies of the 9th Warwickshires on its left. The frontline now comprised companies from four battalions and three brigades, commanded by a general under whom none had previously served. At about 4.30 a.m. on 10 August dense waves of Turks swept over the ridge attacking the units holding the Farm and Rhododendron Ridge. Due to the nature of the struggle, it is difficult to give accurate timing for many of the events as accounts differ. On the extreme right of the line, 80 men of the 10th Hampshires and 5th Wiltshires held on until 9 a.m. when they were forced to give ground when units on Rhododendron Ridge retired.[41]

The Royal Irish Rifles on their left held out for another hour and a half before retiring. The battalion had been accompanied into the frontline by Brigadier-General Cooper and the 29th Brigade staff. Shortly after daybreak command of the British frontline had devolved on Cooper when Baldwin had been killed. Cooper was not to remain in command for long as soon after he was shot through the lungs.

> Lieutenant-Colonel Bradford of the Royal Irish Rifles, upon whom the command [of the brigade] fell, had no sooner been informed of the fact than he too was wounded, as was his second-in-command. Their adjutant was killed. The brigade-major was shot through the face, both the remaining majors of the Rifles severely wounded, and Captain Nugent, staff-captain of the 29th Brigade, killed while leading a charge against some approaching Turks. At 10.30, when the Rifles had lost almost all of their officers, there appears to have been some falling back, and Lieutenant-Colonel Bewsher of the Hampshire, who, though wounded in the head, had taken command, decided that the place was no longer tenable.[42]

The troops at the Farm now retreated down a nullah where they were rallied by two officers and command of the 29th Brigade passed to Jourdain who was not present. Having been rallied, 'the Hampshires on the right under their last officer, the Rifles in the centre and the Wilts and Warwicks on the left, turned their faces again to the Hill of Death and advanced once more', but the Turkish line had been reinforced and the survivors were soon forced back.[43]

Godley sent for the 5th Connaught Rangers, his last reserve, but it did not arrive until late afternoon. When the two companies finally reached the Farm they took up their position but found it untenable due to enfilading fire by the Turks and were ordered to gather up the wounded and withdraw.[44] The estimated casualties of the 29th Brigade on 10 August were 65 officers and 1,195 other ranks.[45] All battalions in the brigade were reinforced on 11 and 12 August by officers and men from their battalions left at Lemnos for that purpose.[46] According to Major L.C. Morley (10th Hampshire Regiment), however, he and the battalion's reinforcements had arrived on the afternoon of 10 August when the remnants of the brigade were in the frontline 'hanging on with their eyelids'.[47] Ordered to take command of the battalion, Morley reported:

> Finally I came across a group of 80 Hampshire men under command of Sergt Lewis, and learnt that Lieut. Hellyer, in command of about 35 men, was holding an under feature in advance of Brigade Headquarters.
>
> At 6 p.m. the Battalion, all that was ever found, was collected behind Brigade Headquarters and numbered with reinforcements about 280 but owing to the lack of cover, casualties were occurring continuously.[48]

Throughout the following weeks, attrition mainly due to sickness reduced the brigade further so that on 21 August when the Hampshires and Connaught Rangers were ordered with other British, Australian and New Zealand units to capture Hill 60 and the wells at Kabak Kuyu, the 10th Hampshires were only able to muster five officers and 330 men.[49] On the left of the line the Connaught Rangers, having captured the wells with little resistance, pushed on and, despite suffering heavy casualties, managed to reach the

Turkish trench on the north-western side of Hill 60 where they dugin. The 10th Hampshires, however, advancing from their position in the reserve, suffered heavily for little effect, were unable to reinforce the leading battalions due to sustained Turkish artillery fire and were reduced to fewer than 200 men of all ranks. A final push involving the Connaught Rangers to capture Hill 60 was made on 27 August and, although gains were made, it was found impossible to capture its summit which remained in Turkish hands for the remainder of the campaign. During two months on the peninsula the 10th (Irish) Division lost almost 75% of its original strength, including over 240 officers killed, wounded or missing.[50]

On 29 September 1915 Bulgaria entered the war on the side of the Central Powers and on 30 September the 10th (Irish) Division left the peninsula for Mudros prior to its dispatch to the Greek port of Salonika. Although partially re-equipped at Mudros, the division was ill prepared for a Balkan winter. Many troops were still wearing light khaki drill uniforms and shorts from Gallipoli and many more lacked greatcoats.[51] The division also landed without artillery which when it arrived lacked the howitzers or mortars necessary for operations in the mountainous Balkanterrain.[52]

On 29 October the 30th Brigade, supported by LXVII Brigade R.F.A., the 31st Field Ambulance, and half the 66th Field Company R.E., began its move from Salonika to Gevegli on the Greco-Serbian border from which it despatched two battalions to relieve French units held in reserve at Hasanli and Čaušli, northwest of Lake Dorian.[53] A further battalion was detached from the brigade to Tatarli on 2 November. Between 7 and 15 November the other two brigades of the division joined the 30th Brigade at Gevegli. During the night of 20/21 November the 10th (Irish) Division relieved French forces on a line running southeast from Kosturino, units of the 30th Brigade occupying frontline trenches to a point just west of Memešli from which battalions of the 31st Brigade defended a two-mile front running through Prsten to where the 29th Brigade extended the line almost to the shores of Lake Dorian. Eight hundred yards to the front of Memešli, and overlooking the British frontline, was an outcrop known as 'Rocky Peak' which was occupied by a company of 5th Royal Irish Fusiliers to deny the position to enemy artillery. The

British battalions were supported by two four 18-pounder batteries; C/LXVII at Kajali and B/LXVII west of Prsten.

Weather conditions in the area were severe with temperatures being experienced as low as minus 22 degrees Centigrade, which resulted in the hospitalisation of 998 frostbite cases.[54] On 1 December, those battalions most affected by the conditions, the 6th Munsters and 6th Dublin Fusiliers, were replaced in the frontline by the 5th Connaught Rangers and the 10th Hampshire Regiment from the 29th Brigade. From 2 December a dense fog descended along the British front restricting their field of vision and allowing the Bulgarians to occupy dead ground from which to fire on British trenches.

Following increased shelling of the Kosturino ridge during the previous two days, the whole line was subjected to intensified artillery and small arms fire on 6 December accompanied by a number of probing attacks which were beaten off. On Rocky Peak the Bulgarians gained a foothold for a time but were driven off by a bayonet charge by the garrison. Although the garrison was reinforced at dusk, at 5 a.m. the next day Bulgarians, under the cover of thick fog, infiltrated the British line in overwhelming numbers forcing the 5th Royal Irish Fusiliers to retreat, which exposed the Connaught Rangers and Hampshire Regiment to enfilading fire from enemy machine guns and mountain artillery. Supported by artillery and machine gun fire from Rocky Peak the enemy launched a series of sustained attacks against the 30th Brigade's front, which despite overwhelming numbers failed to break through. At about 2.30 p.m., however, the first breach in the British line occurred when one of the companies of the 10th Hampshires fell back and could not be rallied until it reached the British second line at Crete Simonet. Here it unfortunately panicked an artillery battery to abandon its guns after removing their sights and breech-blocks. Although believing they were no longer supported on their right flank, the Connaught Rangers continued to fight on until, practically overwhelmed by enemy numbers, the remnants of three of its four companies were forced out of the line. Part of A company, however, remained in the line until approximately 3.30 p.m. when it, together with the left company of the Hampshires, fell back on Crete Simonet. On discovering that the Connaught Rangers had been forced out of the line, Brigadier-General Drage, 7th Royal Munster Fusiliers, turned his right company to protect his exposed flank and maintained his position until 3.40 p.m. when his battalion was ordered to fall back, which it did in good order.

The Bulgarians, having suffered severe casualties in the attack, failed to follow-up their breakthrough and so the 30th Brigade, with the remnants of the Connaught Rangers and the main body of the Hampshires, regrouped on Crete Simonet. With the exception of Rocky Peak and part of the line around Prsten, the 31st Brigade's front line remained intact, but late in the evening, Nicol (who was now acting-divisional commander) ordered the brigade to take up positions extending the defence line at Crete Simonet. During the retreat a battery near Prsten was abandoned in the mistaken belief that the line had collapsed.

Finding that the Bulgarians had failed to occupy the Crete Rivet, a ridge to the front of Crete Simonet, on the morning of 8 December the British occupied the ridge with two companies of the 6th Royal Dublin Fusiliers, protected by a company of French infantry on their left flank,. In dense fog which obscured the intervening ground between the two ridges, the forces on Crete Rivet fought off a series of attacks from the enemy until 2 p.m. when, following the retreat of the French company, the Dublins were ordered to retreat. Fighting their way through the enemy that by now had had almost surrounded their position the two companies rejoined Nicol's defence line on Crete Simonet.

At 3.30 p.m. Nicol received reports that the enemy was attempting to outflank the 31st Brigade, followed at 4 p.m. by information that the 31st Brigade were preparing to retreat thus jeopardising the 30th Brigade's position on Crete Simonet.[55] Disregarding Nicol's protests, Brigadier-General J.G. King-King, commanding the 31st Brigade and fearing they might be surrounded, ordered his brigade to retreat at 5 p.m. forcing Nicol to do likewise.[56] By 12 December all the British units that had entered Serbia had re-crossed the Greek border, the 10th Division continuing its retreat for several more days, the last unit reached Salonika on 18 December.

At the end of December 1915 the division was transferred by land and sea to Stavros at the eastern end of a defensive perimeter being constructed around Salonika and known as the 'Birdcage'.[57]

Following an inspection by the Surgeon-General, the division was withdrawn from the line for four months to recover from the combined effects of their exertions at Gallipoli and Serbia. In the first week of June 1916 units of the 10th Division took over part of the British line in the malarial Struma Valley where between June and October some 6,500 members of the division were admitted to hospital with the disease.[58] Between 30 September and 4 October 1916 elements of the 10th Division crossed the Struma in an action to pin down Bulgarian reserves during the Serbian offensive to recapture Monastir. On 30 September the villages of Karajaköis Bala and Karajaköis Zir were captured by the British 27th Division and, despite several counter-attacks, were held, with the assistance of elements of the 10th Division.[59] The capture of Karajaköis had been greatly facilitated by the construction of a number of bridges across the Struma by the 10th Division's 66th Field Company of the Royal Engineers, the bridgehead having been secured by two composite battalions of the 29th Brigade which had crossed the river by boat.

Early on 3 October, the 30th Brigade, supported by the 6th Royal Irish Rifles, crossed the Struma and at 5.45 a.m., following a thirty-minute bombardment, the 7th Munsters and 6th Dublins, supported by the 6th Munsters and 7th Dublin Fusiliers, advanced on the village of Yeniköi. By 7 a.m. the village had been captured with little loss. At 8.15 a.m. the first of a number of enemy counter-attacks, supported by artillery, commenced, but was broken up by British artillery. Although the British artillery proved effective against Bulgarian infantry it was less so in suppressing enemy artillery, which inflicted heavy casualties on the 6th and 7th Dublin Fusiliers in the middle of the brigade's front line. Following a particularly heavy spell of shelling around 12.45 p.m., when the two battalions had been shelled not only by the enemy but also by their own artillery, they fell back to the cover of a sunken road which ran though the centre of Yeniköi, enabling small groups of Bulgarians to occupy the northern part of the village.

After a slackening of their bombardment, the enemy launched a further counter-attack about 3.45 p.m., during which the two Dublin battalions gave some ground, falling back from the sunken road.[60] As a consequence the 6th Royal Irish Rifles were sent to their aid and together these units retook the sunken road while the British artillery laid down a barrage to prevent the arrival of enemy reinforcements. Due to the confusion surrounding the apparent loss of the village by the Dublins a message was received at 1940 from Colonel A.D. MacPherson, temporary commander of the 30th Brigade, for the brigade to return to the position it had occupied that morning, causing the village to be evacuated by all but one company from each of the Dublin battalions. When the mistake was realised, a counter-attack was organised for the next morning and Yeniköi was retaken without opposition.[61]

In November 1916 each of the division's three brigades was reorganised to reflect the increasing difficulty in obtaining sufficient recruits from Ireland. The 10th Hampshire Regiment left the 29th Brigade to join the 27th Division and was replaced by the 1st battalion the Leinster Regiment. In the 30th Brigade the 6th and 7th Royal Munster Fusiliers amalgamated, as did the 5th and 6th Royal Irish Fusiliers in the 31st Brigade, with the 1st Royal Irish Regiment and 2nd Royal Irish Fusiliers joining, respectively, the two brigades from the 27th Division.

Although the division remained in Macedonia for another eleven months, the capture of Yeniköi was its last major action in the theatre and on 1 September 1917 it was transferred to Allenby's command in Egypt. Over a three-week period the division relocated to the area around Ismailia on the Suez Canal. Compared with their experiences over the previous two years this interlude was like a long-awaited holiday, for the division that arrived in Egypt was but a shadow of the one that had left Ireland; with 3,000 men hospitalised due to malaria, the medical authorities advised that it would be three months before it became operational.[62] Allenby, however, rejected this advice and included the division in his plans for a coming offensive, designating it his army reserve in support of Lieutenant-General Sir Philip Chetwode's XX Corps. Training and reequipping began on 17 September and on 29 September the division began its march to El Kantar, the railhead of the trans-Sinai railway, en route for Palestine.

Allenby's plan was to break through the Turkish defence line which stretched from Gaza on the coast inland for 25 miles to

Beersheba. The attack was planned for 31 October, but to pin down Turkish reserves and suggest the key objective of the assault was to be Gaza, the attack was preceded by a three day artillery and naval bombardment on that end of the line. At the other end of the line were the vital wells at Beersheba, the capture of which was essential if the advance on the right of Allen by's line was to be maintained. In the build-up to the battle, the division's pioneer battalion was involved in the construction of roads, camps and developing water supplies for other divisions, while two battalions of the Leinster Regiment performed the vital but not very glamorous task of loading safe drinking water onto pack animals for transportation to the front.

Between 28 and 30 October the division, less one brigade, undertook a series of night marches to act as reserves for the 60th and 73rd Divisions' attack on Beersheba from the north-east on 31 October. The vital wells at Beersheba, however, were captured by mounted infantry of the Australian Light Horse. Seeing an opportunity to take the Turkish positions by surprise, the 4th and 12th regiments of the Australian Light Horse made a mounted charge, which prevented the destruction of the strategically important wells.[63] To the north of Beersheba the Turks still held a series of earthwork redoubts which could only be taken by a frontal assault to which three of Chetwode's divisions, including the 10th (Irish), were committed. Chetwode deployed his divisions with the 10th Division on the right of the line, with the 31st Brigade in front supported by battalions of the 30th Brigade in the event of a counter-attack. The divisional reserve was provided by the 29th Brigade. On reaching the enemy position the 10th (Irish) evicted them at the point of the bayonet, the Turks falling back to the stronger Hureira Redoubt, whose garrison included 30 machine guns. Chetwode gave the task of turning the garrison out of this position to the 31st Brigade supported by the other brigades of the division, which succeeded in taking the position by turning both its flanks, causing the defenders to withdraw.

On 9 December 1917 British forces entered Jerusalem unopposed, but on 26 December the Turks counter-attacked to retake the city. Chetwode chose the 10th (Irish) Division to repulse the Turkish attack and for the first time since its formation the whole division went into action as a unit under the command of its own divisional commander. Using classic 'fire and movement' tactics, the division, supported by the 74th Division on its right flank, attacked the Zeitun Ridge to the north of Jerusalem. On the division's left flank the 29th Brigade used its Lewis gun sections to suppress enemy fire while its infantry advanced in short rushes. By 11 a.m. the 1st Leinsters had captured their objective but the 5th Connaught Rangers was held up by heavy machine gun fire. Using its two leading companies and its machine gun section, the Rangers swept the high ground south of the village of Kefar Nama before launching a charge by its other two companies at the enemy position from which the enemy flowed away in disorder. The capture of the hill by the 1st Leinsters and 5th Connaught Rangers enabled the 6th Leinsters to take its objective, Shabuny knoll, without opposition.[64]

On the right of the 10th Division's line, the 30th Brigade provided a reserve for the 229th Brigade's attack on Zeitun Ridge, while in the centre the 6th Royal Inniskilling Fusiliers of the 31st Brigade, advancing from the Wadies Sunt, had captured Kereina Peak by 08.30 when a halt was called until units on the brigade's left had captured their objective. At 11.30 a.m. two companies of the 5th Royal Inniskilling Fusiliers attacked a Turkish position that was preventing the movement of artillery along a newly constructed road. The 5th Inniskillings, having occupied this position, the 5th Royal Irish Fusiliers passed along the ridge until they were level with the 229th Brigade. During the action on the Kereina Ridge, Private James Duffy, a stretcher-bearer in the 6th Royal Inniskilling Fusiliers, won the division's only Victoria Cross for conspicuous bravery in rescuing and tending the wounded.[65]

On 28 December, the 30th Brigade's objective was the hills to the north and north-east of the village of 'Ain 'Arik which, according to patrols, were heavily defended. The advance of the brigade up the wadi was slow but when artillery fire began to fall on the enemy position, the enemy commenced their withdrawal so that by 1620 the brigade had captured its objective and thus ended the division's involvement in the operation to defend Jerusalem.[66]

The winter rains largely brought the British offensive to an end and throughout January 1918 much of the division was employed on the construction of roads. In late February British forces captured

Jericho and forced the Turks across the Jordan. The advance then continued on a wide front up the west bank of the Jordan and to the west of the Jerusalem-Nablus Road, through cultivated terrain dominated by high, rolling hills rising to over 2,500 feet and deep valleys. For the forthcoming operation the division was split into two battle groups; a right battle group comprising the 30th and 31st Brigades, each less a battalion kept as a divisional reserve, and supported by LXVII and LXVIII Brigades Royal Field Artillery, while the left battle group comprised the 29th Brigade supported by four batteries of the R.F.A. and a battery from the 7th Indian Divisional Artillery.

On 9 March, the objective for the right battle group was the high ground between the villages of 'Ajul and 'Atara over the steep boulder-strewn depression of the Wadi el Jib. The dominating feature of this objective was Sheikh Kalrawani, a hill to the south-west of 'Atara, which climbed to 2,704 feet. Although delayed by early morning fog, the capture of Sheikh Kalrawani by the 2nd Royal Irish Fusiliers enabled the regiment's 5th battalion to capture 'Atara by 9.30 a.m., while the 1st Royal Irish Regiment, despite heavy artillery fire, captured 'Ajul by 12.30. On the left, the 29th Brigade battle group met little resistance and achieved all its objectives while patrols of the 1st Leinster Regiment pressed forward to Deires Sudan.

With the exception of the 60th Division on the corps' extreme right and the 29th Brigade on the extreme left of the line, XX Corps continued its advance during the night of 9/10 March. On the left bank of the Wadi el Jib the right battle group's position was dominated by two hills on the far bank to the south and south-west of the village of Jilkjliya. During the night, detachments of the 5th Royal Irish Fusiliers and the 1st Royal Irish Regiment descended the 1,100-foot terraced-sided left bank of the wadi but had been unable to complete the ascent before morning when, with the assistance of divisional artillery and two companies of the 5th Royal Inniskilling Fusiliers, the 5th Royal Irish Fusiliers occupied the hill to the south of the village. The enemy, however, were determined to hold their position on the right bank of the wadi and the men of the Royal Irish Regiment encountered stiff opposition that prevented their progress and inflicted over a hundred casualties. It was not until 17.15, and with the vital support of artillery and a company of the 6th Royal Dublin Fusiliers, that they were finally able to take their objective.

To the left of the line the 29th Brigade forced a crossing of the Wadi el Jib,where, despite numerous counter-attacks by the enemy, they consolidated their position, as did the other brigades of the division, bringing to an end the last major offensive action of the 10th (Irish) Division.[67] The German March 1918 offensive increased the need for additional allied divisions on the Western Front. To meet this need, the 10th (Irish) Division was one of those formations 'Indianised' to release British battalions for service in France and Belgium. This process resulted in the retention of the three regular Irish battalions to form a nucleus for the new division, while the division's Irish service battalions were replaced by Indian units. As a consequence of these changes, eight infantry battalions and the 5th Royal Irish Regiment, the divisional pioneer battalion, left the division in the last week of April or first week of May in preparation for their transfer to the Western Front. The three divisional Field Ambulance units, which had accompanied the division to Gallipoli, left the new division in mid-May, while the 29th, 30th and 31st Machine Gun Companies were amalgamated to become the 10th Machine Gun Battalion on 7 May. The Irish Division's remaining service battalion, the 6th Royal Irish Rifles, was disbanded on 15 May 1918 as a result of losses sustained in operations since 9 March.

CHAPTER 6

Gallipoli: The Leadership Deficit

There is no single universally accepted definition of leadership but Gary Sheffield, in his study of leadership in the trenches, has defined it as a 'phenomenon that occurs when the influence of A (the leader) causes B (the group) to perform C (goal-directed behaviour) when B would not have performed C had it not been for the influence of A; the influence of A being generally welcomed by B'.[1] Sheffield notes that the leader's influence is drawn from a number of sources, not just their institutional position, but also from personal qualities and professional competence, the belief that he has the necessary expertise and information that makes him well-equipped to lead the unit.[2]

The United States army defines military leadership as 'the art of direct and indirect influence and the skill of creating the conditions for organizational success to accomplish missions effectively'.[3] The key element of the American definition is the creation of the conditions necessary for success not just the influence of the leader. In 1939 Archibald Wavell, a regimental and staff officer in the Great War who served both on the Western Front and the Middle East, offered the words of Socrates on the virtues necessary for a general as going 'to the real root of the matter':

> The general must know how to get his men their rations
> and every other kind of the stores needed for war. He

must have imagination to originate plans, practical sense and energy to carry them through. ... He should also, as a matter of course, know his tactics; for a disorderly mob is no more an army than a heap of building materials is a house.[4]

Bernard Montgomery, a future Chief of the Imperial General Staff, held similar convictions on the importance of organisation in leadership:

I believe that the task of bringing the force to the fighting point, properly equipped and well-formed in all that it needs is at least as important as the capable leading of the force in the fight itself.

In fact it is indispensable and the combat between hostile forces is more in the preparation than the fight.[5]

In April 1916 an address given at a school for young officers 'somewhere in France' by an unnamed senior officer concerning the duties of an officer was reprinted in *The Times*. In his address on what he termed 'the moral side of the duties of an officer', the senior officer offered the following elements:

You are responsible for the successful leading of your men in battle; you are responsible for their safety, as far as this can be ensured, while gaining success in battle; you are responsible for their health, for their comfort, for their good behaviour and discipline.[6]

Major C.A. Bach of the United States army, addressing the graduating student officers of the Second Training Camp at Fort Sheridan, Illinois, in 1917, reminded the young officers that

Great results are not achieved by cold, passive, unresponsive soldiers. ... Leadership is a composite of a number of qualities. Among the most important I would list self-confidence, moral ascendancy, self-sacrifice, paternalism, fairness, initiative, decision, dignity, and courage.[7]

In the inter-war years Liddell Hart was highly critical of the role played by British senior officers, going so far as to state that 'the decisions which an army commander had to take in the last war, though great in responsibility, were simple in their technical elements compared with those of a battalion commander.'[8] Strachan, however, has suggested that Liddell Hart had 'completely failed to understand that the skills demanded in the leadership of mass armies in an industrialized age were more managerial than heroic'.[9] As John Keegan observed in *The Mask of Command,* the changing nature of warfare has over the centuries changed the characteristics of leadership. Senior commanders are no longer expected to engage the enemy in the frontline like Henry V at Agincourt or risk their life from enemy fire to influence critical phases of a battle as Wellington did at Waterloo; senior officers in the modern age now provided indirect rather than direct leadership.

Although the emphasis on individual leadership qualities may change, depending on their level of command, a number of common leadership elements can be distilled from the above and it is against these that the division's leadership experience will be measured. It is not an exhaustive list but it allows us to draw together the experience of those who led troops at a number of levels during the Great War.

1.	Courage;
2.	Self-confidence;
3.	Technical and tactical proficiency;
4.	Ensuring that tasks are understood, supervised and accomplished;
5.	Sound and timely decision-making;
6.	Employment of forces in accordance with their capabilities;
7.	Provision of the resources necessary for completion of the task;
8.	The confidence of his men; and
9.	Flexibility of mind.

In March 1916 James Edmonds, future author of a number of volumes of the *Official History* of the War on the Western Front, wrote to Spenser Wilkinson, the Chichele Professor of the History of War at Oxford:

> We have not discovered a single good general or staff officer except Sir William Robertson. I believe there is plenty of talent in the army but it does not come to the top. Whenever I look at the list I think of Lincoln [sic] saying 'Well I don't know what effect they have on the enemy but they terrify me'.[10]

It was not only at Gallipoli where the quality of generals and their staff was being questioned. Liddell Hart, who praised Hamilton, despite his lack of success, suggests that it was the nature of the pre-war regular army which was too small and unprepared for a continental scale war in August 1914 rather than the generals or their staff that was to blame for Britain's lack of success in the early years of the war.[11] Pre-war military planning envisaged the dispatch of an expeditionary force of one cavalry and six infantry divisions to the continent in the event of war; few military thinkers could ever have imagined an army of over 60 British divisions, excluding those provided by Australia, Canada, New Zealand, India and South Africa. John Terraine goes further:

> The small size of the pre-war British Army in fact seriously affected the entire British war effort. It not only robbed British generals of necessary training; the small size also robbed the New Armies and Territorials of the regimental officers and NCOs they needed for their training; it robbed the whole Army of munitions because the factories to supply a large army did not exist; and above all it robbed Britain of an independent strategy.[12]

Of the three senior commanders sent to France with the BEF, French, Haig and Smith-Dorian, none had commanded more than a division in action before the war and were the only officers in the British army to have commanded a corps even in peacetime. Not only did its commanders lack experience, but the army lacked enough suitably-qualified staff officers to support its rapid expansion. Terraine has noted that:

> The Regular Army at the time numbered just under 250,000 officers and men, of whom precisely 447 were psc ('passed Staff College'); that is roughly 18% [sic 0.18%], so you can see they were in short supply (and I may add that out of that 219 of the 447 (49.2%) were killed or died of wounds during the war). All other staff officers – and they ran to thousands, were wartime appointments without previous special training, so if the quality was somewhat uneven it is scarcely to be wondered at.[13]

Hussey disputes Terraine's figures for the number of qualified staff officers available to the British army, pointing out that it excludes 'non-psc' officers such as Kitchener and Hamilton who were deemed qualified staff officers by dint of their experience – 'qs'. Hussey's analysis of the *Quarterly* [Army] *List* for June 1914 identified a total of 908 officers, either psc or qs, qualified for staff appointments thus doubling the number of 'qualified' staff officers available to the army on mobilisation.[14] Nevertheless, Terraine's general point on the limited supply of staff officers remains true.

Graduates of the staff colleges at Camberley or Quetta, including Haig and Robertson, obtained the majority of senior command and staff posts in the BEF.[15] By the commencement of the Gallipoli campaign in April 1915, the number of British infantry divisions serving abroad had increased to 22 with a further 18 divisions being dispatched overseas before the 10th (Irish) Division landed on the peninsula at the beginning of August. All required experienced commanders and professional staff officers which the army did not possess. The size of the pre-war army therefore had an on-going impact on the leadership of the wartime army at all levels even to slowing the development of new tactics as the nature of staff college training made graduates particularly suited to provide the leadership and tactical developments needed during the war. At the same time,

Archibald Montgomery, Rawlinson's future chief of staff and future Chief of the Imperial General Staff (CIGS), questioned the quality of pre-war staff training, contending that because so much of the training was undertaken in syndicates few officers were capable of making decisions on their own.[16] Against this, might be set the view that as entrance was by competitive examination and candidates always exceeded the number of places available, 'the intellectual quotient of psc's must have been rather above the average'.[17] Such speculation, however, ignores those officers who were awarded a place through patronage without passing the necessary entrance examination. Setting this argument aside, both Major-General Walter Braithwaite and Brigadier-General Hamilton Reed, Hamilton and Stopford's respective chiefs of staff, were both staff college graduates and in the case of the latter had considerable practical experience as a staff officer, while the former had been commandant of the staff college at Quetta. Reed had also served on Hamilton's staff for a time when Hamilton had been Inspector General, Overseas Force.

Patronage was not confined to staff college entry; it was also found in the use of influence to obtain appointments. While the relationship between French and Haig may be the most famous, one wonders whether Hamilton's request for Rawlinson to command IX Corps was based on his experience in France or because they had served together on Roberts' staff and hence were part of his 'Indian ring'. Hamilton and Rawlinson had also been besieged together at Ladysmith.

By the time the 10th (Irish) Division was 'Indianised' in April/May 1918 it had experienced defeat at Gallipoli, stalemate at Salonika, and success in Palestine. During its almost three years of active service the quality of leadership, undoubtedly, had a profound impact on the experience of the division, particularly at Gallipoli and so, using the criteria identified above, the nature of the leadership provided will be examined.

John Baynes, in his book *Morale*, provides a pen portrait of the ideal regimental officer of the pre-war period and by inference the whole of the British officer class who had progressed through the regimental system:

Calmness in times of stress and danger is one of his main attributes. He is also very brave physically. Of moral courage he also has plenty, and will stand up for his subordinates whatever his seniors may say about them. To his seniors he is sometimes rather aloof, and refuses to be impressed by high rank. He will go to any length to avoid giving even the faintest impression of currying favour.[18]

Of the men who either directly or indirectly led the 10th (Irish) Division, physical courage can almost universally be taken for granted. Sir Ian Hamilton had been recommended twice for the Victoria Cross; Brigadier General Reed, IX Corps' chief of staff, had been awarded the Victoria Cross during the Boer War, while Mahon had taken part in the charge at Omdurman, being for a time reported killed, and was awarded a DSO. Of the division's thirteen battalion commanders, seven were either killed or wounded while leading their battalion into action at Gallipoli, while Cooper, the commanding officer of the 29th Brigade, was wounded while advancing with his staff and two battalions of his brigade on Chunuk Bair.

Examples abound of the courage of officers of all ranks thus making it impossible to record them all here, but the exploits of the 6th Royal Irish Rifles on 9-10 August 1915 provides a superb example. Bean records:

> Lieutenant-Colonel Bradford, of the Royal Irish Rifles, upon whom the command [of the 29th Brigade] fell, had no sooner been informed of the fact than he too was seriously wounded, as was his second-in-command. Their adjutant was killed. The brigade-major was shot through the face, both the remaining majors of the Rifles severely wounded, and Captain Nugent, staff-captain of the 29th Brigade, killed while leading a charge against some approaching Turks.[19]

Bean also records the recollection of an unknown Maori officer concerning his conversation with a company commander of the

Royal Irish Rifles at The Farm who had been ordered to advance – 'Surely you won't do it – it can't be done' said the Maori officer. 'I'm going – I've been told to' came the reply. According to the officer, the Rifles' officer led his men forward but none came back. The bodies of men of the Royal Irish Rifles were later found within 25 yards of the crest of Chunuk Bair.[20]

No less important than physical courage is the moral courage required to be honest with oneself, in dealing with superiors and subordinates, and having the ability to make the right decision no matter how unpalatable. There is no question that Hamilton possessed physical courage, but evidence suggests that he lacked moral courage when dealing with others, and Kitchener in particular, a failing he apparently recognised in himself when he told Churchill that: 'I must not in loyalty tell you too much of my War Office conversation, but I see I shall need some courage in stating my opinions, as well as in attacking the enemy'.[21] He would later record his frustration concerning the constraints placed on him by Kitchener from seeking additional resources.[22] Hamilton even failed to achieve the appointment of Ellison, his chief of staff at Home Command, to the same post with the MEF, accepting Kitchener's appointment of Braithwaite instead, a failure which may well have influenced the outcome of the Gallipoli campaign as Ellison might have encouraged Hamilton to seek bolder solutions to problems rather than the textbook approach of Braithwaite.[23]

Hamilton also bowed to pressure from Kitchener to accept Mahon, if not as corps commander, at least as a divisional commander knowing the complications involved and his belief, rightly or wrongly, of his unsuitability for the type of warfare in which they were engaged at Gallipoli. Hamilton would later claim that he had no choice but to accept Stopford as commander of IX Corps. In truth he could have pressed either for his own choice of commander or, on reflection, have admitted that Mahon would be a better choice. Either way he was in no doubt what Kitchener would have done in similar circumstances: 'imagine Broderick in the South African War nominating the Column Commanders. K. would not have stood it for five minutes'.[24] Hamilton, however, apparently lacked the courage to do the same.

Evidence also suggests Hamilton lacked moral courage when dealing with subordinates. During the initial landings at Helles in April 1915 troops had landed unopposed on Y beach and were in a position to move inland to support the landings on other beaches.

Despite requests for further orders, the divisional commander, Hunter-Weston, failed to take any action other than forward the request to Hamilton's headquarters on *HMS Queen Elizabeth*. Recognising the potential to exploit the lack of resistance at Y beach, Hamilton twice signalled Hunter-Weston offering naval vessels to land more men on the beach. Hunter-Weston ignored the first signal but to the second replied that it was the navy's opinion that diverting naval vessels to land more troops on Y beach would delay disembarkations on other beaches.[25] Thereafter both Hamilton and Hunter-Weston ignored the opportunities presented by the unopposed landing at Y beach, the latter ignoring requests from commanders on Y beach for further orders and so, according to Travers, 'the troops ashore simply sat down and waited for the general advance'.[26] It is clear, however, that the way was opened for an advance from Y beach and only awaited the necessary orders from the divisional commander, as between 07.30 and 11.00 two companies of marines were able to advance about a mile from the beach without opposition.[27] Without doubt Hunter-Weston and his staff had made a major mistake in failing to exploit a weakness in the Turkish defences, but Hamilton's attitude to a failure that would ultimately cost thousands of lives was weak in the extreme. Rather than giving Hunter-Weston a severe reprimand, he concluded 'least said soonest mended'.[28]

In retrospect perhaps the greatest single lack of moral courage, amongst those who led the 10th Division, must be laid at the feet of its corps commander, Sir Frederick Stopford. This man, 61 years old, in poor health, with no experience of command above regimental level, and who had been retired since 1909, accepted a post for which he was totally unsuited. Even accepting that he may have done so for the best of reasons, to serve his country in its time of need, he must have realised the demands of such a post on his already frail health and that his experience was largely confined to staff work in support of others, particularly at a time when many of the old practices were found to be no longer relevant to modern warfare. Nevertheless, Stopford accepted the post which an honest self-assessment would have told him was beyond his capacity to perform to the level required.

From the beginning Hamilton appears to have been confident of his ability to deliver his objective: in his own words '"We have done this sort of thing before, Lord K" I said; "we have run this sort of show before"'.[29] Despite his apparent confidence, he had never commanded more than a division in combat and his confidence tended to be demonstrated in terms of over-optimism. On 27 April 1915 following the landings at Helles and Anzac, and despite a request from Birdwood to evacuate the latter, Hamilton wrote to Kitchener 'Thanks to the weather and the wonderfully fine spirit of our troops all continues to go well', even though he recorded in his diary for the day that 'had our men not been so deadly weary, there was no reason we should not have taken Achi Baba from the Turks, who put up hardly any fight at all'.[30] No doubt Hamilton's optimism was reinforced by those around him. On the same day Hunter-Weston had written to his wife: 'We have managed it, we have achieved the impossible! Wonderful gallantry on the part of Regimental officers and men has done it'.[31] On 10 May Hamilton cabled Kitchener indicating that he could do no more with the resources available, but 'if you could only spare me two fresh divisions organised as a corps I could push on with great hopes of success both from Helles and Gaba Tepe'.[32] At the end of June, Hamilton included a landing south of Suvla Bay as part of his plans for an August offensive and in a telegram to Kitchener again his optimism is evident: 'to summarize, I think I have reasonable prospects of eventual success with three divisions; with four the risks of miscalculation would be minimized; and with five, even if the fifth had little or no gun [artillery] ammunition ... success could be generally assured'.[33] Despite his optimism, the offensive failed, bringing an end to any realistic chance of a successful conclusion to the campaign. Ever the optimist, Hamilton informed Kitchener on 17 August 'he was anxious to try again if provided with adequate men and munitions'.[34] In the opinion of a biographer 'his excessive optimism frequently crossed into the realm of wishful thinking'.[35]

Having no previous experience of commanding troops in action, Stopford might be forgiven for any feelings of self-doubt, though he had the support of Brigadier General H.L. Reed VC, who had seen recent service on the Western Front, as his Chief of Staff. Stopford's lack of command experience makes it difficult to assess his leadership performance against many of the nine-point criteria, in particular physical courage. In his dealings with Hamilton and Braithwaite however, there is evidence to suggest that he had the moral courage to stand up to his superiors when he considered their plans to be too ambitious. On 31 July Stopford forwarded to GHQ for Hamilton's approval a 'proposed plan of operation for the capture and retention of Suvla Bay as a base of operations for the Northern Army' and a copy of the operational orders he proposed to issue.[36] In his proposal Stopford made it quite clear that his first priority was the securing of Suvla Bay and, if possible, the surrounding high ground to prevent its exposure to enemy artillery. In doing so Stopford was effectively limiting his corps' objectives and unilaterally deciding which elements of GHQ's plan were actually deliverable given the resources available. Arguably, Stopford was being more realistic than the GHQ planners. He realised the difficulty for troops in their first action of capturing objectives some five miles away across uncharted country at night. In all likelihood, of course, Stopford's limitation of Braithwaite's original plan for the Suvla landings was prompted by the greater experience of such officers as Reed and Mahon although it has been suggested that because of his limited experience Stopford relied too much on Reed.[37] Hamilton thought that 'Reed, who would be a good staff officer to some Generals, is not well suited to Stopford', while in Carlyon's opinion Stopford had 'become a football, kicked one way by Reed and Mahon (who also disliked the [original] plans) and another by Hamilton and Aspinall becoming more bewildered each time he was kicked. His first battle had not started and he was already a study in mental decline'.[38] That there is a degree of truth in these statements is evidenced by the views he expressed on 22 July regarding Hamilton's original plan for the August offensive: 'this is the plan which I have always hoped he would adopt. It is a good plan. I am sure it will succeed, and I congratulate whoever has been responsible for framing it'. Following discussions with Reed the next day, 'Stopford's early confidence began to evaporate'.[39]

Prior to the war Hamilton had participated in many colonial campaigns, including the Boer War, where he was Kitchener's Chief of Staff, and held a number of important staff and command positions. As a result, in November 1914 he had been considered as a possible replacement for Sir John French as commander of the BEF. In addition to his colonial service, Hamilton had served as Chief of the British Military Mission attached to Japanese Headquarters during the Russo-Japanese War 1904-05 where he observed Japanese forces overcoming entrenched Russian positions by bayonet charge.

On his return from Manchuria, Hamilton was anxious to apply the lessons learned during the Boer and Russo-Japanese Wars to the forces under his command and hence 'he co-ordinated the different arms in manoeuvres, placed special emphasis on indirect artillery fire and the timing of barrages to coincide with the infantry assault, and, as might be expected, made musketry practice a large part of the training'.[40] Nevertheless, Hamilton remained convinced of the superiority of morale and offensive spirit – as represented by the willingness of men to cross a fire-swept zone to impose their will on the enemy – over firepower. [41] This belief, shared by many senior commanders on the Western Front at the beginning of the war, formed the basis of Hamilton's tactics for the Gallipoli campaign and because he had not served on the Western Front he was largely unaware of the devastating effects of modern artillery and machine guns deployed in support of entrenched positions. Hamilton had already lost the element of surprise due to the failure of the navy's attempts to force 'the narrows' and the delay in following up the naval attacks with a landing which had allowed the Turks to reinforce and reorganise the defences. Hunter-Weston, commanding the 29th Division, in an appraisal of the situation written on 25 March 1915, argued that without surprise and with the resources in men and artillery available there was little chance of success and even if the landing was successful troops would be tied up in a trench-war stalemate.[42]

Unmoved in his belief that morale and the offensive spirit were sufficient to overcome Turkish resistance, Hamilton persisted in a number of attacks against the Turkish trenches between April and

July 1915 with little success and high casualties. It appears that by the end of June his belief in this type of tactics was beginning to change. On 2 July Hamilton cabled to Kitchener that:

> The old battle tactics have clean vanished. I have only quite lately realized the new conditions. Whether your entrenchments are on top of a hill or at the bottom of a valley matters precious little .... The only thing is cunning or surprise, skill, or tremendous expenditure of high explosives, or great expenditure of good troops to win some small tactical position which the enemy may be bound, perhaps for military or perhaps political reasons, to attack. Then you can kill them pretty fast.[43]

Despite this revelation, Hamilton and his staff reverted to their established tactics in the planning for the August offensive. Using Helles as a feint, troops supported by naval gun-fire (which had already proved to be ineffective in targeting enemy trenches due to its low trajectory and direct targeting techniques) were to be landed at night to secure Suvla Bay, with the main attack from the Anzac sector to take the Turkish trenches on the heights of Chunuk Bair. Notwithstanding requests from IX Corps for a systematic attack at Suvla supported by artillery, Hamilton and his staff persisted in the same unsuccessful tactics that had failed in previous assaults with the same results.

As noted, Stopford may have had no command experience, but that does not imply that he was totally devoid of all military experience. Having been Sir Redvers Buller's military secretary during the Boer War, he would have been aware of the impact of modern artillery on troops, particularly in the open, and so with Reed, who had served on the Western Front, he pressed for increased artillery support to be made available on the morning after the landings.[44] According to GHQ plans, a total of 56 guns and howitzers were to be available by the night of the 7 August, but in reality only a single battery was available to support the corps' operations at this time.[45] Tactically the Suvla offensive was being conducted in a similar manner to the Western Front where frontal attacks were inadequately supported by artillery.[46] Most of the first day of operations was concentrated on securing the beachhead and attacking the Chocolate and W Hills from the north as a more direct attack from the south or west was expected to incur heavy casualties. While Stopford's plan for capturing Chocolate Hill and its neighbours appeared sound on paper, adequate reconnaissance before the landing or tactical initiative by officers on the ground could have resulted in the early capture of these key objectives thus releasing troops for assaults on other objectives. Major Murray, 9th Sherwood Foresters, who had been landed to the west of these hills, stated they could have been taken early in the day with little loss from that direction:

> This hill [Chocolate Hill] appeared to be quite a short way from where I was that night [6/7 August] and I was sorely tempted to go a bit further and walk on it from our side, but was held back by the knowledge that someone else had orders to take it from the other side and any action from our side might lead to confusion in the dark, especially as there was a thick scrubby undergrowth about it. Besides our orders were very definite. We therefore contented ourselves with occupying the position we had taken up and awaiting daybreak in the confident anticipation that we should receive orders then to advance and would carry all before us.[47]

As a consequence of this lack of initiative and the troops of the 11th Division being pinned down by enemy artillery for most of the day, the Chocolate and W Hills were not captured until 7 pm on 7 August. The repercussions of this were that the 10th and 11th Divisions were scattered and exhausted from a day's fighting and unable to undertake further action on the next day, thus losing the initiative.

With the inability of the navy to land the 30th and 31st Brigades of the 10th Division on their designated beachhead, Stopford's control of the offensive began to unravel. Brigadier-General Hill, who at this time had under his command six battalions of the division, was summoned to meet Stopford at his headquarters on board *HMS Jonquil*. The crux of the orders given to Hill by Stopford was:

You will get into touch with G.O.C., 11th Division, at once if possible, and act under his orders. Failing getting into touch with G.O.C., 11th Division, you must advance and support troops of 11th Division about squares R and S, also make good the ridge running north-east from Ghazi Baba (including that post), and move troops along the top of the ridge to assure our hold on it.

The main objective of G.O.C., IXth Corps, is to secure Suvla Bay as a base for operations, and he does not consider this security will be assured until he is in a position to deny the enemy the heights which connect Anafarta Sagir and Ejelmer Bay.[48]

In giving Hill these orders Stopford was recognising the strategic importance of the Kiretch Tepe range to the achievement of the corps' objectives, so that when Mahon arrived at Suvla later in the morning, when an alternative to 'A' Beach had been discovered, he [Mahon] was ordered to land on the north of the bay and push up the ridge. By this time however, Hill had already begun landing the troops under his command at 'C' beach, just south of Lala Baba. This left Mahon w ith only two battalions of the 30th Brigade, the 5th and 6th Royal Munster Fusiliers, together with the divisional pioneer battalion, the 5th Royal Irish Regiment, under his direct command, although he was later joined by the 5th Royal Inniskilling Fusiliers which was diverted to Ghazi Baba while waiting to land at 'C' beach. As a result, four battalions of the 10th Division were embroiled in operations commanded by Hammersley, GOC 11th Division, while Mahon was required to undertake an attack on troops entrenched on a ridge with four battalions unsupported by artillery that presumably (for no orders had actually been given to the 10th Division before their arrival at Suvla) had been designed as a task for two full brigades.

At the end of the first full day of action at Suvla the battalions of two divisions were intertwined across a five-mile front. Despite a description in the Royal Munster Fusiliers' regimental history of the attack on Kiretch Tepe Sirt on 8 August, that day all across the Suvla front was a day of inactivity, which Aspinall-Oglander later described as 'a wasted day at Suvla'.[49] Stopford recorded that while he realised the importance of pressing on, and his two divisional commanders had assured him they would do all they could:

> they doubted if a further advance was possible as their troops were very much exhausted by continuous fighting for a whole day and night and by lack of water. It is to be noted also that the troops of the 11th Division and 31st Brigade acting with it were very much scattered. The only artillery support available was one Battery R.F.A. and two Mountain Batteries in addition to the Naval guns.[50]

Stopford could have added that 10th Division on Kiretch Tepe had only three under-strength battalions rather than the eight he planned to take that objective.

Mahon had little opportunity to show either his technical or tactical ability at Gallipoli. The Australian writer Robin Prior in *Gallipoli – The End of the Myth*, provides his assessment in just seven words, 'had little in his favour except seniority'. This view was not shared by Hore-Ruthen, one of Hamilton's staff officers in whose opinion Mahon had 'not had quite a fair chance'.[51] Prior's view ignores Mahon's undoubted experience which included command of the column that relieved Mafeking during the Boer War. Field Marshal Lord Roberts, the Commander in Chief in South Africa prior to the appointment of Kitchener, recorded his view of Mahon's tactical ability:

> The operation entrusted to Brigadier-General Mahon was conducted by him with conspicuous ability and energy, and I would draw special attention to the skill he displayed in evading the enemy, who had arranged to dispute his advance along the main road, by deflecting his line of march to the west. Credit is also due to Brigadier-General Mahon for the dispositions which resulted in the defeat of the Boers on 13th and 16th May, and opened the way in to Mafeking.[52]

Roberts at least had confidence in Mahon's tactical ability and energy, as had Kitchener who, despite Hamilton's criticism, was emphatic that Mahon would go to Gallipoli as a divisional commander.

> The 10th Division is complete and commanded by Mahon. Without being methodical, he is a fine leader and has the confidence of his men. He knows his Division thoroughly and has trained them well. He will shine in a tight place or in a hard fight than in ordinary daily work.[53]

In his written statement to the Dardanelles Commission, Mahon stated that, ten days before the landing at Suvla, Stopford showed him in confidence his orders for the plan of campaign for the forthcoming landings. Given the timing of his visit to Stopford, these must have been Braithwaite's instructions of 22 July, before the arrival of his instructions of 29 July. According to Mahon, he

> studied them carefully, and came to the conclusion that they were far too intricate and complicated to have a reasonable chance of success.
> The whole plan of campaign was based on the times when different objectives would be reached and seized by the Anzac troops, and on the assumption that there would be practically no opposition to the troops landing at Suvla.[54]

In Mahon's opinion, the main thrust of the troops from Anzac was being made at night over very difficult terrain, which had not been reconnoitred, and that there was every chance that if any part of the proposed plan went wrong then the whole operation would fail. According to Mahon, he expressed this view to Stopford at the time and became more convinced of his assessment of the situation when:

> the next day I visited Anzac and studied the ground as far as possible from different positions there. I came to

the conclusion that the ground was even more difficult than what I had thought the previous day from the reading it on the map, and the chances of success even more remote.[55]

Of their visit to Anzac, King-King, Mahon's Chief of Staff, recalled:

When we had embarked Gen. Mahon made me write down roughly where I should attack and why, and did the same separately, saying we would compare them afterwards. I must tell you that we spent most of the day in company with Generals Birdwood and Goldby (sic), and had heard all they had to say on the subject. When our two accounts were compared they were identical. An attack on the Kirech Tepe side in strength pushed to the high ridge beyond it, which in our judgement, would have cleared all the ground between that and Anzac as it appeared to dominate it.[56]

Mahon's grasp of strategy appears sound, particularly in light of Orlo Williams' recollection that Dawnay, one of the chief architects of the plan, was 'not very optimistic even about the result of success in our next big push. Seems to think that the best we can hope for would be to get a strong position across the peninsula and build a safe base at Suvla Bay.'[57]

A final word on Mahon's tactical ability, which he was unable to demonstrate at Suvla is given by Sir Charles Monro, who replaced Sir Ian Hamilton as Commander in Chief of the Mediterranean Expeditionary Force in October 1915. In his first *Despatch*, Monro noted his 'desire to give special prominence to the difficulties to which General Sir B. Mahon was exposed from the time of his landing at Salonika, and the ability which he displayed in overcoming them … and the high standard of administrative capacity displayed by the G.O.C. and his Staff'.[58]

In September 1915 Lieutenant-General Byng arrived from France, accompanied by his ADC Captain Basil Brooke, to replace Stopford as commander of IX Corps and proposed a four-day artillery bombardment prior to their attack. Hamilton's response demonstrated his inflexibility of thought and his inability to move with the tactics and technology that modern warfare demanded. Of Byng's proposal for a prolonged preliminary bombardment he complained to Kitchener that 'all these fellows from France come here with this idea' and wished for a last 'dashing assault ... before we subside into this ghastly trench warfare'.[59]

The thrust of the original plan given to Stopford commanding IX Corps on 22 July was that, while the troops at Helles in the south of the peninsula pinned down as many as the enemy as possible, the Australian and New Zealand Army Corps (ANZAC), supplemented by men of the British 13th Division and the 10th Division's 29th Brigade together with the 29th (Indian) Brigade, would push the Turks off Koja Chemen Tepe opening a way to Maidos on the east coast of the peninsula, while the 11th Division from IX Corps was landed at Suvla Bay.[60] On 29 July Braithwaite, Hamilton's chief of staff, issued a second set of instructions from GHQ clarifying the objectives of IX Corps, updating the resources available to it, and containing a further assessment of the enemy forces in the area. Tim Travers suggests that there was a certain degree of ambivalence in Hamilton's instructions:[61]

> Your primary objective will be to secure Suvla Bay as a base for all forces operating in the northern zone. Owing to the difficult nature of the terrain, it is possible that the attainment of this objective will, in the first instance, require the use of the whole of the troops at your disposal. Should, however, you find it possible to achieve this objective with only a portion of force, your next step will be to give such direct assistance as it is in your power to the G.O.C. Anzac in his attack on Hill 305, by an advance on Biyuk Anafarta, with the object of moving up the eastern spur of that hill.[62]

Travers believes that the wording of these orders shows that the General Staff at GHQ were thinking of the operation at Suvla in terms of the capture of a port rather than a realistic means of supporting the operation on the Anzac front. The spur to which the orders refer was steep, rising in places to 900 feet and commencing some four miles from the proposed landing beaches. Travers' view is supported by Major Guy Dawnay, another member of Hamilton's staff, who in a letter to his wife written in early August 1915 stated that 'a force north of the Australian position' would 'seize and hold a fine little natural harbour called Suvla Bay which should serve as a base for the whole of the northern forces, i.e. the Australians and the New Army divisions'.[63]

From the beginning Hamilton and his staff adopted an almost paranoid approach to secrecy concerning their plans for the August offensive. According to Stopford, he asked Hamilton on 11 July if he would tell him anything about the proposed operation but was informed that it was a secret and that he could not be told anything until later.[64] Such was Hamilton's desire for secrecy that he personally visited Stopford at Helles where he had assumed temporary command of VIII Corps when Hunter-Weston fell ill, to deliver and explain the plans. Poett, Stopford's senior administrative staff officer, stated that 'all plans connected with this attack were kept a profound secret and were known only to the Commander in Chief, his Chief of Staff and Sir Frederick'.[65] Hamilton's frame of mind concerning secrecy is revealed in a postscript to a letter to De Robeck, 'You will readily understand that if the Turks get any inkling of our intention, we are done! Neither the bravery of our troops, nor the excellence of the Naval arrangements will save us'.[66] Hamilton's need for secrecy, however, curtailed the navy's preparations for the landing within Suvla Bay as 'the danger of giving away the scheme considerably increased the difficulties of the landings as soundings could not be taken by the Royal Navy, and land reconnaissance was limited to reports furnished by Aeroplanes'.[67] The inability of the navy to survey the bay led directly to the grounding of a number of landing craft and water barges and the abandonment of 'A' beach. Consequently the forces under Hill were disembarked at 'C' beach rather than their designated beachhead, which split Mahon's command and left him with insufficient units to capture Kiretch Tepe Sirt on the first day of the landing when the Turkish positions were at their most vulnerable.

The postscript to Braithwaite's letter of 22 July stated, 'This letter is never to be out of an officer's possession and if, as is possible, you require to send it to your Brig.-Gen. G.S. [General Staff], it must be sent to Mudros in charge of an officer.'[68] Hill, commanding the 31st Brigade of the 10th (Irish) Division, recalled that on 2 August, only five days before their landing at Suvla, Hamilton inspected the troops on board several troop transports at Mitylene, but that 'he would give me no information as to when or where the troops under my command were likely to be employed'.[69] According to Hill, the first he knew where and when his troops were to go into action was 2.30 p.m. on 5 August when he was visited by the captains of *HMS Canopas* and *Euryalus* to inform him of the arrangements for embarking them. It was 'the first and only intimation I received of the intended move and destination of the troops under my command – no orders or instructions of any kind'.[70]

Hill was not alone in his ignorance of how his troops were to be employed. Lieutenant-Colonel Greer commanding the 6th Royal Irish Fusiliers recalled in later life how 'complete secrecy shrouded our future movements. One day [6 August 1915] a destroyer arrived and embarked and I went up on the bridge and asked the commander if he could tell us where we were going. He said I can tell you 12 midnight, not before. At 12 midnight I went up again to the bridge and repeated my request. He said – I have orders to put you ashore at Beach 'C'. I said, where on earth's that? Suvla Bay he said. Where on earth's that? I asked – he showed me a chart'.[71] Recalling this incident some 35 years after the event, Greer's memory may be at fault because the decision to divert his battalion from 'A' beach was not taken until Hill's meeting with Stopford after dawn on 7 August.

Ignorance of their final destination was not just confined to Hill and the 31st Brigade HQ proceeding from Mitylene. It extended even to the 30th Brigade which had travelled from Mudros where both Mahon and Stopford had their headquarters. H.T. Goodland, Staff Captain, recalled in his submission to the official historian that, 'beyond the fact that we knew we were embarking at Mudros for somewhere on the peninsula on August 6, no one knew exactly where. I am convinced General Nicol certainly did not, for when we arrived early in the morning in a bay crowded with shipping he told me find out where we were'.[72]

Hankey, the Secretary of the Committee of Imperial Defence, who was at Gallipoli gathering information for a report to the Cabinet, observed that 'the regimental officers and the rank and file never knew enough of what was expected of them, and what was before them'. In his desire for secrecy Hamilton failed to ensure that his plans were understood by the men who were to undertake them.[73]

According to Terraine, the Great War was 'the only war ever fought without voice control'.[74] By this Terraine meant that it was the first war where commanders were neither on the spot nor had a reliable means of communication with their subordinates, a view that echoes Hamilton's own that 'as armies have grown and the range of firearms has increased the Commander-in-Chief of any considerable force has been withdrawn further and further from the fighting'.[75] While communications limited Hamilton's involvement in the delivery of his plans, totally ignoring the Suvla theatre for days after the landing and to a point where the chances of success in that sector were practically irretrievable, demonstrates that other fronts, in particular the ANZAC sector, were considered of more importance to the overall success of the campaign.

On 31 July Stopford had forwarded to GHQ for Hamilton's approval a 'proposed plan of operation for the capture and retention of Suvla Bay as a base of operations for the Northern Army' and a copy of the operational orders he proposed to issue.[76] This proposal stated that:

> it is unlikely that the attainment of the security of Suvla Bay will so absorb the force under my command as to render it improbable that I shall be able to give direct assistance to the G.O.C., A.N.Z.A.C., in his attack on Hill 305, if however, the operations above referred to meet with such slight opposition as will free a portion of the troops engaged, you may rely on my giving him every assistance in my power.[77]

Stopford's proposal had significantly changed Hamilton's plans for the Suvla sector by effectively limiting the objectives for the landing and yet Hamilton took no steps to redress the situation and hence the capture of the bay itself became the main objective of IX Corps. Although the first troops had landed at Suvla during the night of 6/7 August, it was the morning of 8 August before Aspinall and Hankey were dispatched from GHQ at Imbros to report on the situation. After a meeting with Stopford, who appeared satisfied with the progress his troops had made but who considered that no further advance could be made until his men had rested and more artillery sent ashore, Aspinall reported to GHQ that he had 'just been ashore, ashore where I found all quiet. No rifle fire, no artillery fire, and apparently no Turks. IX Corps resting. Feel confident that golden opportunities are being lost and look upon the situation as serious'.[78]

When Hamilton eventually arrived at Suvla at 6 p.m. on 8 August, having discussed the situation with Admiral De Robeck, Commodore Keys and Aspinall, he visited Stopford who was still of the opinion that all was going well.[79] Not satisfied with the situation, Hamilton ordered a night advance by units of the 11th Division on Tekke Tepe ridge. According to the *Official History*, Hammersley commanding the division, stated that he did not think that anything could be done until daylight because his units were scattered over a wide front, no reconnaissance had been made over the difficult ground, and his troops were too inexperienced for such an operation. Hamilton was, however, insistent and units of the 32nd Brigade were ordered to advance. Unfortunately, in the darkness not all battalions either received the order or had arrived in time to attack at dawn, so that when a battalion of the East Yorkshire Regiment attacked, it found the ridge occupied by the enemy in sufficient strength to repulse its attack.[80] In the opinion of Liman von Sanders, the Turkish commander, 'there can be no doubt that, in view of the great British superiority, complete success would have been possible for them. … We all had the feeling that the British delayed too long on the shore instead of advancing from the landing place at any cost.'[81] It is therefore apparent that by failing to supervise the operations at Suvla to ensure that time was not being wasted and that his plans were being followed, Hamilton materially contributed to the failure of operations in that sector. Furthermore, in his failure to respond to Stopford's understanding of his objectives as expressed in his 'proposed plan of operation' of 31 July, it can be argued that not only had Hamilton removed – albeit unwillingly – a sense of urgency from the task but he had also limited its scope by removing the capture of the strategically important hills surrounding the bay.

Until the arrival of Hamilton at his headquarters late in the afternoon, Stopford had failed to go ashore to see the position for himself, however, it is doubtful given the situation that his presence would have resulted in the taking of the Tekke Tepe Ridge. Meanwhile the main attack from the Anzac front had failed, effectively ending any hope of success for Hamilton's overall plan. Thus, as Travers observed, began the conscious effort to cover up the failure of the Anzac operation by focusing on the failure of Stopford, IX Corps and Suvla.[82] Hamilton was quick to adopt this theme. On 11 August Hamilton's correspondence with Kitchener firmly placed the blame for the failure of the whole offensive on the Suvla operation, a theme that, despite Braithwaite's reminder that Suvla was only one of three operations and 'not even the most important', soon received widespread adoption, ultimately leading to the removal of Stopford on 15 August.[83] That Stopford was a scapegoat for the failure of the whole operation is acknowledged by Godley: 'We are all so dreadfully sorry at F. Stopford having been made a scapegoat – it is so hard to get at the truth or rights of these things but ... the Corps did not push vigorously after it landed'.[84]

Mahon has been criticised for his inability to capture Kiretch Tepe ridge. However, a number of factors should be taken into account, not least the fact that the first time that Mahon was told of his objective was 2.45 p.m. on the day of the landing and that at the time he had only three battalions of inexperienced troops under his command.[85] The objective was the capture of Turkish trenches sited at the top of a 2-mile long ridge and although GHQ's assessment of the number of troops facing Mahon's three battalions was only three companies of the Gallipoli Gendarmerie, approximately 350 men, the strength of their position was such that when the 5th Inniskillings replaced the Manchesters in the front line about 10 p.m. on 7 August, the latter had already lost 15 officers and between 250 and 300 men.[86]

The Gendarmerie on Kiretch Tepe was also supported by artillery on Kidney Hill. The difficulty of the task given to Mahon with the resources available, even before the difficulties of obtaining supplies of water, must not be underestimated. In the words of de Lisle, who was Stopford's temporary replacement in command of IX Corps, 'It must be recognised that on no occasion can good troops with proper trench discipline be surprised, or driven out of a trench even when attacked by vastly superior numbers, five or six times as strong as the defenders'.[87]

After a day of relative inactivity on 8 August, preparations were made to resume the assault on the Turkish positions on Kiretch Tepe the next day.

> About 8 p.m. on the 8th I received an order from the IX Corps that I was to continue the advance along the Ridge the following day and that I would be reinforced by – it might be 1 Bn or 1 brigade. With such vague orders I could make few plans. About mid-night 8/9th I received a further order from the corps that the reinforcements would be 2 battalions and one mountain battery (no mention of their titles) and that Gen. Mahon would arrive at my headquarters at 6 a.m. 9th to make final plans.[88]

Mahon duly arrived as planned and was informed that rations and water for the troops had not arrived and that the men on the ridge had no water in their bottles. At this point troops were seen advancing on the plain below which he took to be his reinforcements. When Nicol indicated to Mahon that he had yet to issue his orders, Mahon replied, 'You must carry on at once and do the best you can'.[89] In sending men off to fight without sufficient food or water, Mahon was demonstrating that 'hint of ruthlessness without a touch of which no leader has ever been successful' of which King-King recalled Stopford was totally devoid.[90] During 9 August Hamilton visited Mahon's headquarters about 2½ - 3 miles along Kiretch Tepe ridge and recalled that 'I was pleased with Mahon and I was pleased with the look of things there'.[91] Of this incident in *Gallipoli Diary* Hamilton wrote 'My talk with Mahon made me happier. Here, at least, was someone who had an idea of what he was doing. The main thing was to attack before more Turks came down the coast'.[92]

Hamilton's leadership style was of considerable importance to the outcome of the Gallipoli campaign. The ability to make a rapid assessment of a situation and arrive at a sound decision is essential to a leader. A good leader must be able to reason logically under the most trying conditions. Samuels in *Command or Control* identifies two mutually contradictory command systems operating within the British army, 'restrictive control' and 'umpiring'.[93] 'Restrictive control' lays out a subordinate's actions in detail which must be followed regardless of circumstances, while in 'umpiring' a commander indicates a general objective and then abdicates responsibility for its method of delivery to his subordinates. While the former removes the ability from the subordinate to use their initiative or respond to changes in circumstances, the latter places all responsibility for timely decision-making on the subordinate rather than the commander. According to Samuels the two most important practitioners of umpiring in the British Army during the First World War were Haig and Hamilton.[94]

Hamilton's non-interventionist views were clearly stated in his book *The Commander*:

> The true commander ... knows the truth of the great maxim: if the subordinate never makes a mistake, he never makes anything. ... against the danger of a subaltern's mistake in the execution of his own job, it is but fair to set the risk of a meddlesome superior failing himself in the performance of another's business. ... the superior is too busy doing someone else's job to attend to his own – too busy with the parts to give his mind to the whole.[95]

The opportunity to exploit the lack of resistance at Y Beach on 25 April has already been noted. Hunter-Weston's decision not to divert troops away from their originally designated landing zone was a mistake, though the responsibility lies not with Hunter-Weston but with Hamilton and his Staff and their non-interventionist philosophy. Hamilton admitted that he saw the opportunity but was advised by Braithwaite, his Chief of Staff, that he did not think it was a sound decision 'to barge into Hunter-Weston's plans, seeing he was executive Commander of the whole of this southern invasion'.[96] Writing of the incident in his diary the next day Hamilton wrote: 'My inclination was to take a hand myself in this affair but Staff [Braithwaite] are clear against interference when I have no knowledge of the facts – and I suppose they are right'.[97] According to Travers, the non-interventionist line adopted by Hamilton was taught at the Staff College when Braithwaite attended and by following the advice Hamilton was simply following War Office instructions.[98] Nevertheless, it is a weak justification for abdicating responsibility for failure to commit reserves to exploit a clear opportunity. In Samuel's opinion, it was Hamilton, from his position on *HMS Queen Elizabeth*, and not Hunter-Weston who had clear 'knowledge of the facts' and what should be done to achieve success. By allowing Braithwaite and Hunter-Weston to override his own inclinations, Hamilton 'gave excessive freedom to his subordinates, even though he knew they were committing serious errors and he had the power to restore the situation'.[99]

As with any plan, success is largely dependent on those who are to put it into operation. Although the main thrust of the August offensive was to be from the Anzac sector, the landing at Suvla was exclusively a 'New Army' operation, supported by a number of Territorial Force divisions, commanded by a general, Sir Frederick Stopford, who had never commanded troops in battle before and was physically unfit. Kitchener had suggested the appointment of Mahon as corps commander but this had been rejected by Hamilton on the grounds that 'I know Mahon well and although he is undoubtedly good up to a certain point as a Corps Commander here he would be quite useless'.[100] Hamilton requested either Byng or Rawlinson as suitable corps commanders as 'only men of good stiff constitution and nerve will be able to do any good. Everything is at close quarters that many men would be useless in somewhat exposed headquarters they would have to occupy on this limited terrain'.[101] Kitchener rejected this suggestion as neither could be spared from their duties on the Western Front and that both were junior to Mahon anyway.[102] Mahon's command of the 10th (Irish) Division effectively limited the choice of corps commanders to the only two lieutenant-generals senior to Mahon not on active service, Ewart and Stopford. Hamilton dismissed the employment of Ewart on the grounds 'he would not, with his build and constitutional habit, last out here for one fortnight' and suggested to Kitchener that Stopford might be preferable 'even though he does not possess the latter's calm'.[103]

So the seeds of command failure were sown for the Suvla operation by the choice of Stopford. There is no evidence to suggest that Mahon would not have made a more effective commander of IX Corps. On the contrary, Mahon had the command experience that Stopford lacked and had been commended for his 'conspicuous ability and energy' following his relief of Mafeking by no less than Field Marshal Lord Roberts, then the Commander in Chief in South Africa.[104] Kitchener expressed his opinion of Mahon in a letter to Roberts as 'very good' while Sir John French, the future commander of the BEF, wrote 'I wish once again to bring forward Brigadier General Mahon to the favourable attention of the Field Marshal Commander in Chief. I consider he handled his troops with great skill and judgement in a somewhat critical situation'.[105] Despite what Hamilton may have considered to be Mahon's failings, he had rejected a commander of known experience and tactical ability for an unknown quantity who, as noted above, had no previous experience as a frontline commander and was in poor physical condition.

In his written submission to the Dardanelles Commission, Mahon stated that ten days before the landing at Suvla Stopford showed him in confidence his orders and plan of campaign for the forthcoming landings, after which he came to the conclusion that 'they were far too intricate and complicated to have a reasonable chance of success. The whole plan of campaign was based on the times when different objectives would be reached and seized by the Anzac troops, and on the assumption that there would be practically no opposition to the troops landing at Suvla'.[106]

In Mahon's opinion the main thrust of the troops from Anzac was being made at night over very difficult terrain which had not been reconnoitred and that there was every chance that if any part of the proposed plan went wrong then the whole operation would fail, a view he expressed to Stopford at the time. Mahon became more convinced of the soundness of his assessment following his visit to Anzac.[107] His assessment was based on a combination of experience and his knowledge of the troops he had been training for almost a year.

The failure of the August offensive led very quickly to the search for a scapegoat which was quickly found in Stopford and the New Army and Territorial Force divisions under his command at Suvla. The historiography of the August campaign at Gallipoli has been overshadowed by the Suvla Bay landing, thus deflecting criticism away from the failure of the main thrust of the campaign from the Anzac sector. It has even been used as an excuse for tactical failures by the Australians in Peter Weir's film, *Gallipoli*, and in the *Official History*, where Aspinall-Oglander reserved his strongest criticism for the lack of leadership in the Suvla sector.[108] That Hamilton was implicit in directing attention away from the failure of the Anzac offensive is demonstrated by Braithwaite's need to remind him that Suvla was only one of three operations and 'was not even the most important'.[109]

Putting this aside, however, it is evident that the complexity of the plans for the August offensive was, in retrospect at least, beyond the capability of the troops required to undertake them. Guy Dawnay, a staff officer at GHQ, wrote of the August offensive:

> The original landing was nothing to the complexity of this operation, which has involved a great attack from Cape Helles in the south; the breaking out of the Australian position in the north, and the carrying out of one of the most difficult of all military operations – a long night march on the arc of a circle and a night attack in the most exceedingly rough and difficult country, and finally – most intricate of all – another landing on an open beach by night.[110]

Following the failure of the Suvla landings, Dawnay wrote that 'to say the task set to the New Army divisions was, as it turned out, rather beyond their powers, owing to the fact that their officers are insufficiently trained. It is no one's fault – but officers can't be made good company leaders even after a year'.[111] As Dawnay observed, it was not just that the officers were insufficiently trained that led to the failure of the new divisions to take their objectives, 'the truth is that these new armies will have to be taken quite gradually into actual fighting. Fine fellows as they are, they are not well enough led to enable them to compete with all the difficulties and confusion of an attack until they have gradually become accustomed to being in action against the enemy'.[112]

Of the 11th Division which undertook the initial landing at Suvla, Arthur Beecroft, Divisional Signal Officer, wrote:

> they were as fine a body of men as ever put on khaki, and in France would doubtless have excelled themselves; but they never had a vestige of training in any other field of warfare. In early 1915 home training was already on the lines of trench warfare, with musketry practice for repelling counter-attacks etc. The Division knew little or nothing about open order attack, nothing about taking advantage of cover, could not creep up in attack, and knew nothing of sniping.[113]

At Anzac, where the 10th Division's 29th Brigade had been deployed with the 13th Division in support of the ANZACs, the situation was no different because, in the opinion of Temperley, 'the immaturity of the New Army and their natural inability to stand up to either climate or geographic conditions, to both of which they were utterly unaccustomed and untrained. They were quite useless except in one or two conspicuous cases and even dangerous after the first forty-eight hours.'[114]

As early as 12 August Orlo Williams recorded in his diary, 'Everyone here pretty down on the 9th Corps though perhaps we expect too much of them'.[115] Some members of Hamilton's staff had their own views of why the operation at Suvla had failed – 'confusion of night landing/water etc; T[erritorial] F[orce] Divs no good; battn commanders might have done more. The scheme, though well conceived; was probably too extensive for the troops which were at our disposal'.[116] According to Williams, 'Aspinall complained tonight [23 August 1915] how failure of attack on 21st wholly due to bad company leading in 11th div'.[117] In short the reason for failure was the troops not the plan; at least in the opinion of the planners.

Brigadier-General Hill, commanding the 31st Brigade, perhaps summed the situation up best:

> When one considers that these New Army Battalions put on shore at Suvla Bay had under a year's training as Battalions and that under great difficulties, it is a wonder to me that they were even as good as they were. ... Is it to be wondered at that movements were slow? & officers and men inclined to hesitate – if it was all so new and nearly everyone so inexperienced in open warfare. I have often thought that had I under the circumstances disregarded the normal system of attack & sent them off hell for leather like a mob after a pickpocket that we should have captured Chocolate Hill in a couple of hours.
>
> Possibly no heavier casualties but what about after results?[118]

Not only were the New Armies being asked to undertake a complex attack beyond their capabilities and experience, it has been claimed that Hamilton and his staff failed to provide the resources necessary to undertake the task. Credit must be given to Hamilton for the provision of armoured landing craft for the Suvla landings in August rather than the open boats used in the initial landings in April. These undoubtedly reduced the number of casualties in the actual landing itself. Nevertheless, Hamilton and GHQ staff failed to provide a number of resources essential to the success of the campaign, particularly at Suvla. The most essential of these was an adequate water supply. Although arrangements had been made for lighters to bring water from Egypt, a number did not arrive in time and those that did were unable to supply the needs of the men ashore who never 'knew what it was to be thirsty, so could not be expected to eke out a small supply'.[119] The need for water became a major preoccupation for many, as witnessed by Verschoyle of the Royal Inniskilling Fusiliers:

> Looking down you could see a mob of our chaps all round the beaches trying to get water. We were fortunate in our position because the destroyer Grampus cut one of its own water tanks loose and floated it ashore and supplied us from that. Of course the quantity of water was very little, you got about a pint a day which with temperatures verging on a hundred degrees isn't very much.[120]

The lack of water at Suvla in the days immediately following the landing is a theme taken up by many writing on the campaign and water arrangements came in for specific criticism by the Dardanelles Commission:

> We think that want of water was not the sole cause of the failure of the troops to advance further on the 7th; but on the 8th, with the exception of the 34th Brigade, the troops had been so long without water that they could hardly have been expected to undertake any serious operation. There is some reason to suppose that if the objectives had been gained on the 7th more water would have been obtainable from wells and springs, and the sniping of the known wells would have been much reduced, if not stopped altogether.[121]

The shortage of water was a recurring theme in many of the letters to the official historian when the official history of the campaign was being prepared, as it was in a number of letters at the time. Lord Granard, commanding the 5th Royal Irish Regiment, wrote to his wife that 'the troops have suffered very much from the want of water and they have been much more uncomfortable than conditions demanded'.[122]

Despite representations made by Stopford and Reed, Hamilton failed to supply artillery support for the Suvla landings. In his submission to the Dardanelles Commission Stopford responded:

> He [Hamilton] states that at my disposal was placed the IXth Army Corps, less the 13th Division, and the 29th Brigade of the 10th Division. He should have stated that the 10th Division had no artillery and that of the artillery of the 11th Division only one brigade of artillery was available until 12th August, and of it only one battery was available for the fighting of August 7th – 8th.[123]

According to the table accompanying the instructions given to Stopford on 22 July, he would have had an expectation of having some 56 artillery pieces from the 11th Division at his disposal within twenty four hours of the initial landing.[124] Due to the lack of artillery support, the landing divisions were pinned down for most of 7 August in the area around the Salt Lake until at 5 p.m. the support of a single battery on Lala Baba and naval gunfire enabled a successful attack on Chocolate Hill, an objective designated to be captured at dawn.[125]

During cross examination at the Dardanelles Commission, Hamilton admitted that, in the context of lack of artillery support, 'The vital thing was to make good, and to make good we ought to have had ample artillery, especially howitzers. We had not, and there was nothing for it but to try and get on, as you say by a sacrifice of human lives'.[126]

Over time, and in the case of the 10th Division quite a short period, Hamilton lost the confidence of those under his command. As early as 10 August Granard was writing home expressing his lack of confidence in Hamilton's ability to deliver the objectives of the August offensive:

> Our losses in the fighting after the landing have been very heavy and I attribute this to the stupidity of Ian

Hamilton in starting operations before he had sufficient troops and what was more criminal starting operations without any artillery whatever. If this campaign had been properly run we ought to have gained the positions we are [now] attacking and cut off a great proportion of the Turkish army.[127]

On hearing of Mahon's decision to 'resign' rather than serve under De Lisle, Granard considered doing the same given the treatment afforded to the division, presumably by Hamilton and GHQ. Referring to the casualties experienced by the division in just a week, some 114 officers and 3,000 men killed and wounded, Granard concluded:

> Ian Hamilton is entirely responsible for the state of things and the sooner he is recalled the better. He has run this whole show like a madman. He will take no advice and unless he is soon recalled it is difficult to know what will happen. As usual we have underrated the Turk and now owing to General Hamilton's action we have not the number of troops necessary for an advance. ... This could have been avoided by proper generalship.[128]

Granard was, however, not content with just sharing his opinions with his wife as a message sent to Hamilton, a copy of which Hamilton forwarded to Kitchener, showed:

> Dear General, I should have felt I had violated my oath, as a Member of HM Privy Council, if I had not informed The King, and other of my colleagues, my opinion of the circumstances as they appear to me out here. These views are not in accord with the present policy. I may, however, add that both the Corps and 10th Divisional Commanders have the entire confidence of all ranks.[129]

In a letter forwarded to Hankey, an anonymous officer of the 10th Division expressed the view that the New Army divisions at Suvla had been sacrificed to protect the Australian [sic] attack, 'the success of the whole movement depending on the ability of the Australians to move over impossible country and take a certain hill by night'. Pessimistically the officer concluded that the army's current position was as a result of 'bad generalship and inadequate arrangements'. He concluded:

> We want a [new] policy and a general who can carry it out. This one can't and has shown incompetence in every particular since we came under his orders. We are losing prestige for every minute he remains and none of us have the slightest confidence in him or his staff. [130]

Others had come to the same conclusion, including some of Hamilton's staff officers, for on 1 September Dawnay was sent to London ostensibly to seek more reinforcements, but in reality to apprise Kitchener of the need to end the campaign. According to Dawnay, it was apparent that during his second meeting with Kitchener he too was convinced that the campaign had been badly managed.[131] Ultimately this loss of confidence led to Hamilton's recall on 15 October.

Due to the amphibious nature of the April and August offensives at Gallipoli the campaign is often viewed as different from that of the Western Front, but in truth the development of tactics was in many ways similar and this theme will be developed further in the next chapter. Hamilton, his staff, and the corps and divisional commanders initially subscribed to a need to achieve moral dominance over the enemy by employing offensive tactics, essentially the frontal attack.[132] Although by the beginning of July he would write 'the old battle tactics have clean vanished', Hamilton had learned little from his mistakes as the plan for the August landings was essentially no different from that of the landings at Helles or Anzac.[133] Troops were landed at Suvla without adequate artillery support and with the intention of overwhelming the Turkish positions by sheer weight of numbers.

Despite continued leadership failures by Hunter-Weston in July 1915, Hamilton once again refused to remove him from command even though 'there was practically a mutiny out there, and a great number of Brigadier-Generals openly refused to take any further orders from Gen. Hunter-Weston, who was responsible for the muddle'.[134] Hunter-Weston was later removed from command as a result of sunstroke.

It would appear from the above analysis that Hamilton does not score well against the nine-point leadership framework, but was this leadership failure from GHQ entirely his alone? Orlo Williams, the cipher officer at Hamilton's Headquarters wrote 'I fear the General [Hamilton] is run by the CGS [Braithwaite], who may be a good soldier, but a stupid man, with no ideas ... fond of his own way. CGS relies almost wholly on Aspinall and Dawnay'.[135] Bean puts this down to Hamilton's inability to control his staff: 'It is rather a fault of character than of intellect that has caused him [Hamilton] to fail. He has not the strength to command his staff – they command him; especially Braithwaite; his chief of staff, with whom he is on the worst of terms, I believe has commanded this expedition'.[136] Bean continued, 'Hamilton has not the strength to give those with whom he is surrounded a straight out blow from the shoulder'.[137] That Bean's comments reflect a degree of truth is illustrated by Hamilton's non-intervention at Y beach on 25 April where an opportunity to exploit an unopposed landing existed. Writing in his diary Hamilton recorded: 'My inclination was to take a hand myself in this affair [Y beach] but the Staff [Braithwaite] are clear against interference when I have no knowledge of the facts'.[138] It is obvious that Hamilton knew the right thing to do but allowed himself to be overruled by Braithwaite who was a staff college graduate and was following what was at the time accepted policy. In the last annual conference of staff officers held before the Great War, Brigadier General John Gough addressed the question of what could be done to make officers competent commanders in war. He concluded 'the practical difficulty, however, is that some commanders are so anxious to leave subordinates a free hand that they forget their own duty of control and guidance, while others go to the opposite extreme and interfere with the methods of their subordinates'.[139] Evidence suggests that Hamilton at Gallipoli vacillated between these two extremes and on more than one occasion made the wrong choice.

Perhaps there is an element of truth in the 'Peter Principle' that everyone is promoted to a level above their level of ability. After a career of unbroken success at regimental and staff level and outwardly possessing all the qualifications for the job, Hamilton was appointed to senior military command which ultimately proved to be beyond his capability. Perhaps one of Hamilton's biographers sums him up most succinctly:

> He had personal charm, integrity, more experience of war than any of his contemporaries, intellectual detachment, and physical courage. His flaws were not as visible but they proved fatal. He lacked mental toughness, basic common sense, and sufficient ruthlessness to dismiss an incompetent subordinate. He underestimated the enemy, a cardinal sin in war, and his excessive optimism frequently crossed into the realm of wishful thinking. While it was theoretically sound to refrain from interfering in field operations once in progress, it was unwise to adhere to that principle when subordinates were unproven or inadequate. The plain truth was that throughout the Gallipoli campaign he never acted like a commander-in-chief.[140]

Cassar's summation appears fair in light of the evidence. Williams records in his diary that 'really Sir Ian does not impress me. He can't say a thing direct, nor bring himself to stand up to K'. He then proceeds to give details of a flaw in his character which may help to explain the underlying reason why Stopford was appointed to command IX Corps.[141] According to Williams, an officer at Hamilton's Headquarters had been promised by the Quartermaster-General when he left England that he would be given a particular post when it was created, to which Kitchener subsequently appointed another officer. Rather than insist that the post be given to the original officer as promised, Hamilton began to suggest things against Kitchener's appointee, 'which quite fail to put K off'.[142] Parallels exist with the proposal to appoint Mahon to command IX Corps following Kitchener's refusal to appoint either Rawlinson or Byng who had been requested by Hamilton. Having failed to get his way, Hamilton began to suggest things against Mahon to Kitchener such as his alleged limitations. In doing so, however, Hamilton was hoist with his own petard – succeeding in having Mahon replaced by Stopford, a man of lesser experience and ability.

Stopford was certainly not the best man for the job, but given Hamilton's rejection of Mahon as corps commander, Kitchener's insistence that Mahon should accompany the 10th (Irish) Division to Gallipoli and French's refusal to release Byng and Rawlinson from the Western Front, he was the only officer available. Stopford's lack of experience was to some extent mitigated by the appointment of Reed, with recent experience on the Western Front, as his Chief of Staff, who according to Hamilton 'is calm and tough, exactly the sub-strata most lacking in Stopford's otherwise complete outfit'.[143] Stopford recognised the need for effective artillery support while Hamilton was still convinced of the superiority of morale and offensive spirit. That Stopford, and Reed, were more in touch with current tactical thinking is demonstrated by the adoption of the preliminary bombardment by Byng, Stopford's replacement as corps commander and Hamilton's original choice to command IX Corps.

Arguably, Stopford's decision to limit the corps' objectives to securing Suvla as a supply base was more realistic than GHQ's original plans given the resources, especially inexperienced troops, available to him. This certainly appears to be the view taken by the Deputy Chief of the Imperial General Staff who wrote:

> From a careful study of the Orders and Instructions so far as they are available and bearing in mind the nature of the terrain and also the quality of the troops and the fact they had just come straight off board ship, I incline to the belief that the whole series of tasks as planned for the IX Corps was somewhat of a risky business and not a thoroughly sound practical operation of war.[144]

What Stopford and IX Corps achieved immediately after the landing was precisely what Stopford had informed Hamilton he would deliver, a supply base for the northern peninsula. This is an incontestable fact as Suvla provided this function until its eventual evacuation in December 1915. While Stopford and his staff were not dynamic they were not the blunderers that Aspinall-Oglander's official history and Hamilton's *Gallipoli Diary* tend to paint.

Hamilton's diary entry for 13 August shows that he considered removing Stopford from command of IX Corps, 'were not my hands tied by Mahon's seniority. Mahon is next senior – in the whole force he stands next to myself'. That evening he cabled Kitchener expressing his disappointment at the progress made by the corps, stating 'the generals are unfit for it'.[145] The following day Kitchener replied giving permission for the removal of Stopford, Hammersley and Mahon and asking for suggestions for possible replacements. Kitchener ended his reply, 'This is a young man's war, and we must have commanding officers that will take full advantage of opportunities which occur but seldom'.[146] Having once again suggested Byng as a possible replacement for Stopford, Hamilton recorded:

> Between them, these two messages have cleared the air. Mahon's seniority has been at the root of this evil. K.'s conscience tells him so and therefore, he pricks his name upon the fatal list. *But he did not know, when he cabled, that Mahon had done well.* [my italics] I shall replace Stopford forthwith by de Lisle and chance Mahon's seniority.[147]

Mahon, however, refused to waive his seniority and serve under de Lisle and asked to be replaced as commander of the 10th Division.[148] According to Nicol:

> General Mahon in his note of farewell says he believed it better for the 10th Div for him to leave. General De Lisle, I believe owed him a grudge & General Mahon knew his man and expected that grudge to be repaid on his division.
>
> My experience proved that he was right – I knew what I had to expect from Gen De Lisle after the events of the 16th [August] from what I heard of him but did

not expect that my Brigade would be victimised too for the responsibility was mine alone; but Gen. Mahon was right – every one of my recommendations for recognition in the Brigade was quashed and not one soul was mentioned.[149]

What grudge de Lisle held against Mahon is unknown, but Mahon could have refused to serve under him on the grounds of seniority and experience alone. Joining the army in the same year, Mahon's advancement had been much swifter and experience of command wider than de Lisle who had on mobilisation commanded a cavalry brigade in France, while Mahon was already a Lieutenant-General. Any suggestion that de Lisle was given command of the corps because of his age (he was 3 years younger than Mahon) or his supposed greater experience of command on the peninsula (he had taken command of the 29th Division on 4 June) is a fallacy. In the Third Battle of Krithia he had demonstrated no original thought following the tactics of the previous offensives at Helles. According to Prior, de Lisle 'is often thought of as a new breed at Gallipoli, but there is no evidence that he performed with greater skill than his predecessors' and he made no further progress than Stopford at Suvla.[150] On the basis of this evidence there was no reason why de Lisle should have replaced Stopford, even temporarily, rather than Mahon. However, Mahon's grounds for declining to serve under de Lisle appear to be for reasons other than experience or seniority. His reply to Hamilton's message stated that he declined to 'waive my seniority and to serve under the officer you name', thus suggesting the reason was more personal. While it may not be possible to know the real reason for Mahon's refusal, perhaps Birdwood provides a clue in his comment on de Lisle's character: 'everyone hates him as he is a brute, with no thoughts for others, rude to everyone and has no principles'.[151]

Informing Kitchener of Mahon's decision not to serve under de Lisle, Hamilton wrote, 'From this correspondence it will be seen that there never has been any question affecting Lieutenant General Mahon's efficiency as a Divisional Commander; indeed, the only time I have mentioned his name to you has been in terms of commendation'.[152] It may be the nature of the British army at the time but Mahon's decision to relinquish his command in the middle of an offensive was not criticised either in the report of the Dardanelles Commission or the official history. There appears to be no complaint about Mahon within the 10th (Irish) Division and no mention of the event in Cooper's *The Tenth (Irish) Division in Gallipoli*. Only Hamilton refers to the incident in his diary and then mildly as 'a very unhappy affair' and describing Mahon as a fighter who given time to think would return to his command.[153] In this Hamilton was correct. On the arrival of Byng to take command of IX Corps on 23 August, Mahon returned to command the 10th (Irish) Division. As Mahon was senior to Byng this demonstrates that Mahon's problem with de Lisle was purely personal and not a matter of seniority or annoyance at not getting command of the corps.

※

The leadership provided to the 10th (Irish) Division at Gallipoli at the most senior level was poor and this stemmed from Hamilton himself. Of the nine leadership principles identified at the beginning of this chapter, Hamilton failed on most counts. In truth Hamilton's mind-set was that of a previous era not dominated by trenches, machine guns and artillery, and where an enemy could be overcome by the moral ascendancy of the bayonet charge. In this he was not alone. On the Western Front the British army was only at the beginning of a long learning curve. Hamilton's problem and that of his staff was that they were not open to recent developments elsewhere. Byng favoured the systematic use of artillery to support the offensive at Suvla, as had Stopford and Reed previously, which extracted the complaint from Hamilton 'all these fellows from France come here with this idea'.

Contrary to popular belief and not in line with his role of scapegoat for the failure of the August offensive, Stopford's leadership was adequate within his limitations. He had no combat command experience, yet with the support of Reed he recognised that Hamilton's plan for the Suvla landing was beyond the capability of his troops and forced an amendment of the original plan to cover more realistic objectives. Despite attempts by Hamilton and others to portray him as the reason for the failure of the August campaign, he achieved his overriding objective of securing Suvla Bay as a base for troops in the northern sector of the peninsula, which arguably was the only aspect of Hamilton's original plan to be achieved. It is undoubtedly true that Stopford missed the opportunity to capture Tekke Teppe ridge due to being out of touch with his command and allowing the troops to rest on 8 August. In reality, even had the ridge been captured it would have been difficult to hold given the fact it was over 5 miles from the beach.

As observed by Hore-Ruthven, Mahon was given little chance at Gallipoli to demonstrate his leadership ability.[154] Past performance, and the endorsement of previous commanders under whom he had served such as Kitchener, French and Roberts, show that he was regarded as an able tactician with the skill and ability to handle troops in critical situations. Even Hamilton during the Boer war is known to have sought Mahon's agreement on his planned course of action.[155] It is unfortunate that Mahon chose to relinquish his command in the middle of the battle for Kiretch Tepe and did not return until after the key battle of 21 August as it robs history of the opportunity to assess his tactical ability. Nevertheless his comments on Hamilton's plans show that he had a strong grasp of strategy and a realistic understanding of the capabilities of the inexperienced soldiers of IX Corps. In Hamilton's opinion he was a fighting soldier and 'someone who had an idea of what he was doing' and 'there never has been any question affecting Lieutenant-General Mahon's efficiency as a Divisional Commander'.[156] That Hamilton was wrong not to have accepted Mahon rather than Stopford to command IX Corps is demonstrated by Sir Charles Monroe's endorsement of his performance during the early months of his command of British forces in Salonika and in particular during the retreat from Serbia. Sir Charles also noted the organisational difficulties that faced Mahon and his staff caused by the unplanned nature of the initial allied involvement in Salonika. In his opinion, Mahon's ability to overcome these demonstrated 'the high standard of administrative capacity displayed by the G.O.C. and his Staff'.[157]

CHAPTER 7

Morale and Discipline

Although the pre-war army eschewed the adoption of a formal military doctrine, the majority, particularly of senior officers, subscribed informally to a belief that the offensive was the solution to modern warfare and increased firepower. Fundamentally the offensive was viewed in terms of the need to achieve a moral ascendancy over the enemy on what was termed a 'psychological battlefield'; essentially the willingness of attacking troops to cross a fire-zone, regardless of losses, to close with the enemy and by so doing demoralise them by their willingness to accept casualties.[1] Sir Ian Hamilton wrote in 1910:

> Blindness to moral forces and worship of material forces inevitably lead in war to destruction. All that exaggerated reliance placed on chassepots and mitrailleuses by France before '70; all that trash written by M. Bloch before 1904 about zones of fire across which no living being could pass, heralded nothing but disaster. War is essentially the triumph, not of the chassepot over a needle-gun, not of a line of men entrenched behind wire entanglements and fireswept zones over men exposing themselves in the open, but of one will over another weaker will.[2]

In the closing years of the nineteenth century Jean de Bloch, a financier, banker and railway contractor and amateur military theorist, wrote a series of volumes entitled *The War of the Future*. Bloch believed that improvements in weaponry had enormously increased the power of the defensive, which could only be overcome by a vast numerical superiority and even then at the cost of heavy casualties.[3] The British army's experience in the Boer War appeared to justify Bloch's views on firepower, and although the musketry skills of individual infantrymen were improved following the war, the success of Japanese forces against entrenched troops in the Russo-Japanese War led many to believe that the solution to the problem of modern firepower was to emphasise the moral/psychological qualities necessary for success in war. This view was supported by the War Office because it believed that the experience of modern firepower in the Boer War had caused long-term damage to the offensive spirit of junior officers.[4] As a result, the *Field Service Regulations* and the *Training and Manoeuvre Regulations* of 1909 placed more emphasis on moral rather than physical force than its predecessor, which had been more cautious about assaults across open ground at decisive ranges.[5] In the years immediately preceding the Great War, however, there was a gradual acceptance of the increased impact of firepower and that more realistic tactics were needed if it was to be addressed. It has even been suggested that 'if the outbreak of war had been delayed for another two years or so, the British army might well have moved toward both more realistic and more imaginative tactics'.[6] Nevertheless, despite the experience of two world wars, Charles Moran, who had served as a regimental medical officer with the 1st Royal Fusiliers during the First World War and was Churchill's personal physician in the Second, observed that 'it has always been a military axiom, that a man's will to fight is the ultimate arbiter of battles and that this is governed by the thoughts however elementary which pass through his head. ... It is not the number of soldiers, but their will to win which decides battles'.[7]

To achieve moral ascendancy attacking troops had to have instilled in them, corporately and individually, a belief in their superiority and ability to win. To the majority of pre-war officers this was achieved by a combination of morale and discipline. John Baynes in his study of the 2nd Scottish Rifles gives the *Webster's Dictionary* definition of morale as being:

> a confident, resolute, willing, often self-sacrificing and courageous attitude of an individual to the functions or tasks demanded or expected of him by a group of which he is a part that is based upon such factors as pride in the achievements and aims of the group, faith in its leadership and ultimate success, a sense of fruitful personal participation in its work, and a devotion and loyalty to the other members of the group.[8]

Baynes distils his years of experience as an officer in a regular battalion and commander of a Territorial Army regiment to describe the importance of morale:

> High morale is the most important quality of a soldier. It is a quality of mind and spirit which combines courage, self-discipline, and endurance. It springs from infinitely varying and sometime contradictory sources.... At its highest peak it is seen as an individual's readiness to accept his fate willingly even to the point of death, and to refuse all roads that lead to safety at the price of his conscience.[9]

Timothy Bowman, in his study of discipline and morale in Irish regiments during the Great War, adopted a more basic definition of these terms. Morale he suggests 'is the force which comes from within which makes a soldier carry out his duty but which can be influenced by external factors such as regimental loyalty, efficient administration, good leadership and patriotism', while 'discipline is an external force which carries out the same function'.[10] Bowman recognises the difficulties involved in measuring morale and that a number of quantifiable and unquantifiable criteria were used during the Great War. These include the quantifiable cases of trench foot, shell shock and courts martial, and the unquantifiable dress, cleanliness, frequency of saluting and the degree of formality, particularly between officers and other ranks, within units.[11]

Bowman's study of discipline and morale was based on soldiers in Irish units on the Western Front who were tried by courts martial between August 1914 and 11 November 1918, supplemented by the courts martial records of a sample of Irish battalions serving on other fronts. This chapter extends this study to cover the courtsmartial records of all soldiers serving in the infantry battalions of the 10th (Irish) Division from its raising in September 1914 to its 'Indianisation' in May 1918. The courts martial records of the infantry battalions of the 13th (Western) Division, as the only other active division never to serve on the Western Front, were also extracted for the same period for comparison purposes. Bowman's analysis of courts-martial records for the 16th (Irish) and 36th (Ulster) Divisions have been used to provide a comparison between the 10th Division and other Irish New Army battalions.

The creation of New Army battalions not only broadened the social spectrum from which recruits were drawn but also exposed many volunteers to an environment beyond their previous experience. For the working-class recruit, however, the regimented system of the army differed little from that of the factory floor and they would have been used to the subordination and tedium involved in military service.[12] It would therefore be expected that volunteers from industrial areas would adapt more quickly to military discipline than those from a rural background and thus the level of offences as demonstrated by the number of courts martial would be lower for battalions recruited in urban rather than rural areas. Analysis of the 10th Division's 13 battalions (Table 7.1, Annex 2), however, shows that 40% of all courtsmartial offences perpetrated during training were committed by men from two of the three battalions with recruiting districts in large urban areas, i.e. 6th Royal Irish Rifles and 6th Royal Dublin Fusiliers.[13] By contrast the third battalion, namely the 7th Royal Dublin Fusiliers, which was mostly recruited from the Irish urban working class, largely conforms to Beckett's hypothesis regarding the compliance of urban working-class recruits as it had one of the lowest level of courts martial within the division during their period of training in the United Kingdom. The only apparent difference between this battalion and the other two is that it was formed around a nucleus of middle-class recruits in D company, collectively known as 'The Pals', approximately 20% of whom were commissioned from the ranks during and after Gallipoli. Excluding those promoted from D company the other companies of the 7th Royal Dublin Fusiliers also had a higher proportion of men commissioned from the ranks than any other battalion of the division. This higher proportion of middle-class recruits in the 7th Royal Dublin Fusiliers may therefore have had an impact on discipline throughout the battalion.

Recruitment from the urban working class, however, was not confined to the towns and cities of Ireland. Major Geoffrey Drage, 7th Royal Munster Fusiliers, acquired over 1,000 Yorkshire men at the regimental depot of the York and Lancaster Regiment at Pontefract; while Verschoyle, 5th Royal Inniskilling Fusiliers, noted the presence of 100 Glasgow shipyard workers in his battalion, while almost a third of the men in his company were from London.[14] There is no evidence, however, to suggest that in the 10th (Irish) Division recruits from the urban working class from other parts of the United Kingdom were more amenable to discipline than their Irish counterparts, particularly when three of the battalions that received significant numbers of urban working-class volunteers from Great Britain had a level of courts martial above the divisional average.

The experience of the 107th Brigade, 36th (Ulster) Division, which was mainly recruited from working-class areas of Belfast, casts further doubt on the validity of Beckett's hypothesis on the acceptance of military discipline. In a letter to his wife, the divisional commander wrote: 'I am not too happy about the Ulster Division for it cannot be denied that some of them have very little discipline. The Belfast Brigade is awful. They have absolutely no discipline and their officers are awful. I am very much disturbed about them. I don't think they are fit for service and should be very sorry to have to trust them'.[15] Having been given the opportunity to exchange a brigade with another division, ostensibly to enable it to obtain frontline experience, Nugent used it to discard his troublesome brigade and made it quite clear to its officers that it was a punishment for indiscipline.[16] It is doubtful if this banishment did much to improve the discipline of the brigade for Major Crozier, 9th Royal Irish Rifles, recalled that when the time came for the brigade to return to the division it was 'reformed perhaps but by no means penitent'.[17] Both qualitative and quantitative evidence therefore suggest that Beckett's hypotheses regarding the amenability to discipline of the industrialised working class does not necessarily hold true in relation to the Irish working class.

Not all disciplinary problems experienced by the 10th Division during training were due to morale or resulted in formal disciplinary action. Cooper recorded of the Englishmen of the division that

> They had enlisted purely from patriotic motives, and were inclined to dislike the delay in getting to grips with the Germans; and being, for the most part, strong Trade Unionists, with acute suspicion of any non-elected authority, they were disposed to resent the restraints of discipline, and found it hard to place complete confidence in their officers. They also felt the alteration in their incomes very keenly. Many of them, before en- listment, had been miners earning from two to three pounds a week, and the drop from this to seven shillings, or in the case of married men 3s.6d., came very hard. The deduction for their wives was particularly unwelcome, not because they grudged the money, but because when they had enlisted they had not been told that this stoppage was compulsory, and so they considered that they had been taken advantage of. However, they had plenty of sense, and soon began to realise the necessity of discipline.[18]

A comparison of the total number of offences tried by courts martial while the three Irish divisions were training in the United Kingdom provides an interesting contrast of their disciplinary records. Table 7.2 combines Bowman's analysis of the sample of disciplinary records extracted for the 16th and 36th Divisions with those of their regimental equivalents in the 10th Division.[19] The table shows that, although the 10th Division trained for a shorter period in the United Kingdom (ten months compared with the thirteen and eleven months of the 16th and 36th Divisions respectively), with the exceptions of the 5th Royal Inniskilling and the 7th Royal Dublin Fusiliers, all battalions of regiments serving in the 10th Division had higher levels of offences warranting courts martial than their battalions in the other two divisions.

The level of offences that occurred in the 6th Royal Dublin Fusiliers is unparalleled in any battalion of the three divisions during their period of training. It has been suggested that the difference between the courts martial records of the 6th (150 cases) and 7th Royal Dublin Fusiliers (18 cases) is partly due to their differing social background and partly the former's proximity to their homes when stationed in Dublin because the battalion's most prevalent offence was going absent without leave (89 cases).[20] This view is supported by Captain Hervey de Montmorency serving with the 7th Royal Dublin Fusiliers:

> It is quite true that the Irishmen in my battalion have been recruited from the poorest, unskilled casual labourers of Dublin, the lowest strata of our society – and there has been undoubtedly a great deal of absence without leave, but absence without leave is a purely military offence, it is not immoral, besides the prevalence of this 'crime' is, in no small measure due to the men being stationed within reach of Dublin i.e. within reach of temptation.[21]

De Montmorency's comment is interesting for a number of reasons. As an officer of the 7th Royal Dublin Fusiliers, he stated that his battalion had 'been recruited from the poorest, unskilled casual labourers of Dublin, the lowest strata of our society' without making any reference to the 'Pals' company of the battalion which was largely drawn from a stratum of society that in other battalions would have provided the officer class. Given, however, that the majority of the battalion's other ranks may have come from the same background as those of the 6th battalion, it is noteworthy that only 20 cases of absence without leave were tried in the 7th battalion during training. De Montmorency gave no reason for this disparity between men largely recruited from the same area. A number of possible reasons, however, present themselves: either all absences in the 7th battalion were not recorded - as in the case of the 14th Royal Irish Rifles of the Ulster Division whose Adjutant, Captain Bentley, refused to refer occurrences of absence without leave to courts martial – or the internal management of the 6th battalion was seriously flawed.[22]

De Montmorency's assertion that the battalion's proximity to Dublin was a contributory factor to the high number of cases of men from the battalion going absent without leave bears some discussion. Analysis of the 6th Royal Dublin Fusiliers' courts martial records reveals that half the cases tried for absence without leave occurred while the battalion was stationed at the Curragh while the other 50% occurred while it was stationed in Dublin. The validity of de Montmorency's explanation fails to hold water when compared to the 13th Royal Irish Rifles of the 36th (Ulster) Division, which was stationed on the Clandeboye estate, within walking distance of the homes of many of its soldiers, and experienced only one case of absence without leave while training in the United Kingdom. It is possible, however, that the battalion adopted a similar approach to absences without leave as that of the 14th Royal Irish Rifles.

An offence prevalent in both the 16th (Irish) and 36th (Ulster) Divisions but apparently absent from the 10th (Irish) Division is that of mutiny. The *Manual of Military Law*, paraphrases 'mutiny', defined in section 7 of *The Army Act 1881*, as the 'collective insubordination, or a combination of two or more persons to resist or to induce others to resist lawful military authority'.[23] Only eight cases of mutiny, all in the 16th (Irish) Division, were tried in the three Irish divisions during their period of training in the United Kingdom. Eyewitness accounts, however, testify to mutiny in the 16th and 36th Divisions for which no charges were brought against the participants. Seven members of the 8th Royal Inniskilling Fusiliers were each sentenced to one year's hard labour following their trial on 6 September 1915 for mutiny and drunkenness. At the same time, no charges resulted from a mutiny in the 6th Connaught Rangers of the same division, which contributed to the deaths of two soldiers.[24] While this was the most serious occurrence, Staniforth in his letters to his parents suggests that this was neither the first nor the last mutiny involving the 6th Connaught Rangers during training, although the final incident on either Christmas Eve or Christmas Day 1914, which involved a number of men invading the Officers' Mess during dinner, was regarded as seasonal high-jinks.[25]

The indiscipline of the 10th (Irish) Division was not only high in comparison with that of the other Irish divisions but also with the 13th (Western) Division. In absolute terms the number of cases tried by courts martial in respect of offences occurring in the United Kingdom in the 10th Division (618) was 68% higher than the number of cases in the 13th Division (367). Figure 7.1 (Annex 1) shows the relative frequency of courts martial between the two divisions and shows quite clearly that with one exception, the level of courts martial cases in the 10th Division exceed that of the 13th in each of the nine months for which records exist.[26]

Comparison of the courts martial records reveals that while desertion was a greater problem for the 13th Division (81 compared to 63 cases in the 10th), the level of drunkenness and absence without leave in the 10th (Irish) Division were 150% and 210% higher respectively. Higher levels of drunkenness in the 10th (Irish) Division might be seen as a reflection of the hard-drinking Irish stereotype believed to be prevalent in Victorian society. Roger Swift's observation of civil criminality in Great Britain in the latter half of the nineteenth century noted that 'Irish criminality was highly concentrated in the often inter-related categories of drunkenness, disorderly conduct and assault'.[27] J. V. O'Brien in his study of early twentieth-century Dublin suggests that drunkenness and associated criminal behaviour was not confined to Irish immigrants in Great Britain but that the situation in towns and rural communities of Ireland was little different.[28] These observations tend to suggest that higher levels of drunkenness in Irish regiments merely reflected Irish society as a whole. Comparison of the two battalions within the 10th Division with the highest levels of charges for drunkenness, the 6th Royal Irish Rifles and 5th Royal Irish Fusiliers, appear to contradict the hypothesis. The former battalion comprised mainly Irishmen, including reservists, while the latter was one with a high proportion of volunteers from England. What these battalions have in common is that they were both the senior service battalion of their respective regiments. Accordingly they would have been commanded by the promoted major of the regimental depot or a regular who with more recent experience of military discipline may have been less lenient with drunken offenders than officers from the Reserve of Officers commanding other battalions.[29] Indeed, only in the case of the 5th Royal Inniskilling Fusiliers does the senior service battalion of regiments in the division not have a higher proportion of courts martial for drunkenness than their more junior counterpart.

Figure 7.2 in Annex 1 shows the relative proportion of crimes by category as a total percentage of all crimes committed by each division.[30] This analysis shows that absence without leave, loss of property and miscellaneous military offences formed the bulk of offences committed by the 10th (Irish) Division. It is notable that those crimes that Swift associated with drunkenness amongst the Irish civil population in Great Britain, such as disorderly conduct and assault, were less a feature of the Irish 10th division than the English 13th, as were the civil crimes of fraud and theft.

Although the number of offences committed by members of the 10th Division was almost 70% higher than the number committed by the 13th Division over the same period, an analysis of the percentage of offences committed per month during training (see Figure 7.3 below) shows that there is no significant difference in the pattern of offending over the period. This suggests that if the 13th (Western) Division is viewed as a typical New Army division, the 10th (Irish) Division's disciplinary record, and hence how well the men of the division adjusted to military life, largely conforms to that of the rest of Kitchener's K1 divisions.

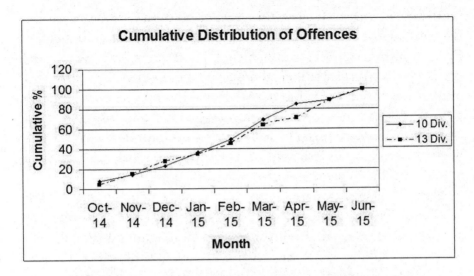

Figure 7.3: Cumulative percentage distribution of offences tried by courts martial in the 10th (Irish) and 13th (Western) Divisions between 1 October 1914 and 30 June 1915.[31]

Bowman provides a series of tables giving details of sentences passed by courts martial. These tables equate the number of sentences to a similar number of offences. However, analysis of courts martial records show that multiple offences could result in a single sentence whereas the outcome of a single offence might lead to a sentence with a number of elements. As a consequence the number of offences shown in Table 7.1 does not match the number of sentences passed during the period shown in Table 7.3 (Annex 2).[32]

As previously observed, the battalions with the highest level of courts martial in the 10th Division were the 6th battalions of the Royal Irish Rifles and Royal Dublin Fusiliers, whilst the units with the lowest level of recorded offences were the 5th Royal Inniskilling Fusiliers and 10th Hampshire Regiment. It might be expected that the severity of sentences passed on offenders in these units might proportionately reflect the seriousness of the crime. Table 7.3 (Annex 2) shows that while this supposition is reflected by the courts martial records of the 10th Hampshires, evidence from the records of the other battalions show that offenders in the 5th Royal Inniskilling Fusiliers were proportionately more likely to be sentenced to detention or hard labour than in any other battalion in the division and almost twice as likely to be sentenced to hard labour than the division's most offending battalion, the 6th Royal Dublin Fusiliers. Field Punishment (FP2) was imposed on offenders in eleven of the division's thirteen battalions, although the more severe punishment of FP1 was only awarded in the 5th Royal Irish Fusiliers, a unit also with the highest proportion of stoppages, fines and loss of pay. Of the battalions awarding FP2, offenders were proportionately more likely to have it awarded in the 6th Royal Munster Fusiliers, a battalion in the lower quartile of offending units.[33]

Table 7.3 also shows that in the 5th Royal Irish Regiment and the 7th Royal Dublin Fusiliers, over 25% of courts martial resulted in a sentence of 'discharge with ignominy' while the 6th Royal Irish Rifles, the battalion with the second highest level of offences, had proportionately more 'not guilty' verdicts than any other battalion. If it is assumed that the punishments listed in Table 7.3, which follow the order they appear in the War Office records, represent a descending hierarchy of severity, it might be concluded that discipline in the 5th Royal Inniskilling Fusiliers was more strictly administered than in other battalions of the division and this was the reason why it had fewer offences than any of the other Irish battalions. It might also help explain why the 6th Royal Dublin Fusiliers and the 6th Royal Irish Rifles, with significantly lower proportions of the most severe punishments being awarded, had the highest levels of offences tried by courts martial in the division.

A comparison of the severity of sentences passed by courts martial across the three Irish divisions during training shows that while the 10th Division had a significantly higher level of offences tried by courts martial they were proportionately less severely dealt with than in the other two divisions. Table 7.4 (Annex 2) compares Bowman's analysis of the sample of disciplinary records extracted for the 16th and 36th Divisions with those of their regimental equivalents in the 10th Division and the sentences passed.[34] This table clearly shows that – with the exception of the 5th Royal Inniskilling Fusiliers, (already identified as the most severely administered battalion in the division) and the 6th Royal Dublin Fusiliers, (the unit with an unprecedented level of courts martial of any Irish New Army battalion) – the proportion of the most severe categories

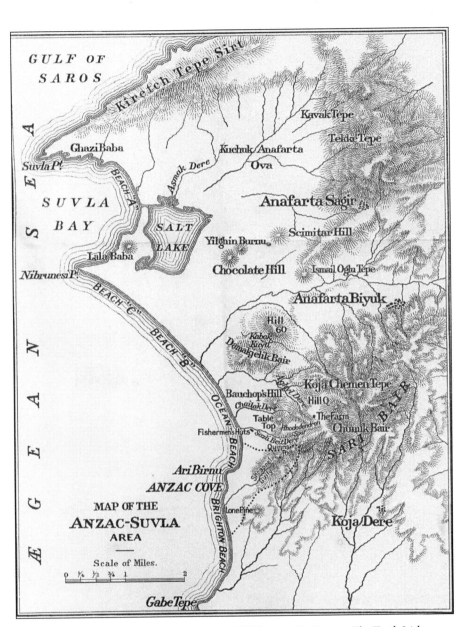

Map 1. Map of the Anzac-Suvla area, August 1915 (source: B. Cooper, *The Tenth Irish Division in Gallipoli*, London, 1918).

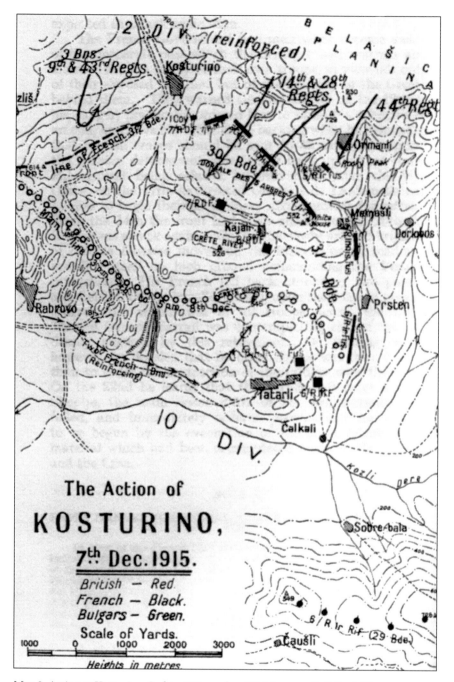

Map 2. Action at Kosturino, Serbia, 7 December 1915 (source: C. Falls, *Military Operations Macedonia*, I, London, 1933).

1. Private Frederick Croad, 6th Royal Munster Fusiliers, of Tonyrefail, Glamorgan (Graham Croad).

2. Private John David Purcell (seated) and one of the 'Colne Pals', 5th Royal Irish Fusiliers. (Margaret Purcell)

3. Officers of the 10th Hampshire Regiment, Basingstoke, 1915 (Royal Hampshire Regiment Trust)

I.H. German L.A. Shone L. Whittome P.L. Bell

P.C. Williams G. Clement G.H. Tanner R.W. Lamb O.S. Whaley F.W. Parry P.H. Hudson
C. Grellin W.J. Saunders

G. Nicholson G. C. R. Black-Hawkins T. Faith L. C. Morley W. D. Bewsher A. L. Pilleau
W. H. Savage F. M. Hicks C. B. Hayes

E. Dupree G.L. Cheeseman O.A. Scott W.A. Lowey G.S. de Gaury

4. 5th Royal Inniskilling Fusiliers, Basingstoke, 1915 (Hampshire County Council Museums Service P2002.674).

5. The King's Escort of 10th Division Mounted Military Police commanded by Lord Powerscourt Assistant Provost Marshal. (Hampshire County Council Museums Service P2002.639).

6. Men of the 6th Royal Inniskilling Fusiliers, Basingstoke, Spring 1915 (Hugh Lamont/John Thompson)

7. Kitchener reviewing the 10th (Irish) Division at Basingstoke, June 1915 (Hampshire County Council Museums Service P2002.640).

8. 5th Royal Irish Fusiliers landing at Suvla 7 August 1915 (Royal Irish Fusiliers Museum, Armagh)

9. Private James Lamont, 6th
Royal Inniskilling Fusiliers (Hugh
Lamont/John Thompson).

10. Private James Lamont (second from right back row) and fellow members of 31st Machine Gun
Company, Egypt 1917 (Hugh Lamont/John Thompson).

of punishment awarded to battalions of the 10th Division was significantly lower than that meted out in the 16th (Irish) Division and – with the exception of the 13th Royal Irish Rifles – the 36th (Ulster) Division. It would therefore appear that while indiscipline was higher in the 10th (Irish) Division, it was dealt with less severely than it was in the other two Irish divisions.

It has been shown that the 10th (Irish) Division had a higher level of recorded indiscipline than a comparable non-Irish K1 division, but were offenders treated more harshly than their English counterparts as suggested by such writers as Gerald Oram?[35] Figure 7.4 (Annex 1) illustrates the distribution of sentences in each of the two divisions. It is apparent from a comparison of the sentencing pattern that there was no significant difference in the proportion of offenders awarded detention or a more severe punishment in the two divisions (10th Division: 54%; 13th Division: 56%). However, if Field Punishment (which represented only 1% of the sentences awarded in the 13th Division) is included, then the relative proportion of the most severe punishments becomes more significant (10th Division: 67%; 13th Division: 57%).[36]

The sentence of a court martial required to be confirmed by a higher authority and as a result the final award could differ markedly from the original sentence. An analysis of courts martial records show that over 10% of offenders in the 10th (Irish) Division had either all or part of their sentence remitted while a further 12% had their sentence commuted. In total over 25% of the division's offenders had their sentence for an offence committed during training remitted, quashed, commuted, varied, or not confirmed. Compared to the 10th Division, 29% of offenders from the 13th Division had their sentence reduced although almost double the number of offenders in the division had had their sentence remitted than in the 10th Division.

Although no officers from the 10th Division were court-martialled during their period in the United Kingdom, this does not mean that no disciplinary problems existed among the division's officers. Personnel files show that at least two officers committed offences contrary to military law. The contraction of a venereal disease was considered by the army as a disciplinary offence, equivalent to a self-inflicted wound or making oneself unfit for duty. According to Bowman, however, venereal disease was practically unknown in Irish New Army divisions while training in Ireland and cases prosecuted by courtsmartial are not apparent in War Records. It is possible nevertheless that such cases were concealed under the heading 'Miscellaneous Military Offences' as Bowman observed that soldiers were frequently not charged with a specific offence but under a section of the Army Act.[37] According to his personnel file, 2nd Lieutenant R.A.F. Gill, 5th Royal Irish Regiment, contracted the disease while training in England but rather than being charged was given leave to have treatment privately before departing for Gallipoli.[38] A second officer, Lieutenant H.G. Montagu, 7th Royal Munster Fusiliers, allegedly dishonoured a number of cheques, which in 1914 was both a military and civil offence, and although there is no evidence that Montagu was charged by either authority, the nature of the allegations were such that Mahon recommended his removal before the division left for Gallipoli. Mahon's recommendation was not implemented, however, as Montagu accompanied his battalion overseas.[39]

Incidences of drunkenness were not confined to the other ranks although a blind eye was usually turned in respect of officers as long as they were capable of undertaking their duties. Drury records that Captain Newton, 6th Royal Dublin Fusiliers, 'has always been too fond of the drink and since he has been here he has gone too far and has finally been kicked out altogether'.[40] There is no evidence amongst the courts martial papers to indicate that Newton's dismissal was a result of any formal proceedings and it must be assumed that he was asked to resign.

It may be concluded that as the 10th (Irish) Division prepared to embark on active service for the first time, it did so with an undeniably poor disciplinary record, even compared with other New Army formations. But what of morale: that internal motivation that compels a man to his duty and more? Unlike the other two Irish divisions, the 10th (Irish) was not associated with a political cause, although it is evident that a number of men enlisted in response to appeals made by Carson and Redmond. Nor given the difficulties experienced in filling the division's ranks is there any suggestion that a majority of its members, except possibly those that joined in other parts of the United Kingdom or the 'pals' of D company, 7th Royal Dublin Fusiliers, were swept into its ranks by the early war euphoria that filled other K1 divisions. How then was good morale created in the division?

The basic building block of good morale in the 10th (Irish) Division, or indeed any other division, was not the division itself but the regiment and the battalion to which a man belongs. Writing of the British army at 'First Ypres', Liddell Hart records that, 'the family spirit was its keynote, and the key to the apparent miracle by which, when formations were broken up and regiments reduced to remnants, those remnants still held together'.[41] Nowhere is the importance of regiment over division better demonstrated than in the 36th (Ulster) Division where for political reasons a divisional cap badge displaying the Red Hand of Ulster was issued. As Crozier recalled, 'protests reached Divisional Headquarters in such large numbers, in the regulation manner, that within a week the Royal Irish Rifles badge was again in every cap'.[42] It is therefore around the regiment, and more specifically the battalion, where measures to develop unit morale and *esprit de corps* can be seen.

Evidence shows that battalions used established methods for promoting morale and encouraging a sense of belonging. In the spring of 1915 the 6th Royal Dublin Fusiliers held a sports day, at which both officers and men competed against each other, culminating in a tug-of-war competition between the officers and sergeants.[43] Similar sporting events were held on board ship en route to Gallipoli, including a boxing tournament and an inter-battalion tug-of-war competition.[44] The purpose of such sporting events was, according to Cooper, to make the men 'feel at home'.[45]

Regimental tradition was also important in building and maintaining *esprit de corps*. Drury wrote that on St. Patrick's Day it was the regimental custom for all officers to accompany the men to the Roman Catholic service at mid-day and so in keeping with the custom 'Good Presbyterians like myself paraded and marched off to the tune of the "Boys of Wexford" and "A Nation Once Again" and went to chapel for the first and, probably, the only time in our lives'.[46] No matter how disconcerting this may have been for Drury, regimental tradition had been maintained and he appeared aware of the role it played in maintaining morale. He noted with regret that the battalion would not be allowed to exercise the ancient right of the Royal Dublin Fusiliers 'to march through the city with fixed bayonets and show ourselves off a bit to the delight of the onlookers and our own secret satisfaction'.[47] In Drury's opinion the battalion's 'martial ardour was somewhat damped' by this decision and that 'it would have been worth 100 recruits at least to have marched the first service battalion of the first Kitchener Division through the city with bands playing, but no, we sneaked off unsung in pours of rain, everyone looking rather miserable'.[48] It is not recorded what Drury's view, or that of the 6th Royal Dublin Fusiliers, was when the 7th battalion, and hence its junior, of the regiment was allowed to exercise its rights to march through the city on its way to embark on overseas service.

Regimental pride had been so inculcated into the division that, when at a rehearsal for an inspection by a senior officer the Dublin Fusiliers tried to vary the monotony of the band playing the 'British Grenadiers' (a march common to all fusilier regiments) by playing 'St Patrick's Day' the Connaught Rangers, who shared the right to play the march with the Irish Guards, objected so intensely that it had to abandoned.[49]

The provision of entertainment and recreational facilities also contributed to the maintenance of morale. Sergeant J. C. Dart of the 10th Division Signalling Company recalled in later life that 'the people of Carlow were very good to us. The church hall was open in the evenings for the rank and file and on a couple of nights concerts were arranged there; the performers being from the Company. The Sergeants' Mess had a piano, a good pianist and some fine singers to keep them pleased and amused'.[50] Concerts appear to be a feature of many units with the officers often taking the lead. Drury recorded one such concert on St Patrick's Day 1915 when he brought down a friend from the Trinity Dramatic Club to help entertain the battalion. He provides great detail of the act performed by the battalion Quartermaster who 'dressed like a stage Irishman gone mad', much to the approval of all present who joined in the chorus. Drury concluded that 'altogether it was a great evening, with a good long interval for the men to go out and have a drink to wet their parched throats'.[51] A similar concert was held for the more socially elite 7th Royal Dublin Fusiliers in December 1915 on the Woodbrook estate 'where during the afternoon and evening they were royally entertained by their host [Lieutenant Sir Stanley Cochrane Bt., an officer in the battalion] at both dinner and tea'.[52] Sir Stanley was a patron of the arts and had built his own theatre on his estate and so it is possible the concert was held there. The same source recorded that en route to Gallipoli 'once or twice a week they had a very good concert on board, generally got up by Lieutenant and Quartermaster Byrne of the 6th Royal Dublin Fusiliers, who acted as master of ceremonies and obtained the services of some excellent artistic talent which was on board'.[53]

The welfare of the troops and their families was essential to the maintenance of morale. The resentment of the men towards compulsory stoppages has already been noted but the reduction in income also had an impact on their families, and officers often spent hours at the end of the working day trying to rectify grievances such as non-payment of separation allowance.[54] Army bureaucracy often exacerbated the impact on families, as until October 1914 separation allowances were paid monthly unlike the weekly wages to which they were accustomed, which in many cases resulted in severe hardship. Such was the hardship caused to many families that up to 31 December 1914 branches of the Soldiers' and Sailors' Families Association had collectively dealt with 279,019 cases concerning wives' and 653,266 children's separation allowances, resulting in expenditure of over £1 million from its funds for the relief of distress.[55]

Writing of the role of the regimental depot of the Royal Dublin Fusiliers, the *Irish Times* noted:

> But the depot is not merely a recruiting depot. Colonel Cronin superintends an establishment of many activities. It is largely an inquiry bureau for the dependents of men who have enlisted in the Royal Dublin Fusiliers. Not a day passes but some women are guided to sources from which they may obtain relief. When a man enlists

he supplies information about his dependents (if any), which is registered and passed on to the Ladies Committee, two members of which are on all day duty at the bureau. In this way the ladies have been able to render much help to necessitous dependents of our soldiers. [56]

Such *noblesse oblige* by the ladies of the regiment was also evidenced at battalion level. A letter in the *Irish Times* from Mrs Yates, the wife of Captain L. W. P. Yates, a former District Inspector in the Royal Irish Constabulary, now serving in the 6th Royal Inniskilling Fusiliers asked that 'As the regiment is shortly for the front, I will be grateful for contributions of shirts, socks, mitts, etc. for B Company. These are urgently needed'.[57]

Individual officers were also mindful of the welfare and morale of their men. In a letter to his family, Lieutenant R.C. Broun, 6th Royal Dublin Fusiliers, who joined the battalion after Gallipoli wrote 'I wonder if you could send me some little thing for each [sic] man in my Platoon (I have 50 men) for Xmas, any little thing, cigarettes, sweets or any little thing. They are a fine crowd, and stick the cold weather well'.[58] It seems unlikely that the gifts requested by Lieutenant Broun were ever received by his platoon as he was killed in action on 8 December 1915.

At the beginning of July 1915 the 10th (Irish) Division boarded transports, not for the Western Front, but for the Dardanelles. Cooper described their departure from Basingstoke:

The men paraded in the dark, marched through the empty echoing streets of the silent town, sometimes singing, but more often thoughtful. The memory of recent farewells, the complete uncertainty of the future, the risks that lay before us, alike induced a mood that if not gloomy was certainly not hilarious. The cheerful songs of the training period were silent, and when a few voices broke the silence, the tune they chose was 'God Save Ireland'. We were resolved that Ireland would not be ashamed of us, but we were beginning to realise that our task would be a stiff one.[59]

The voyage east was largely uneventful but the time spent aboard ship took the edge off many of the men's standard of fitness. It also split many of the division's formations which were unable to regroup until, in some cases, days after they had gone into action and, in the case of the 29th Brigade meant that it was detached from the division for the whole of its Gallipoli service. The time taken to transport the division from the United Kingdom meant that the division had little time to either acclimatise to the heat of a Turkish summer or obtain experience from gradual exposure to frontline conditions granted to the other Irish divisions on the Western Front.

Bowman's examination of the incidence of courts martial in Irish divisions during their first twelve months in an active theatre of war concentrates primarily on the two divisions serving on the Western Front and excludes any comparison with the third Irish division serving at Gallipoli or in the Balkans. The study, while providing in-depth coverage of the prevalence of courts martial, omits any analysis of the nature of the offences involved or whether their pattern differed from those committed during their period of training in the United Kingdom. Table 7.5 (Annex 2) summarises, at brigade level, the number of men tried by courts martial in the 16th (Irish) and 36th (Ulster) Divisions while serving on the Western Front during the period 1 October 1915 to 30 September 1916.[60]

In passing, considering Beckett's hypothesis regarding the better acceptance of military discipline of the urban working class, it may be noted that of the three brigades in the Ulster Division, the 107th (Belfast) Brigade continued to have the worst disciplinary record in the division, even after more than twelve months training and a year's active service. In the 16th (Irish) Division, the number of courts martial in each brigade is for the period consistently higher than that of the 36th Division, and in the context of Beckett's hypothesis, only one battalion in the 16th Division had a higher level of indiscipline than the 6th Connaught Rangers which was mainly raised in west Belfast.

The number tried by courts martial in the division's first twelve full months of active service confirms the general level of indiscipline in comparison with the other two Irish formations previously identified during training. Table 7.6 shows that the incidence of courts martial in the 10th Division was more than double that of the Ulster Division during the same period.[61] While Bowman's analysis of courts martial in the 16th (Irish) Division only provides data for its first ten months of active service, its extrapolation to cover a full year reveals that the number of courts martial in the first twelve months of active service of the 10th (Irish) is only 10% higher than that of the 16th Division.[62]

During training, the division's 29th Brigade committed significantly more courts martial offences than either of the other two brigades in the division, a situation that remained unchanged during its first year of active service when 46% of the division's courts martial occurred in the brigade. The occurrence of courts martial in the 31st Brigade remained at a level consistent with that experienced in the United Kingdom, but it was in the 30th Brigade and particularly the 6th Royal Dublin Fusiliers, that the greatest improvement in discipline is apparent. The 6th Royal Dublin Fusiliers, which had the highest level of offending in the division during training, improved its disciplinary record to bring it below the divisional average, although the average is heavily skewed by the level of courts martial in the 29th Brigade, which in the twelve month period was higher than that for the whole Ulster Division.

Comparing the numbers tried by courts martial in the 10th (Irish) Division during its first twelve months of active service with the 13th (Western) Division which had been dispatched to Gallipoli a month earlier, one finds (as was the case during training) that the incidence of indiscipline in the former division was significantly higher, 570 courtsmartial compared with 312. Figure 7.5 in Annex 1 shows the relative incidence of courts martial between the two divisions.[63] For the purposes of comparison the 10th Division's first month of active service is August 1915 when it arrived at Gallipoli while that of the 13th Division is July 1915 as it arrived and saw action in the theatre a month earlier. Although there appears to be little similarity between the patterns of courts martial in the two divisions, it is possible to identify from the level of courts martial when a division was in the front line or had been just withdrawn. From the graph it is possible to see that the Irish Division had high levels of courts martial in periods one and two while engaged at Gallipoli and periods three to six when in the frontline in Salonika before being withdrawn from the line at the beginning of their period six (January 1916). By contrast, the 13th Division remained at Gallipoli until the final evacuation during their period seven, also January 1916, when they were shipped to a rest camp in Egypt before being transferred to a quiet sector in the Canal Zone when courts martial in the division almost ceased to exist.

Although Noel Drury gives the impression that morale in the division was good, it would be surprising if following its experience at Gallipoli that morale had not suffered.[64] During its months at Gallipoli, the division never fought as a unified command, and this appears to have had a particularly detrimental impact on the detached 29th Brigade whose disciplinary record soared in the months following the evacuation (see Figure7.6, Annex 1). Officer casualties in particular during the Gallipoli campaign had been high and included Brigadier Cooper and all the staff of the 29th Brigade. Seven of the division's thirteen battalion commanders and a total of 233 other officers had been killed or wounded, while numerous officers, including the commanding officer of the 7th Royal Munster Fusiliers, were hospitalised due to illness.[65] Individual battalions also suffered high rates of attrition. The 6th Royal Irish Rifles landed at Anzac on 5 August 1915 with 743 other ranks, yet following the action on 10 August, and having received 139 reinforcements from Lemnos, was only able to field 490 other ranks the next day; an attrition rate of 44%.[66] At the end of September 1915, 30th Brigade, despite receiving reinforcements from the United Kingdom, could only muster 43 officers and 1,706 other ranks and to bring two of its battalions up to strength drafts were required from non-Irish regiments; the 6th Royal Munster Fusiliers receiving a draft of 6 officers and 293 other ranks from the Oxfordshire and Buckinghamshire Light Infantry while the regiment's 7th battalion received 10 officers and 498 men from the Dorset Regiment.[67] Cross-posting of drafts was unpopular with all concerned and had an impact on morale.[68]

The 6th Royal Dublin Fusiliers, a week or so after their arrival in Salonika, received a draft of eight officers and 388 other ranks intended for the Norfolk Regiment and neither the Fusiliers nor the Norfolks appear to have been enthusiastic about the arrangement. Cox, the commanding officer of the 6th Dublins, insisted that the bulk of the replacements should be accommodated together in D Company or in their own platoons in other companies. Drury was obviously unimpressed by the new arrivals whom he considered 'a bit uppish':

> I have overheard a few remarks about their 'hard luck' in being attached to an Irish Regiment. By the Lord, I'll make them have sense. It isn't everyone has the honour to be in the oldest Regiment in the Army [sic], making Empire history since 1641. I have a little booklet which I must read them extracts from on parade, and make them learn our battle honours.[69]

Sensing animosity between the original men of the company and the Norfolks, Drury issued orders to his Company Sergeant Major to 'take the greatest care that all duties and fatigues are evenly divided'.[70] Time did nothing to ameliorate Drury's initial opinion of the Norfolk Regiment officers and men. On 10 December 1915 he recorded in his diary that 'Captain Horner who rejoined yesterday after practically deserting us on Crete Simonet, went sick today with a sore toe! I'd like to give him the weight of mine for a rotten scrimshanker. Parish also went off sick. Most of the people who have gone off sick have been Norfolks and soon we will be shut [sic] of the whole crowd'.[71]

Other battalions of the division, such as the Connaught Rangers and Royal Irish Rifles, however, continued to receive reinforcements from their regimental depots.[72] Sheffield notes that 'the need to maintain discipline on active service depended on the survival of personnel to pass on the tradition and spirit of the original unit to replacements, or on receiving replacement officers sympathetic to the original ethos'. As a consequence, in 1915-16 a system was introduced of holding back about 10% of its personnel when a unit went into action to form a cadre around which the unit could be rebuilt.[73] Unfortunately in the case of the 10th (Irish) Division, the cadre left behind at Lemnos as first line reinforcements, were thrown into action within days of the division landing at Gallipoli, leaving units with no reinforcements nearer than the United Kingdom.

Table 7.7 (Annex 2) shows the distribution of courts martial offences in the 10th Division during the division's first 12 months of active service while Figure 7.6 (Annex 1) provides a graphical comparison of the percentage distribution of offences between the 10th and 13th Divisions. The comparison shows that in both divisions approximately 25% of all offences tried by courts martial during the period were in respect of drunkenness. However, the level of miscellaneous military offences and the serious offence of sleeping or quitting a post on active service were significantly higher in the 13th Division. It also shows that soldiers in the 10th (Irish) Division had a greater tendency towards disobedience and insubordination, although their greater propensity to absent themselves from camp is probably more a reflection on the locations of the two divisions for most of the year and their relative proximity to a civilian population. Alternatively, the tendency for men of the 10th Division to absent themselves from camp may be explained by Captain G. Nicholson, the Adjutant of the 10th Hampshires who, in a description of military life in Salonika, wrote ' perhaps we didn't go into action as frequently as our troops in France, but when we did, we used to have a good "fill of it". Afterwards we merely went back to a mosquito-ridden camp, or at best, a dirty camp in the foothills where water in all probability was scarce'.[74]

It was not just the unofficial absences from camp that had an impact on the behaviour of the men of the 10th Division. The 29th Brigade's War Diary entry of 23 October 1915 notes that 'since passes were allowed into Salonika, crime has been very prevalent and a large number of courts martial (averaging two per day) chiefly for drunkenness – absence – selling kit etc. The Royal Irish Rifles have by far the largest proportion of these'.[75] Although Table 7.7 confirms the opinion of Brigade Headquarters, no mention is made of it in the battalion's war diary. The Irish Rifles were not the only battalion of the brigade that took advantage of the availability of alcohol. CQMS John McIlwain, 5th Connaught Rangers, recorded that on 20 January 1916, 22 men of 'A' company were tried by Field Court Martial for drunkenness having pilfered spirits during the unloading of supply ships at Stavros.[76] Wakefield and Moody's book on the Salonika campaign states that 'the punishment given to these men consisted of hard labouring tasks such as sinking wells and road building'.[77] Official records, however, show that no men of the 5th Connaught Rangers were court-martialled on 20 January 1916 although twelve were tried and convicted of drunkenness on 27 January, of which eleven were sentenced to imprisonment with hard labour. Of the eleven sentenced to imprisonment with hard labour, nine had their sentence commuted to three months FP1 and the remaining two had the hard labour portion of their sentence remitted.[78] That the number of men court-martialled recorded by McIlwain differs from the official records may be a result of a transcription error as the typed copy of McIlwain's diary held by the Imperial War Museum states 'this part has been copied from the original book (into which it was entered from rough notes) by John McIlwain, the youngest son of the writer'.[79]

Information regarding the sentences passed by courts martial within the 10th (Irish) Division, see Table 7.8 (Annex 2), when taken with Figure 7.7 (Annex 1), illustrates the relative distribution of sentences in the two divisions and allows further consideration of Oram's belief that Irish soldiers were more harshly treated then their English counterparts. Analysis of the sentences handed down shows that although 82% more courts martial took place in the 10th (Irish) than the 13th (Western) Division during their first 12 months on active service, only 18 men in the former were sentenced to death compared with 51 in the latter, a ratio of approximately 1:3, while as a percentage of all offences, the death sentence represented less than 3% of all sentences in the 10th Division compared with almost 16% in the 13th Division. Despite the high number of death sentences passed in the two divisions, only one death sentence was carried out in the 10th Division and two in the 13th Division during the period. Beckett noted that only 10.8% of death sentences imposed by British courts martial on white soldiers were actually confirmed.[80] As the 10th division's single execution represents only 5.6% of all death sentences imposed on the division during the period, there is no reason to suggest that members of the division were more severely treated because of their ethnic background.

The sole member of the 10th Division to be executed was Private Patrick Downey, 6th Leinsters, who was found guilty of disobedience on 1 December 1915, having been previously awarded 84 days FP1 on 12 November. The court's unanimous recommendation was referred to Sir Bryan Mahon, then commanding all British forces in Greece, for submission to the Commander-in-Chief Mediterranean Expeditionary Force for confirmation. In submitting the recommendation Mahon added:

> Under ordinary circumstances I would have hesitated to recommend that the Capital Sentence awarded be put into effect as a plea of guilty has erroneously been accepted by the Court, but the condition of discipline in the Battalion is such as to render an exemplary punishment highly desirable and I therefore hope that the Commander in Chief will see fit to approve the sentence of death in this instance.[81]

There are a number of factors concerning the Downey case that are of interest. The original wording of the charge against Downey was that 'on active service disobeying a lawful command given personally by his superior officer in the execution of his office'. This was amended by Brigadier-General Vandeleur commanding the 29th Brigade to read 'on active service disobeying a lawful command in such a manner as to show wilful disobedience of authority given personally by his superior officer in the execution of his office', which changed the offence from a non-capital to a capital offence. Myles Dungan claims that Downey's commanding officer, Colonel F.W.S. Jourdain promulgated the charge claiming that Downey had refused to enter the trenches.[82] In this Dungan is incorrect as this officer never served with the division and had not even been commissioned at the time of Downey's execution on 27 December 1915.[83] There is no reference in the papers relating to the Downey case to any submission made by Downey's commanding officer, Major J.C. Colquhoun. Five other members of the 6th Leinsters were also tried for unrelated offences at the same time as Downey, three with disobeying a lawful order and two with insubordination. Of the three charged with disobedience, all were sentenced to various terms of Field Punishment No. 2 although the sentences of two of the offenders were not confirmed.

Although the courtmartial panel was properly constituted, its composition barely met the minimum required by military law. Section 106 of *The Rules of Procedure 1907* required that a field general court martial should comprise a panel of at least three members of which the president of the court should be a field officer (Major or above) and that all members should have held a commission for a minimum of one year, although officers with commissions of more than three years were to be appointed if available. Provision was also made under the same section for a captain to be appointed as president if a field officer was unavailable. Despite Downey's court-martial taking place at 5th Royal Irish Regiment headquarters, Captain (Temporary Major) R.O. Mansergh, 6th Royal Irish Rifles, was appointed president of the court rather than a field officer because according to Vandeleur 'none can be spared'.[84] The other two members of the court, Lieutenant J.K. Starkie, 6th Royal Irish Rifles and 2nd Lieutenant Ivor Powell, 13th Hampshires, had only held commissions from 16 November and 20 October 1914 respectively. None of the members of the court had any legal background and appear to have been unaware of an instruction issued by the Adjutant General regarding capital cases stipulating that a not guilty plea had to be entered on behalf of a defendant, and thus had accepted Downey's guilty plea.[85]

Finally, in making his recommendation, Mahon stated 'the condition of discipline in the Battalion is such as to render an exemplary punishment highly desirable'. Yet analysis of courts martial records shows that at the beginning of December 1915, the 6th Leinster Regiment's disciplinary record while on active service was no worse than that of the 5th Connaught Rangers, 27 and 25 courts martial respectively, and less than 50% of that of the 6th Royal Irish Rifles, all serving in the same brigade. During December 1915 a total of ten members of the 10th (Irish) Division, including Downey, were sentenced to death including four for sleeping at their post, one for insubordination and one for desertion, yet only

Downey was executed. Of the ten sentenced to death, apart from Downey only Private J. Creegan, also of the 6th Leinsters, had any previous convictions. Private Creegan was tried for his first offence, that of disobedience, on the same day as Downey, receiving 56 days FP1 for his crime. On 20 December, Creegan was charged with insubordination and was sentenced to death, later commuted to ten years penal servitude.[86]

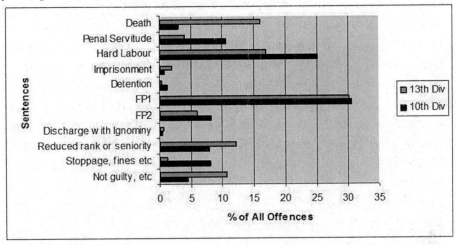

Figure 7.7: Distribution of sentences passed by courts martial in the 10th (Irish) and 13th (Western) Divisions during their first 12 months of active service.[87]

Although Downey was the only serving member of the 10th (Irish) Division to be executed, Private George Hanna, Royal Irish Fusiliers, who had previously served with the 6th Royal Irish Fusiliers and had landed with the battalion at Suvla on 7 August 1915, was executed on 6 November 1917 at Metz-en-Couture in northern France for desertion.[88] Hanna had previously attempted to desert but was quickly arrested, court-martialled and sentenced to death but on the recommendation of Mahon the sentence was commuted to 10-years imprisonment, which was subsequently suspended and Hanna was returned to duty. Despite an apparent improvement in Hanna's behaviour over the following months, at some point during the retreat from Kosturino in Serbia, Hanna again left the ranks and for a second time was charged with desertion and sentenced to death. Again Hanna's sentence was commuted and he was sentenced to seven years imprisonment. In August 1917, while serving his sentence at Maidstone Prison, he was released and sent to his regiment in France where on being ordered to parade for duty in the frontline on 28 September, he again deserted, which led to his execution.[89] What the case of Private Hanna demonstrates is that the 10th (Irish) Division, with the aid of Sir Bryan Mahon, both as divisional commander and while commanding the British Salonika Force, made every effort to avoid the ultimate sanction when possible.

John Fuller has demonstrated the importance that popular culture had in maintaining the morale of British and Dominion forces during the war and how the replication of popular civilian pastimes such as sport, concert parties, cinemas and even social drinking were used by the authorities to redress the monotony and horror of trench warfare on the Western Front by providing a sense of normality when out of the line through the provision of familiar activities.[90] To a certain extent similar measures were employed to maintain morale on other fronts although their very remoteness had an impact on what could be provided.

The music hall and to a growing extent the cinema was a feature of pre-war civilian popular culture amongst the lower and middle classes in Britain. Consequently some divisions sought to replicate these popular forms of amusement to entertain the troops when out of the line. Although both the Irish divisions in France formed concert parties and General Nugent commanding the Ulster Division even purchased a mobile cinema to entertain the troops, there is no record of the 10th (Irish) Division, or indeed the 13th, participating in such activities.[91] Why these divisions chose not to use such forms of entertainment to maintain morale is not known. It was not due to their location as, both the 26th and 28th Divisions serving in Salonika constructed substantial theatres a few miles behind the frontline at Kalinova and Kopriva respectively and Rattray, writing of a performance of the 26th Division's concert party, testified that 'it certainly helped to take one "away from the war" even if only for a few hours'.[92] While the 10th Division had neither its own concert party nor cinema, efforts were still made to entertain the troops when out of the line. Drury records a 'lantern show with a racy yarn by a padre', while the war diary of the 6th Leinsters records that 'a concert was given tonight, commencing at 18.15 in the Y.M.C.A. tent at Karm station [Palestine], to this battalion, hot cocoa & cigarettes were distributed and the men had a jolly evening. About 12 officers and 350 other ranks attending'.[93]

Social drinking was, as now, a key element of social interaction for both civilians and servicemen in the years prior to 1914, providing for many their only means of escaping for a time the grinding poverty in which many lived. Unlike the Western Front where estaminets serving alcohol were accessible to the men while in rest areas, the nature of the Gallipoli or Salonika fronts, meant that, with the exception of the city of Salonika itself, there was an absence of similar establishments near the frontlines resulting in more limited opportunities for drinking for the ordinary soldier than for his counterpart on the Western Front, which perhaps explains the cases of pilfering official stores and the selling of kit to obtain alcohol.

Although Bowman provides no details of the number of courts martial in the Irish divisions on the Western Front during their first year of active service, he provides details for a number of Irish battalions for a 17-month period covering October 1916 to February 1918 against which a comparison can be made.[94] This comparison reveals that the average ratio of courts martial per month in Irish battalions on the Western Front compared with the average of battalions serving with the 10th (Irish) Division at Gallipoli and Salonika was 1:2.5, which may reflect either a greater tolerance towards drunkenness by authorities on the Western Front or a tendency by troops in other theatres to drink to excess during their less frequent sessions of social drinking. An account by McIlwain of a corporal of the Munsters being hospitalised with alcoholic poisoning would tend to support the latter view.[95]

To troops serving away from home, the prospect of leave was an important factor in the maintenance of morale. Fuller suggests that 'it would be hard to overstate the eagerness with which a spell of leave was awaited by troops of every nationality. For all its disorientations, leave offered a chance to see loved ones, a release from discipline, and an intense interval of pleasure'.[96] Despite this in June and July 1917 107,000 soldiers on the Western Front had had no leave for eighteen months while over 400,000 had had no leave for a year.[97] In the view of a serving soldier, the greater frequency of leave for officers created 'a very definite and serious current of discontent and dissatisfaction'.[98] Because of the distances involved, it appears unlikely that many of the other ranks of the 10th (Irish) Division obtained home leave while serving in the Balkans or Middle-East, if the experience of other troops in the theatre is typical. According to Cyril Falls, the official historian for the Macedonian theatre, 'leave had been given only in individual cases, small parties having been occasionally sent, by arrangement with the French, to Toulon. The first leave ship, with approximately 113 officers and 1,282 other ranks, sailed in November [1916], and thereafter similar parties were sent home once a month'.[99] Even this level of home leave was unsustainable, as due to a shortage of shipping, only two leave parties sailed for the United Kingdom between May and October 1917.[100] Even had all the available shipping been dedicated to the 10th (Irish) Division, it would have been October 1917 before all the infantry of the division received home leave, by which time the division had been transferred to another theatre of operations. Nevertheless, some home leave for the men of the division must have been possible as the war diary of the 6th Royal Dublin Fusiliers records the return of RSM Foster and seven other ranks from leave in England.[101]

Given the distances involved, the duration of absence from their unit was substantial and the early experiences of those concerned must have proved unsatisfactory as the War Office felt it necessary in April 1917 to change the existing arrangements as follows:

> In future Officers, non-commissioned officers and men proceeding on and returning from furlough in England will receive free messing on board ship and be rationed across France. They will be entitled to 18 days ration allowance for the period of leave in the United Kingdom. Officers Commanding units will show in their Casualty Return (A.F. B.213) that such men are entitled to the allowance for the period at 1/9d a day.[102]

Lieutenant Melville Rattray, Royal Engineers, whose experience and that of his men, appears to have been typical of many who served outside France and Belgium, recorded:

> naturally the great topic was leave and demobilisation. We had many who had not had a single leave home during the war. Now that the war was over, we expected and hoped things would be better, though up to our arrival in Silistra, we had sent only a few small parties on leave … it was a weary wait for men who had never seen home since August 1915, who for many years had talked of, and yearned for leave to 'Blighty,' and still in the beginning of January 1919, it seemed almost as far away as ever.[103]

An undated analysis of leave due to members of the 6th Royal Inniskilling Fusiliers by the battalion's commanding officer, probably compiled in late 1918, shows that five officers and 640 men of the battalion had not had home leave in over 18 months while one officer and 156 men had not had home leave for over three years.[104]

Morale could also be determined by the relationship with the civilian population behind the lines. It was at times difficult enough in France and Belgium with allies, but in Salonika it could be hostile and dangerous. According to Simkins, 'men who had volunteered for the army in the belief that they would be helping to deliver beleaguered France and Belgium were understandably bitter when they were made to feel unwelcome'.[105] Captain Reginald Cockburn, 10th King's Royal Rifle Corps, recorded the difficulties of obtaining billets for 'as a rule, all they wanted was money; the Belgians were worse in that respect. They robbed the soldier even more unscrupulously than did the French, who themselves were bad enough in all conscience'.[106] Cockburn was willing to concede that 'I often wondered whether, if our country were swarming with foreigners, our poor peasant and country folk would not, even if they were making money out of them, sooner grow tired and impatient of their harassing guests. At times one has felt such an intolerable nuisance, and able to do so little'.[107]

By comparison, the Greeks were at best unenthusiastic allies but more often displayed outright hostility. The Reverend John Crozier, the son of the Archbishop of Armagh and a chaplain to the 10th (Irish) Division, recalled that 'everything possible was done to hinder our troops leaving Salonika for Serbia and eventually things became so bad that no further troops could be spared to go North, and the Navy cleared for action in the harbour because of the evident hostility of the Greek Authorities'.[108] McIlwain's initial view of the inhabitants of Salonika as he marched through the city was that they were 'quiet and undemonstrative'. They soon recognised an opportunity for making money as 'our fellows making fools of themselves buying Koniak [*sic*] and kindred spirits from hawkers who in hundreds follow us up'.[109] The people of Salonika, despite their complete indifference to the arrival of the troops, recognised a captive market which sent prices soaring.[110] Greeks did not have a monopoly on increasing prices but at least troops in Salonika did not have to pay inflated prices caused by large numbers of better-paid Dominion troops. As Archie Surfleet, a private of the 13th East Yorkshire Regiment, wrote, 'as soon as they appear in a place everything goes up in price and we hate to follow them into billets'.[111] The effect on morale of such anomalies was not lost on all senior officers. General Ivor Phillips M.P. raised the issue in the House of Commons:

> the subject of low pay is talked about every day by the soldiers. The Division with which I was connected in France was posted near a Colonial Division ... These Colonial men had 5s and 6s a day, and they drank coffee and beer and went out to buy butter, cheese, and eggs for themselves in the town just close behind the lines. What chance had my men with their shilling-a-day? They had no chance in a public house to get attended to, nor could they purchase provisions like those with the 6s a day.[112]

The reaction of the inhabitants was not confined to the Greek authorities or a desire by civilians to exploit the troops financially. An unnamed member of the 10th Division's Signal Company later recalled, 'when we first reached Salonika the natives were hostile to us, and several men of the Division found eternal rest via a knife thrust in the ribs! In one way, this was hardly to be wondered at, as prior to 1912, Salonika was Turkish territory, and the Turks formed a goodly percentage of the population'.[113] Although no source has been found to substantiate this claim, Drury in his diary asserts that 'going around in the dark is not pleasant as there are a lot of blooming cut-throats about so I kept my revolver handy'.[114]

A high level of sickness is ruinous to the morale of any organisation. The first incidence of large scale illness in the division began to manifest itself while it awaited its landing on the Gallipoli peninsula and was caused by swarms of flies alighting on food. Due to a shortage of disinfectant, it was impossible to either check their increase or prevent the spread of disease. This together with the heat and lack of drinking water on Mudros and Mitylene led to soldiers purchasing large quantities of local produce from hawkers resulting in enteritis becoming rife among the troops. According to Cooper:

> Though this was not very severe, this affliction was widespread, hardly anyone being free from it. A few went sick, but for every man who reported himself to the doctor, there were ten who were doing their duty without complaining that they were indisposed. Naturally, men were reluctant to report sick just before going into action for the first time; but though they were able to carry on, yet there was a general lowering of vitality and loss of energy due to this cause, which acted as a serious handicap in the difficult days to come.[115]

Such were the debilitating effects of illness that an officer from another division claimed:

> Suvla was already lost in Imbros. We had hell in that island. We knew little about sanitation or the dangers of a tropical climate, and water was so scarce that armed guards had to be detailed for water carts. Discipline was difficult to maintain even there because of such official

mistakes, and instead of training the troops in open warfare, COs spent there [sic] time trying to get sufficient water, and trying to cope with diarrhoea.

We had a crude saying that the 11th Division went into battle grasping a rifle in one hand, and holding up its trousers with the other. There was hardly a man who was not so troubled.[116]

The situation did not improve following the landing on the peninsula, 'the heat was intense, the biscuit was dry and the bully beef very salty, while many men were suffering from dysentery or enteritis and were parched with fever though they were unwilling to report sick in the face of the enemy. In such times surface civilisation vanishes, and man becomes a primitive savage'.[117] An indication of the virulence of disease within the division is provided by the 6th Leinsters which had 157 other ranks hospitalised by sickness between 24 August and 30 September 1915. According to the battalion's war diary, only two appear to have returned to duty while the battalion was on the peninsula.[118] When the division arrived at Salonika the health of many of its men had been undermined by its experiences at Gallipoli and its overall fitness was not aided by many of its new drafts having been made up of men invalided from France.[119] The division's health was further undermined by being inadequately equipped for a move from the dry sub-tropical heat of the Gallipoli summer to the cold and heavy rain of a Balkan autumn.

In early November 1915 the division, with many men still inadequately equipped, advanced into the mountains of Serbia where at the end of the month the heavy rain turned to snow with a heavy frost at night. Such was the cold that the men began to suffer from frostbite and exposure in increasing numbers. Knott of the division's 32nd Field Ambulance recorded 'the snow has ceased and frozen hard, consequently frostbite cases streamed in some in the worst stages, over 100 being admitted before three o'clock'.[120] In a letter to a friend in Londonderry dated 30 December 1915, Lieutenant G.A.P. Dickson, 6th Royal Inniskilling Fusiliers, wrote of their period in Serbia that 'we lost quite one-third of the effective strength of the battalion from frostbite and exposure'.[121] Between 26

November and 8 December, 23 officers and 1,663 men of the division were evacuated to Salonika as a result of complete physical collapse, frostbite, and general debility.[122]

In the early decades of the twentieth century, malaria was endemic in the marshlands and river valleys of Macedonia and as a result the disease began to have a major impact on the division and the allied armies as a whole from the summer of 1916. Such was the impact of malaria on the division that in August 1916 the 29th Brigade could only field a composite battalion of four companies.[123] During the course of the Salonika campaign, non-battlefield casualties were twenty-times those of battlefield casualties and of the 481,262 non-battlefield casualties, 162,517 were as result of malaria.[124] The military authorities in Salonika have been castigated for taking little interest in promoting knowledge of malaria among the troops as attendance at malaria prevention lectures was optional.[125] The editorial of the *British Medical Journal* of March 1918 noted that several military operations in Salonika had been cancelled because of the high incidence of the disease.[126] While it had a debilitating effect on the body and morale, the unpleasant side effects of quinine was almost as bad, as it 'seemed to upset most peoples [sic] digestion and livers, and tempers were frequently on the short side'.[127] The results obtained by the use of quinine to prevent malaria were also inconclusive. Major C.H. Tredgold, RAMC, serving in Salonika noticed that while some men in his division who received quinine were resistant to the disease many still fell ill, while Cecil Alport, regard its use as an 'absolute failure', a view largely supported by the Director of Medical Service General H.R. Whitehead.[128]

It has been argued that religion had little influence in the maintenance of morale in the British army as only between 6% and 9% of soldiers were active Christians.[129] Such generalisations ignore the significance of religion in civilian life in pre-war Ireland among Catholics, Protestants and Dissenters, which to some extent carried over into the three Irish New Army Divisions. Wilfrid Spender, GSO2, and Cyril Falls, the divisional historian, among others testified to the importance of religion to many men of the Ulster Division. Falls, alluding to the Scots Covenanter heritage of many in the division, recorded that 'something of the old covenanting spirit, the old sense of the alliance of "Bible and Sword", was reborn in these men'.[130]

Cooper recorded the importance of religion to the men of the 10th Division at Gallipoli:

> Before dawn, each of the two chaplains attached to the Brigade held a service. The Church of England chaplain, the Revd J.W. Crozier, celebrated Holy Communion in the operating tent of the 30th Field Ambulance, while Father O'Connor said Mass in the open air just outside the camp. It had been decided that the chaplains were not to come with the Brigade, but were to remain with the Field Ambulance. This decision caused much regret, not only to the chaplains themselves, but to all the ranks of the Brigade. The Roman Catholics in particular disliked losing Father O'Connor even temporarily, for he was personally loved by the men, and in addition the Irish soldier faces death twice as cheerfully when fortified by the ministrations of his Church.[131]

Drury recalled that the two chaplains attached to the 30th Brigade bolstered the men's morale not only through their devotion but also in practical ways:

> Of course, Father Murphy is a regular and it his job to be up here, but the dear old Canon [McClean] just does it because he thinks he ought to. He is really too old for this climate and rough life, and we notice a considerable change in him since he came out, but he is as cheery as ever, and loves going along the line and chatting to the men. I hear he goes off to the Hospital ships and spins such terrible yarns about the hardships of the men that he seldom, if ever, goes away empty handed![132]

To many men in the division, religion and its observance were very personal. John Crozier, chaplain with the 5th Connaught Rangers, wrote of 2nd Lieutenant Norman Lucas, an officer with the 6th Royal Irish Rifles that, 'he was often at my services and took a great interest in them, and many a time was a communicant at my Holy Communion services'.[133] In a moment of self-reflection Lucas recorded, 'I think I must be developing a very clerical appearance. During the whole of my visit to the Connaughts, their new Commanding Officer addressed me as the new Church of England padre, much to everybody's secret amusement. This ought to be a compliment, for the padres are an awfully decent lot here'.[134] Some soldiers seemed to have found a meaning for their suffering in their religion. An anonymous private of the 6th Royal Irish Rifles wrote from Salonika: 'I do wish this horrible conflict was over. But we must not give up hope, but press forward doing the right, and trusting in the Lord, for he made the earth and is controlling it in His own wise way'.[135]

The evidence suggests that if Beckett's assertion is correct, then the importance of religion to Irish regiments appears to be atypical and that Cooper's comments in particular point towards religion being an essential element in the maintenance of morale in the division. Cooper, of course, was writing of his experience at Gallipoli in August–September 1915 at a time when the division was experiencing combat for the first time. In December 1917, when the division had become both battle-hardened and more dependent on replacements from outside Ireland, Drury recorded an incident in Egypt when 'Padre O'Connell held a RC service in the gulley this morning and there was not a single person there, but he seemed quite oblivious of the fact as he kept his back turned to where they should have been, all the time of the service'.[136] Such an occurrence suggests that either religious observance had declined or become less important than it had been to the original members of the division.

Finally contact with home was an important element in the maintenance of the morale of troops serving overseas. During the war the General Post Office and the Army Postal Service transported up to 7,000 sacks of mail and 60,000 parcels across the English Channel every day. A detailed record book of the postal activity between Thomas Glover and his son serving in France shows that on average it took only three days for letters and postcards to arrive from France. The efficiency of the postal system was remarkable as Glover's record book revealed that out of 373 items sent, his son failed to receive only three over a period of 34 months, at a total of some 22 different addresses.[137]

No similar record is available for those serving at Gallipoli or Salonika but evidence exists that the postal service was more erratic but nevertheless welcomed. On 15 August 1915 Drury recorded:

> There was great excitement this afternoon as some letters arrived up – the first we have had since leaving home on the 10th July. I got several including one from 1st Leith Company Boys Brigade in Camp at Cloan Perthshire, written by Corporal LIVESSEY in reply to a cable I sent them from VALETTA (Malta) [17 July] … I also got a badly needed jacket from tailors.[138]

With reference to Drury's telegram, it appears that mail from the United Kingdom to units in the eastern Mediterranean took between three to four weeks to arrive. This is confirmed by a letter from Corporal R.A. Semmence, 6th Royal Dublin Fusiliers, to his mother from a hospital in Egypt, dated 22 August, which stated that he had received papers from his father dated 14 and 21 July 1915. Corporal Semmence's letter also provides a clue as to how long it took for letters to reach home as it was reproduced in the *Kildare Observer* on 15 September. Not everyone appears to have felt the need to write home. On 9 December 1915, Drury received an enquiry from the MEF records office in Alexandria concerning Private, 6/12181, J. Richardson who had never written home.[139]

Drury also recorded a less satisfactory aspect of the postal service which did nothing to improve morale:

> When we left Basingstoke we had ordered and paid for a small box of supplies to be sent to the mess each week, and some whiskey. The first consignment arrived tonight. … at last the case was opened and a cork whipped out of one of the bottles and some of the contents poured into a mug. The smell seemed queer and when we examined it we found the stuff was salt water! Every one of the bottles had been emptied and filled with sea water. We

then examined the box of provisions and found it cleared
and filled with tins of bully beef. I wish I could catch the
culprit. I think we could almost have forgiven him if he
had put stones into the box but Bully beef!![140]

Apparently pilfering from parcels sent to troops in the Middle East
was not uncommon. A letter of 2 September 1915 from Private Richard
Murphy, 7th Royal Dublin Fusiliers, recorded, 'I unfortunately did
not get the cigarettes you mentioned so I am afraid they must have
gone astray or someone appropriated them before they got this far.
It is very annoying because they are the greatest want out here'.[141]

Not all news took 3–4 weeks to reach the 10th Division. On 27
April 1916 Noel Drury recorded in his diary that:

We got the most astounding news on the 27th that a
rebellion has broken out in Ireland [Easter Sunday, 24th
April]. Isn't it awful. Goodness knows what they think
they are going to gain by it. It's a regular stab in the back
for our fellows out there [sic], who don't know how their
people at home are. I don't know how we will be able to
hold our heads up here … as we are sure to be looked
upon with suspicion. The men are mad about it all, but
don't understand who is mixed up in the affair. I am sure
Germany is at the bottom somehow.[142]

Bowman views the period from October 1916 to February 1918 as
vital to understanding the development of morale and discipline in
Irish Regiments. By the end of July 1916, some 74% of the 140,460
men who enlisted in Ireland during the war had already done so.
By October 1916 it was apparent that following the serious losses
experienced by the 16th (Irish) and 36th (Ulster) divisions and
numerous Irish regular battalions on the Somme, that insufficient
recruits were available from Ireland to bring these units up to
strength.[143] In a minute to the Army Council in September 1916, Sir
Nevil Macready, the Adjutant General, stated that Irish Infantry
units were 17,194 men below strength. It is not clear whether this
relates solely to units on the Western Front or included units on

other fronts such as the 10th (Irish) Division but this deficiency was more than the total enlistments in Ireland in the following twelve months.[144] Macready offered a number of solutions to this problem, but the preferred choice of the Army Council to amalgamate the two Irish divisions serving on the Western Front was vetoed for political reasons. As discussed in Chapter 5, to retain the 16th (Irish) and 36th (Ulster) divisions, a series of amalgamations of service battalions and the transfer of Irish regular battalions to the divisions took place. Ultimately a manpower shortage across the whole of the army led to the number of infantry battalions in a division being reduced from twelve to nine, which resulted in a number of service battalions in each division being amalgamated or disbanded. Similar changes began in the 10th Division with the arrival of three Irish regular battalions in November 1916, the departure of the 10th Hampshires and the amalgamation of the two battalions of the Royal Munster Fusiliers. Although by February 1918 the division included three regular battalions, it still retained its twelve battalion structure.

The restructuring of the three Irish divisions brought a greater reliance on men enlisted in other parts of the United Kingdom to maintain manpower levels. As already noted, the 10th Division received a number of drafts from English regiments immediately after Gallipoli, which may have been as much a matter of expediency as a reflection on declining recruitment in Ireland at the time. However, the latter situation was officially recognised in October 1916 when GHQ in France received 'approval from WO [War Office] for reinforcing Irish units with Englishmen, keeping the Regular Irish Bns supplied with Irishmen'.[145] As there was no conscription in Ireland, this effectively consigned men conscripted in England to serve in Irish service battalions.

Having examined the nature of structural changes in the three Irish divisions it is now possible to explore the effect, if any, these changes had on discipline and morale, particularly in the context of the 10th (Irish) Division. As the 13th Division was transferred to Mesopotamia during this period, no further comparison with this division is possible.

A comparison between Tables 7.6 and 7.9 (Annex 2) shows that the number of courts martial in two of the division's three brigades fell in the latter period compared with the division's first twelve months on active service despite the upheaval caused by changes from amalgamations, transfer of units, and increased number of conscripts in the ranks. Even in the 30th Brigade, where the number of courts martial increased between October 1916 and February 1918, the increase, when adjusted to take account of the longer time period, is less than one extra court martial per month. It is noticeable however that, with the exception of the 7th Royal Dublin Fusiliers, the number of courts martial fell in all the division's original battalions not subject to amalgamation. There is no definitive reason why the 7th Royal Dublin Fusiliers should be an exception. At least 48 members of the battalion's D company, originally largely composed of middle class recruits, had been commissioned since going on active service which, with the number lost to enemy action and other causes, would have reduced the steadying influence of this group on the rest of the battalion. In addition, during this period the 7th Royal Munster Fusiliers merged with the regiment's 6th battalion and the 6th Royal Irish Fusiliers merged with its 5th battalion. In the case of the Munster Fusiliers this was followed by an increase in the number of courts martial in the 6th battalion, but as the number fell with the merger of the Irish Fusiliers battalions, it is not possible to say whether amalgamations had a causal effect on indiscipline.

Bowman observes that the level of courts martial for drunkenness rose sharply during the period October 1916 to February 1918 and that levels of drunkenness appeared to be higher in regular infantry battalions than in service battalions.[146] While the latter may be true of units serving on the Western Front, Table 7.10 (Annex 2) shows that there is little evidence of this in the 10th Division where two of the three regular battalions have a lower than average level of courts martial for drunkenness while the level of the third, 1st Leinsters, still had fewer charges of drunkenness than two of the division's service battalions.[147] The number of courts martial for drunkenness of the division's three regular battalions ranged from 9 to 22 while two sample regular battalions of the 16th and 36th Divisions examined by Bowman had 19 and 15 courtsmartial for this offence respectively. Therefore, it appears that there is no significant difference between the levels of drunkenness in the regular battalions across the three divisions. With regard to Bowman's observation 'that the number of men tried for drunkenness rose sharply during the period October 1916 to February 1918', the evidence regarding the 10th (Irish) Division is inconclusive.[148] Although the incidence of drunkenness increased in absolute terms over the period when adjustment is made for the variation in time period, only three battalions had increased levels of drunkenness while the level of charges for this offence in the 6th Royal Irish Rifles reduced by more than half. Overall, the level of courts martial for drunkenness amongst the original battalions of the division when adjusted for the differing time periods fell by some 21%.

Bowman has observed that during this period battalions of the 36th (Ulster) Division had fewer men court-martialled than their counterparts in the 16th (Irish) Division. Table 7.11 (Annex 2) would tend to support this assertion, at least in terms of the Service battalions which now largely comprised English conscripts formed around a nucleus of the battalion's original Irish members. It is notable, however, in both divisions that the highest level of courts martial in the sample occurred in the regular battalions which were still largely Irishmen.[149] A similar pattern is not so easily discernible in the 10th Division where the level of courtsmartial remained higher than either of the other Irish Divisions. Tables 7.10 and 7.11 show that the level of courts martial in the regular battalions of the division were, with the exception of the 2nd Royal Irish Fusiliers, on a par with those in the Ulster Division, with both having significantly fewer courts martial than the sample Regular battalion of the 16th Division. Finally, although the overall level of courts martial in the division's Service battalions fell after its first twelve months of active service, there appears to be no evidence that this was due to any reluctance to prosecute by the military establishment. The evidence suggests that, as a whole, the level of courts martial in the 10th Division remained higher than those of the two Irish divisions on the Western Front. It also suggests that the gap, at least in comparison with the 16th (Irish) Division, was closing.

David Englander has suggested that during this period punishment under the British courts martial system became more severe, citing the twenty executions on the Western Front in

September 1917 to support his view.[150] Table 7.12 in Annex 2 shows the sentences of courts martial for members of the 10th (Irish) Division in the 17-month period from October 1916 to February 1918.[151] Comparison with the 12-month period, August 1915 to July 1916 (Table 7.8) shows that the number of death sentences in the later period fell from 18 to 15 while the number of men sentenced to penal servitude also fell from 65 to 52. It should be noted, however, that none of the death sentences awarded during the latter period were carried out. Of the 52 awards of penal servitude, 13 had part of their sentence remitted, 7 had their sentence suspended, 21 sentences were commuted, and 1 sentence was not confirmed. As a consequence, less than 20% of men originally sentenced to penal servitude in the division between October 1916 and February 1918 had their full sentence confirmed.

Bowman observes that executions and penal servitude were imposed very rarely in Irish units on the Western Front and that field punishment number one was the main form of sanction, although a higher number of NCOs were reduced to the ranks following courts martial during this period than formerly.[152] Comparison of courts martial records for the 10th Division for the period October 1916 to February 1918, when adjusted for the 17-month period, shows that the number of awards of FP1 compared with the division's first 12-months actually fell by 6% while the number of reductions in rank fell by 25%. Analysis of the numbers being sentenced across all categories of punishment, when adjusted for the differing time periods involved, shows fewer men of the 10th Division were sentenced in each category between October 1916 and February 1918, than in the period August 1915 to July 1916.

If Englander's suggestion that there was a tightening of the British courts martial system is true in respect of those serving on the Western Front, analysis of the courts martial records of the 10th (Irish) Division provides no evidence of any similar changes on other fronts. The evidence indicates that while indiscipline may have been at higher levels than Irish units on the Western Front, it was not viewed as either a matter of concern or as an indicator of a morale problem, nor did the authorities feel the need to have increased courts martial sanctions as appears to be the case on the Western

Front. Jourdain, while commanding the 6th Connaught Rangers in France, provides an unflattering, and perhaps not unbiased, comparison with his former unit.

> The men were very young indeed ... their bearing was good but they were too inexperienced. Their officers were good as far as I could see but the Battalion was not fit for service in an offensive. I was much depressed by the knocked about appearance of all ranks. What a change from my 5th Battalion at Salonika![153]

Before concluding this chapter on corporate morale and discipline it is necessary to acknowledge that morale has an impact, not just on a body of men, but on individuals which sometimes manifested itself in self-inflicted wounds and attempted suicide. Whether these are considered to be a matter of morale or discipline is open to further discussion, although both were regarded at the time as military offences. In the opinion of Mitchell and Smith, the incidence of self-inflicted wounds was extremely low as

> only 1% of all courts martial offences were due to self-mutilation, and it seems unlikely that this represents a low detection rate. Of the more than one million casualties analysed by the official medical historians 273, or less than 1%, fell within this category.[154]

This appears a reasonable estimation given that only three men were court-martialled for the offence in the 10th Division between July 1915 and May 1918. The three, two members of 6th Leinsters and one from the 6th Royal Irish Rifles, although the latter had previously served in the 6th Leinsters, received sentences ranging from 3 months FP1 to 2 year's hard labour, although in the latter case, that of Private Hunt, the charge was quashed in February 1919.[155] By comparison between July 1915 and March 1917, ten similar cases in the 13th (Eastern) Division were tried by courts martial, equivalent to 3% of all cases tried in the division during the period, suggesting a more serious morale problem.[156]

There are no records, in either the 10th or 13th Divisions, regarding any courts martial for attempted suicide, although this may be because all attempts proved successful. An entry in the war diary of the 5th Connaught Rangers records on 29 December 1915 'one casualty by gunshot wound (fatal) self-inflicted'.[157] That this was not an isolated incident is supported by an entry in the war diary of LXVII Brigade RFA: 'A Bombardier of A/67 attempted to commit suicide by cutting his throat, he was taken to the 30th Field Ambulance and died during the afternoon. A most regrettable incident'.[158] Nor were incidence of suicide among members of the 10th Division confined to either those on active service or the rank and file. Jasper Brett, an Irish rugby international and officer in the 7th Royal Dublin Fusiliers, took his own life on 4 February 1917 after being discharged from Latchmere Military Hospital, Richmond, Surrey.[159]

At the end of April 1918 the 10th Division lost its 'Irish' designation when it was decided to 'Indianise' the formation by replacing all but the three Irish regular battalions of the division with Indian infantry battalions. Due to heavy losses the 6th Royal Irish Rifles was disbanded and its men transferred to the three regular battalions remaining with the division, while the remaining six Irish Service battalions were transferred to the Western Front where manpower was in great demand. On arrival in France the 6th Royal Munster Fusiliers and the 7th Royal Dublin Fusiliers were absorbed by the 2nd battalions of their respective regiments while the other battalions were distributed to a number of divisions.

CHAPTER 8

From the Curragh to the Judean Hills – The Lessons Learned

Writers including Travers and Griffith have characterised the development of the British army during the Great War as a learning curve.[1] Rather than a single curve, however, the process might be more realistically described as a series of different curves, including technical, tactical and strategic development, that really only intersected in the last 100 days of the war. Most of these developments first became apparent in the main theatre of operations on the Western Front before their adoption in other theatres. This chapter will examine the relevance and impact of these developments on the 10th (Irish) Division which never served on the Western Front.

In the previous chapter it was noted that the pre-war army had eschewed the adoption of a formal military doctrine on how battles should be fought although the majority of senior officers at the time, including Haig and Hamilton, subscribed informally to a belief in the offensive and moral superiority as the solution to the increased firepower that had transformed the modern battlefield. What this group appeared to have ignored however is the caveat contained in *Field Service Regulations* that 'the assault is made possible by superiority of fire'.[2]

During the Boer War the British army experienced for the first time the effects of modern firearms and their greatly increased range. Since before Waterloo it had been the practice of the artillery to provide close support to the infantry; with guns being laid by line of sight. At Colenso, however, a number of guns were lost when their crews were killed by Boer riflemen at ranges of over 1,000 yards and infantry seeking to close on the enemy in line were shot down from long range. Its experience in South Africa taught the army, particularly the infantry, a number of valuable lessons such as marksmanship and an increased understanding of field craft and minor tactics, which were put into immediate effect. The war also demonstrated the need for more modern artillery which led to the introduction of Quick Firing (QF) guns similar to those introduced by the French in 1895. The QF system was based on a hydrostatic buffer and recuperator system which absorbed the gun's recoil thus removing the need to re-sight the gun after each shot.[3]

Apart from the famous sieges of Ladysmith and Mafeking and a few set piece battles such as Colenso (15 December 1899), the Boer War was largely one of movement but the Russo-Japanese war, which also had a profound effect on the British military, was essentially static in nature. British observers, including Hamilton, reported on a very different battlefield from that of South Africa; a battlefield of trenches, machine guns and barbed wire, and, of most importance to the artillery, a battlefield of indirect fire. At the battle of Sha-ho in September 1904 the Japanese artillery deployed on the reverse slope and used forward observers to report on the fall of shot enabling them to fire on an enemy they could not see. Despite the developments of such tactics, however, the Russian trenches were eventually captured, at great cost by infantry which led to some erroneous conclusions by some senior officers. Kiggell, Director Staff Duties at the War Office 1910-1913, observed:

> After the Boer War the general opinion was that the result of the battle would for the future depend on fire-arms alone, and that the sword and bayonet were played out. But this idea is erroneous and was proved to be so in the late war in Manchuria. Everyone admits that. Victory is won actually by the bayonet, or by the fear of it, which

amounts to the same thing as far as the actual conduct of the attack is concerned. This fact was proved beyond doubt in the late war. I think the whole question rather hangs on that, and if we accept the view that victory is actually won by the bayonet, it settles the point.[4]

Britain's most successful commander, the Duke of Wellington, would not have been impressed by Kiggell's analysis having demonstrated on numerous occasions the superiority of firepower, properly used, over an army whose belief in its moral superiority had defeated every other army in Europe.[5]

In the years preceding the outbreak of war, the army underwent a series of changes to its structure, training, and equipment. Between 1908 and 1911 three new artillery pieces were introduced to replace the obsolete equipment of the Boer war: 13 and 18-pounder (QF) guns to support the cavalry and infantry respectively, and a 4.5-inch howitzer firing a 34lb shrapnel, or high explosive (HE), shell. By the beginning of 1914 the infantry had been reorganised into four company battalions armed with the new .303 bolt-action Short Magazine Lee-Enfield (SMLE) rifle, with its 10-round magazine loaded by a 5-round charger. With the improved Mark VII ammunition, this enabled a trained regular to fire at a rate of 15 aimed shots per minute at an effective range of 800 yards. In addition to its rifle strength, each battalion also possessed two Maxim machine guns which, on the outbreak of war, were in the process of being replaced by the lighter and more effective Vickers. Despite its increased firepower, the ultimate task of the infantry remained the imposition of its moral superiority on the enemy, in pursuit of which the pre-war British infantryman was trained in the tactics of fire and movement. Fire and movement, still a basic of British infantry training today, consists of one group providing suppressing fire while a second group advances towards their objective. The second group then halts to provide covering fire to allow the first group to advance and the process is repeated until both groups are close enough to the enemy position to form an assault line from which a bayonet charge may be launched. It was by such tactics that moral superiority could overcome modern firepower. The army went as far as to express the belief that casualties actually decreased with a steady advance because of its morale effect on the enemy.[6] One has only to observe the repulse of the 'Old Guard' by Maitland's brigade at Waterloo to realise the belief that the morale of well-trained and led troops, in a strong defence position, would fall to such an extent as to cause panic on the approach of the enemy even in overwhelming numbers was a fallacy. The role of artillery in fire and movement was to provide fire support during the assault to 'help the infantry to maintain its mobility and offensive power'.[7] The British belief in the moral superiority of the offensive over firepower, however, totally ignored the serious imbalance between offensive and defensive firepower. Writing in retrospect, in a work of at least partial self-justification, Sir John French claimed to have recognised this imbalance early in the war, 'as, day by day, the trench fighting developed I came to realise more and more the greater relative power which modern weapons had given to the defence ... and so, day by day, I began dimly to realise what the future might have in store for us'.[8]

At the beginning of the war, only the British had their cavalry entirely armed with an infantry weapon rather than a shorter and less effective carbine, a tactical doctrine based on dismounted firepower, and on synchronizing a mounted charge with flanking or supporting fire.[9] That the role of the cavalry was changing was not accepted by all. Erskine Childers wrote in 1910 that 'mounted men not only can pass through a fire-zone unscathed, but making genuine and destructive attacks against riflemen and guns', while Haig in his evidence to the Elgin Commission in 1903, stated that 'the ideal cavalry is one which can attack on foot, and attack on horseback'.[10]

While each of the three main arms of the British army had undergone considerable change since the end of the Boer War; little had been done to co-ordinate these changes. More modern artillery pieces had been introduced to reflect developments in artillery usage rather than the needs of the infantry it was to support or the nature of the battlefield on which it was to be used. The size of the infantry arm, and its lack of agreed doctrine, was still based on its primary role of colonial policeman, while future wars were seen as wars of manoeuvre, which was reflected in training. Bidwell and Graham have termed the development of the British army in the period before the commencement of the Great War as the tactics of separate tables, with each of the three arms developing their tactics in isolation from the others, with no clear doctrine on how they should operate together in battle. Nevertheless, Sir James Edmonds would describe the British Expeditionary Force (BEF) of 1914 as 'the best-trained, best-organised and best-equipped British Army that ever went forth to war' but added the caveat that:

> In the matter of co-operation between aeroplanes and artillery and the use of machine-guns … in heavy guns and howitzers, high explosive shells, trench mortars, hand grenades, and much of the subsidiary material required for trench warfare it was almost totally deficient. Further, no steps had been taken to instruct the Army in knowledge of the probable theatre of war or of the German Army.[11]

Before discussing the British army's experience of its first conflict on the continent since Waterloo, it would be unfair to ignore two subordinate arms on which the lessons of the Russo-Japanese war had not been totally lost, the Royal Garrison Artillery (RGA) and the Royal Engineers (RE). Although the Japanese had used 11-inch howitzers to neutralize the fortifications of Port Arthur and siege guns were used widely against Russian trenches, most British officers viewed this as only an aberration. The RGA however, rewrote its manual about sieges while the Royal Engineers were in the process of doing so when war was declared.

Despite the initial retreat from Mons, the opening months of the conflict largely conformed to the war of manoeuvre for which the British army had trained. On 9 August 1914 the four infantry and single cavalry divisions of the BEF began crossing the channel to aid the French and Belgian armies already being pressed by a German army equipped and organised for this specific conflict, even down to siege guns for the demolition of the Belgian frontier defences. Each British infantry division of 12 battalions was supported by a cavalry squadron and its own artillery of 54 18-pounders, organised in three brigades of three batteries each with six guns, a three battery brigade of 18 4.5-inch howitzers, and a single battery of 4 long range 60-pounder heavy field guns. No siege guns accompanied the BEF to France and its 18-pounders were only supplied with shrapnel rounds. In essence British artillery was designed to fight an enemy in the open and at medium to close range; effectively the army's experience of pre-Boer war colonial warfare.

The retreat from Mons until the beginning of the 'race to the sea' provided the British regulars with few opportunities to demonstrate their belief in the offensive and its moral superiority over firepower. This period, however, demonstrated the infantry's marked super-iority in musketry and field craft over the regular, reserve and Landwehr regiments of the German army.[12] The opening manoeuvre phase of the war on the Western Front also demonstrated that a number of lessons of South Africa had been forgotten and threw up for the first time the difficulties of communication and co-ordination involved in controlling what was, at that time, the largest army Britain had ever put into the field. The opening battles demonstrated clearly how different continental warfare was from fighting untrained natives or even Boers on the veldt.

At Mons, a coalmining town in southern Belgium, the British army experienced its first battle in Europe for almost 100 years. Fought among the slagheaps of the town the British infantry fought doggedly against superior enemy numbers but the artillery, particularly the 18-pounders with their flat trajectory, found it difficult to find suitable positions to deploy in support of the infantry due to the close nature of the terrain. The terrain also provided communication difficulties when the time came for the army to withdraw when a number of units failed to receive their orders in time or in some cases at all. As a result a number of units were cut off when the rest of the army retreated.

During the retreat from Mons the lessons of the Boer War regarding the effects of modern firepower were clearly forgotten as, although the *Field Artillery Training* manual emphasised indirect fire as 'the normal method employed in the field', artillery continued to provide close support to the infantry. At Le Cateau, the 5th Division deployed its guns in full sight of the Germans and lost almost half its artillery when German fire prevented their withdrawal. For the neighbouring 3rd Division, deployed on a reverse slope, the effectiveness of the division's indirect fire was limited due to inadequate communication.[13] During the Peninsula War and at Waterloo, the Duke of Wellington had eschewed counter-battery duels with French gunners on the twin grounds that the main aim of artillery was to support his infantry and that there was never enough artillery pieces available.[14] In the Boer War a limited amount of counter-battery fire had taken place, usually at long range. The retreat from Mons, however, involved a number of incidents of counter-battery fire at close range and in the open when the Royal Artillery engaged their German counterparts. The most famous of these engagements was at Néry where 'L' Battery RHA engaged a German battery at point-blank range in the open but in the process lost heavily in men and guns. However, such incidents were rare and the Germans soon switched to engaging British artillery by indirect fire to which the Royal Artillery had little response. This change in tactics highlighted the deficiency of the British pre-war planning process that had chosen as its main infantry support weapon a field gun specifically designed with a flat trajectory and limited range to optimise the effects of shrapnel. The effectiveness of the shrapnel rounds fired from British 18-pounders diminished significantly at longer ranges while their flat trajectory limited its use against targets in cover.

It is perhaps appropriate to mention here the role of the army's newest arm, the aircraft of the Royal Flying Corps (RFC), which had crossed to France with the BEF. Not yet a fighting weapon, the aircraft of the RFC provided the army with useful information during the retreat from Mons on the location of enemy units and indeed on some occasions its own. At an early stage in the war Haig saw the potential of the aeroplane and appointed Major-General Horne, his Corps' senior artillery officer, to organise co-operation between artillery and aeroplanes.[15] As the war developed, this arm would expand its role both in support of ground forces and as an independent fighting force.

After the allied victory on the Marne, the German army withdrew towards the Aisne where the nature of the war began to change. On the Aisne the Germans found a series of ridges which they could defend and from which their artillery could dominate the allied positions below, and began to dig in leaving the allied armies little choice but to try to eject them. When this failed they too began to dig trenches to shelter from the enemy's devastating artillery fire and thus began the creation of a continuous line of trenches from the Swiss border to the Channel coast, the breaking of which would dominate military operations on the Western Front for the next four years.

It soon became obvious to the allies that protection from enemy shell fire was more important than good fields of fire. The best defensive positions were those on the reverse slopes of hills where the effect of falling shot from German howitzers firing high explosive shells could be minimised. High ground not only provided good observation, but its reverse slopes sheltered artillery and supply lines from the effects of direct fire. From the beginning, however, the allied choice of where their trenches were sited was to a large extent determined by the Germans who were able to fall back to positions that offered the greatest defensive advantage leaving the allies to construct their defence line in inferior positions often on lower slopes overlooked by the enemy and from which any assault was made more difficult.

On 6 October the British army left the area of the Aisne, taking up a line from Givenchy to the Belgium town of Ypres. Ypres lies at the centre of a saucer shaped depression overlooked by higher ground on three sides which in October 1914 was held by the German army. Troops in the Ypres salient had the added problem that in places the water table made the digging of trenches impossible and as a result defensive breastworks had to be built up. The official historian, Sir James Edmonds, records the failure of an early attempt to break out of the salient thus:

> They were called on to attempt the impossible. Without adequate artillery preparation and support, over ground unknown and unreconnoitred, they were sent to turn out an enemy well provided with machine-guns out of

a position which had ready-made cover in houses and a wood, and splendid artillery observation from high ground behind it.[16]

The beginning of trench warfare completely changed the nature of the war from that anticipated by the British army; there was now no chance of a quick war of manoeuvre that would be over by Christmas. The change emphasised deficiencies in the army's equipment. Unlike the Germans the BEF had no siege train and few heavy guns; neither had it any of the trench equipment such as barbed wire, grenades and trench mortars that the Germans possessed, nor the high explosive shells essential to destroy trenches.

Although trained with a view to deployment on the Western Front, the 10th (Irish) Division was ultimately sent to reinforce Hamilton's campaign on the Gallipoli peninsula. According to Travers, the Gallipoli campaign, which is often viewed as being unique because of its amphibious elements and geographical location, should really be viewed in the context of the Western Front.[17] As such the campaign took place early in the army's learning curve and, as a secondary theatre with low priority for men and matériel, a time lag often existed between the implementation of new methods on the Western Front and their adoption by the Mediterranean Expeditionary Force. When the division landed in August 1915, however, it encountered many of the problems faced by the BEF on the Western Front. In many ways the area around the landing beaches of Suvla was similar to the Ypres salient. The bay was surrounded on three sides by hills occupied by an enemy with a view overlooking the whole plain. Although initially the Turks were not great in numbers, they were quickly reinforced and occupied positions where the terrain favoured the defenders which enabled them to dominate the British positions. Just as the BEF had to site its trenches in inferior positions, so the 10th Division 'had to dig in anywhere we happened to be whether it was well sited or not'.[18]

Static warfare demanded new approaches to both defence and attack. On the Western Front the trenches soon developed from the single line of hastily dug trenches into a series of lines of mutually supporting trenches connected by communication trenches. In these trench systems the fire trench, with its machine gun emplacements, formed the frontline, which except at morning stand-to, was lightly defended. The majority of men lived during their period in the line in the second line trench from which they would reinforce the fire trench if attacked.[19] To minimise the effects of shellfire, trenches were not built in straight lines but broken up into a series of bays.

In Salonika the 10th Division made every effort to take advantage of the high ground to create an effective position. According to Drury, 'The line consisted of a series of detached trenches or rifle pits along the forward slope of the hill [Simonet Ridge] 50 or 80 yards down from the top, and extending about a mile in a slight arc. There was a fine field of fire and no dead ground for the enemy to collect in except on the right flank where I made a detached post on a separate knoll held by one platoon and 1 MG (Vickers)'.[20] As was the practice on the Western Front, the forward trench was lightly manned during the day – 'everything was quiet during the night, and we stood to Arms at 04.45 and at 05.30. I withdrew most of the men behind the crest, leaving two main posts and various sentries along the front but keeping the 1 platoon complete in the detached post on the right'.[21] As at Ypres, the division also encountered ground where it was impossible to dig sufficiently deep trenches and therefore had to adopt measures similar to the French to provide adequate cover:

> We have made big improvements in the line since we have been here, and I find that the trenches are almost invisible from the front, in great contrast to the French stone sangars which can be seen for miles around. They give no protection from shell fire and the flying stones only increase the casualties. We moved 50 yards or so down the forward slope, and dug trenches as deep as the ground would let us, building up low breast works of stone and sods, and covered thickly with earth and scrub on the front and also up behind, so that from the front no break appeared. They are not deep but give good protection to men kneeling or lying and they are well traversed to localize the effects of shells.[22]

Barbed wire had become a feature of defence on the Western Front as early as 28 September 1914.[23] At first these entanglements 'were made of two or three strands, at the most, of agricultural wire picked up where they could find it'.[24] By contrast in November 1915 Drury could write 'we have managed to get a good deal of barbed wire and have made low entanglements, knee deep in the undergrowth, and twisted between the trees. There are no stakes to be seen and no sign of wire can be seen from the front'.[25] As the months passed the amount of barbed wire being used increased, and Drury recorded that 'the wire entanglements are wonderful and I hear that we have used no less than 1,000 miles of wire per mile of front'.[26] On the Western Front belts of barbed wire were placed 50-100 yards in front of the defender's trench in order to break the attacker's momentum and holding them under the defender's fire. At the same time the attackers would be prevented from getting close enough to throw grenades. Wire entanglements were to be 'so placed that the enemy will come upon them as a surprise'.[27] Following their retreat from Serbia in December 1915, the 6th Royal Dublin Fusiliers had the opportunity, seldom given to the BEF, to choose an advantageous defensive position to site their trenches. These trenches were described as providing 'a magnificent field of fire everywhere and every range is carefully checked and noted down on boards in every platoon sector. The wire entanglements are designed to make troops bunch together in spots covered by the cross fire of many machine guns'.[28]

In the period following the Boer War there was considerable discussion of the value, role and use of the machine gun and this, and financial constraints, delayed until 1913 the delivery of the lighter Vickers medium machine gun to replace the army's Maxims. Aylmer Haldane, who had been an observer during the Russo-Japanese War in Manchuria in 1904 and 1905, told the 1909 General Staff conference that in his opinion it was 'impossible to take a position which is well defended by machine-guns until these guns have been put out of action'. However, he expressed this view with the caveat that an attack could still be pressed home but only if the attacker was willing to accept heavy losses.[29] This had been the experience of the

Japanese in Manchuria and in the opening months of the Great War also the experience of the British army, which led many to believe that the enemy possessed many more machine guns than the British Army. In truth a German division deployed no more machine guns in 1914 than a British division. However, the German army deployed its eight machine guns in a single company attached to each four-battalion regiment rather than two to each battalion as the British did. This had the effect of creating a powerful source of massed firepower and also allowed the creation of interlocking zones of fire, which increased the already deadly effect of the weapon. In an unsigned minute of 24 November 1914, it was proposed to double the number of Vickers machine guns per battalion and 'give each division and brigade a machine gun battery of 6 guns'. The minute continued that it was hoped that 100 Lewis guns per week would be delivered to the army commencing March 1915.[30] The delivery of additional Vickers machine guns to battalions on the Western Front did not begin until February 1915, due to industry's inability to produce sufficient numbers at this stage of the war. A minute of 24 November 1914 stated that the sole factory producing the Vickers could only produce 50 pieces per week and consequently battalions of the 10th Division did not receive their additional allocation of machine guns until late November 1915.[31]

On the Western Front a number of proponents of the machine gun, in particular Captain George M. Lindsay an instructor of musketry at Hythe, were examining how machine guns might be used to their full potential. Following his analysis of battlefield practice, Lindsay came to the conclusion that individual infantry units could not be trusted to use their machine guns to provide mutual support that would produce an interlocking and enfilading defensive belt that would effectively cover their own and neighbouring units' frontline. Lindsay's answer to this problem was the central control of the deployment of all machine guns across a section of the frontline.[32] To facilitate this role and increase the effectiveness achieved by massing the number of machine guns firing on the same target, the Machine Gun Corps (MGC) was formed in October 1915. This removed the four machine guns from each battalion of a brigade and combined them into a single brigade machine gun company of 16 guns. In the

10th (Irish) Division, the nucleus of 30th Machine Gun Company was formed in April 1916 from those attending a Brigade machine gun class and certain other officers and men from units of the brigade, although the new unit was not officially recognised until 10 May 1916.[33] Evidence suggests that following initial problems of obtaining equipment, the company first went into action as a unit on 1 October when 12 guns were deployed along the river bank at Karadzakaj in anticipation of an enemy attack. Two days later a half section was lost while covering the withdrawal of the 6th RDF.[34]

It is claimed that the formation of the MGC resulted in dramatic developments in machine gun tactics. First the curving trajectory of the ammunition used by the Vickers was exploited to develop a system for firing over the heads of friendly troops. Secondly, indirect fire was developed to enable guns to fire at targets they could not see. By the time of the Battle of the Somme in July 1916 these techniques were being combined to create machine gun barrages fired by groups of guns.[35] Before the creation of the MGC, Lindsay had been concerned about the lack of interlocking and enfilading fire support between neighbouring sections of the frontline. The 30th Machine Gun Company war diary entry for 1 January 1917 records cooperation with 81st MG Coy in the 27th Division who agreed to establish mutual zones of fire between guns on respective flanks so demonstrating that the lessons of the Western Front were being applied by the division in Salonika. On 15 May 1917 two guns of B section, 29th Machine Gun Company, covered the infantry advance on Kupri with indirect overhead fire, while on 27-28 July 1917 the 30th company's war diary recorded that it was undertaking 'barrage lifting practice' which was put into practice on 3 August the war diary recording 'ranging and barraging left bank of river [Struma]'.[36] These were major advances in the use of the machine gun which, according to Hutchinson, the German army only began to experiment with in November 1917.[37]

As the Western Front descended into siege warfare, weapons of earlier siege eras were reintroduced by both sides. On 31 October 1914 the BEF encountered a German 'Minenwerfer', a weapon capable of lobbing a shell with a high trajectory, similar to a howitzer, over a much shorter range. Lacking a similar weapon, the British army resorted to makeshift solutions such as the Leach catapult and the West spring gun, a cross between a Roman ballista and medieval French trebuchet. Neither of these was in any real sense a trench mortar but were essentially bomb throwers, the former being capable of propelling a two pound hand grenade for up to 160 yards while the latter had a range of around 250 yards. The supply of both these weapons was officially discontinued in July 1916 when sufficient numbers of the 3-inch Stokes Mortar became available.

Trench warfare brought the return of the hand grenade [bomb], which had largely fallen out of use by the British army, the availability of which was limited to a few of the notoriously dangerous 1908 No. 1 Mark 1 stick type model used by the Royal Engineers. Due to limited supplies of suitable detonators, the British munitions industry struggled to supply even half the 10,000 grenades per week required by the BEF by the end of 1914, the shortfall being met during 1914/15 in the form of the improvised jam tin bomb; the antique ball grenade and other experimental grenades until the arrival of the M5 Mark 1 Mills Bomb late in 1915. Dependent on the skill and strength of the thrower, the hand grenade is a relatively short range weapon and so on 4 November, 1914, a consignment of 1,000 rifle grenades were sent to the BEF, although there is no indication of how effective they were at this stage of the war.[38]

Due to the competing demands of the Western Front, when Hamilton's five divisions landed at Gallipoli on 25 April 1915 they had only 118 artillery pieces each, a third of their quota, and almost totally lacked howitzers, trench mortars, hand grenades and high-explosive shells.[39] There appears to have been little improvement by the time the 10th (Irish) Division landed on the peninsula. According to the Australian official history, 'it was not until May 12th that the first rudimentary trench-mortar was introduced at Anzac, and even this was but an improvised weapon of doubtful precision, consisting merely of a length of tube or pipe, from which, by the explosion of diminutive bags of black powder, a "jam-tin" bomb could be fired'. These improvised mortars were later supplemented on 20 May by four Japanese manufactured trench mortars, which fired a 30lb. bomb.[40] While the Japanese mortars were more effective than their improvised counterparts, their usefulness was curtailed by ammunition shortages because additional supplies, beyond the 2,000 rounds originally landed, had to be specially manufactured and shipped from Japan. Bean also records the introduction of two or three catapult like weapons which although having the advantage of being noiseless had only the same effect as a hand-grenade.[41]

As on the Western Front during this stage of the war, hand-grenades at Gallipoli were still largely of improvised manufacture, the chief engineer of the New Zealand and Australian Division noting on 31 May the 'manufacture of hand-grenades well organised and going satisfactorily' although only when the supply of grenades increased and the men became more accustomed to handling them did Turkish dominance of this area of trench warfare cease.[42] The 10th Division's experience of these new weapons when they arrived on the peninsula was negligible. Their training in the use of grenades (see chapter 4) was minimal while there is no mention at all in regimental histories, diaries or memoirs of any training in the use of mortars.

At 08.40 on 15 August, Mahon's two brigades on Kiretch Tepe Sirt received preparatory orders for an attack at 13.00 hours. Despite the initial success of the attack, which drove the enemy out of their forward trenches, the 10th Division was unable to clear the entire ridge. Although they resisted a series of counter-attacks throughout the day and night of 15/16 August, due to heavy losses, particularly officers, they were ordered at 21.00 on 16 August to withdraw to their old frontline of the previous day. Together with lack of reinforcements, Nicol commanding the division's 30th Brigade, placed the real reason for the withdrawal on the 'want of bombs'.[43] The lack of these by now essential weapons of trench warfare had put the division at a severe disadvantage. As Drury recorded:

> Early in the morning [16 August] the Turks counterattacked using bombs and I think some kind of trench mortar. We have practically no bombs to reply with. I only saw one box sent in reply to requests for some. ... There were very heavy casualties from the Turk bombs which they lobbed up over the rocks. We couldn't get at them as we had no bombs and if one stretched

up to shoot down behind the rocks, they got potted by M.G.s further back. I saw Fitz Cullen doing great work today - was actually fielding Turk bombs and hurling them back before they could burst.[44]

Even when available, the bombs provided still had their limitations:

> An attack was carried out on the morning of the 13th inst [August] to secure a hostile trench. The attack was preceded by a bombing party of the R.E. but the only bombs available were those which have to be lit by a fuse. The result was that on getting near the trench the assaulting party were greeted with a brisk rifle fire. The bombing party lay down under a bush and endeavoured to light the fuses. There was a considerable delay which, (unavoidably) detracted from the dash and élan of the infantry assaulting party, and by the time the fuses were lit and the bombs thrown the Turks had bolted. These bombs are utterly unsuited for an operation of this nature. The only suitable bombs are of percussion pattern which can be thrown instantaneously without checking the infantry advance.[45]

Possibly in response to this criticism, the division's Commander Royal Engineers (CRE) instructed 66 and 85 companies Royal Engineers to:

> visit each Battn in their area and instruct in the manipulation of bombs; also to test each of the six patterns of bombs and withdraw any found unsuitable. There are now six patterns of bombs and in view of the fact they have to be used by more or less unskilled men it would appear preferable to have only two types one percussion and the other fuse. [46]

Although the divisional CRE is noted as visiting Chocolate Hill that afternoon and 'supervised testing and instruction in manipulating trench mortars and hand-grenades', it was not until a week before the division left the peninsula that the availability of trench mortars is mentioned.[47] On 31 August the CRE reported that the division's estimated requirement for bombs was 600 per week. Despite rifle grenades now being available, the nature and supply of grenades had not improved by mid-September when those attending bomb throwing instruction were each asked to bring a cricket-ball bomb with him including detonator and fuse, 'as there are none left in the R.E. Park'.[48]

The situation concerning the training and availability of grenades in the 10th Division appears to have improved early in 1916 as Drury's company had sufficient bombs to allow the use of 150 for practice.[49] That bombing tactics were now beginning to be taken seriously by the army is demonstrated by the appointment of battalion bombing officers in January 1916 and the arrival of four officers posted from the 5th (Extra Reserve) Battalion Royal Dublin Fusiliers to the 6th Battalion RDF all of whom had certificates in bombing.[50] Towards the end of February 1916 at least some battalions of the division had created specialist bombing sections within companies similar to the practice already adopted on the Western Front.[51]

While brigade trench mortar batteries (TMBs) had been formed on the Western Front prior to the Somme and Drury mentions that 'a trench mortar school has been started and we sent 2/Lt Dunwoody and some other ranks away this week to learn how to poof them off' in the last week of March 1916, trench mortar batteries attached to each brigade of the 10th Division were not formed until 28 September 1916.[52] Unlike the officers and men of machine gun companies who became part of the new MGC, members of trench mortar batteries remained members of their parent regiment. Initially TMBs were formed around a nucleus of officers and NCOs from other divisions. The 8th Stokes Trench Mortar Battery, later 30th Brigade TMB, was originally commanded by Captain A.J. Horrocks, 7th Manchester Regiment, who had brought with him 7 NCOs and other ranks as 'trained men' from the same battalion.[53]

On 22 April 1915, the Germans launched a poison gas attack against Algerian troops of the French army in an attempt to break through the allied trench lines during the 2nd Battle of Ypres.

Although no breakthrough was achieved, within weeks Churchill, as First Lord of the Admiralty, had established a committee to 'consider use of asphyxiating and life destroying gases', instructing that 'preparations for war with poisonous gases of the above nature are to be made forthwith on the largest possible scale'.[54] On 15 May 1915 Churchill cabled de Robeck, the allied naval commander at Gallipoli, suggesting that he and Hamilton might consider using gas against Turkish forces on the peninsula as '[t]he Turks will very likely use it against you'.[55] Both commanders responded in similar vein, that they were against initiating the use of gas in the campaign, though de Robeck informed Churchill that they would welcome gas bombs as a retaliatory weapon.[56] Hamilton's cable of 18 May included a request for anti-gas defences such as respirators, which was followed by an Admiralty letter asking 'whether any protective [gas] helmets have been sent out for the use of Allied Forces there [Gallipoli]'. The War Office immediately replied that '50,000 respirators have been despatched for the use of the Mediterranean Expeditionary Force, and that a further 50,000 [gas] helmets are now being sent in addition'.[57]

Following a meeting of the Dardanelles Committee on 24 July 1915, Kitchener informed Hamilton that 'a certain amount' of chlorine gas was on its way by sea to Gallipoli and asked him to 'let me know if you think of using it, as it may lead to retaliation. I understand that the Turks, although supplied with German gas, have refused to use it'. Hamilton was adamant that he would not use the new weapon, perhaps because as, Kitchener suggested, it might lead to Turkish retaliation, which might jeopardize the coming offensives.[58] Prior to the landing, Brigadier-General H.L. Reed, Brigadier-General, General Staff (BGGS) at IX Corps HQ issued a memorandum to the 10th Division stating that 'the Turks have lately been reported using some shells the contents of which, although probably not asphyxiating, are poisonous and inflammable'. Reed, however, reassured the division that 'gas helmets are a complete protection, but the compound should be got rid of as quickly as possible, as otherwise the gas may continue to be given off by the compound for some days and though the helmets would be proof against it, it would be impossible to wear them for so long a period'.[59] It was into this air of uncertainty that units of the 10th (Irish) Division, equipped with primitive respirators issued before their landing, disembarked at Anzac and Suvla on 6-7 August 1915.[60]

There is no evidence in divisional war diaries that the 10th Division either used or experienced a gas attack at Gallipoli or in any other theatre in which it served, although gas was used by both sides in Salonika and by the British in Palestine. The threat of gas and its changing nature, however, was always present, as was noted by Drury in July 1916:

> We have just had a very interesting lecture by Major Cluny McPherson of the Newfoundland RAMC on Gas, explaining the latest method of use and means of protection. I'm thankful we hav'nt [sic] had any out here so far, but the Germans are sure to use it and we must be ready for it. I believe we have supplies at the base ready for issue but don't intend to use it unless they do it first. Our helmets give better protection from German gas than theirs do against ours. There is a gas chamber at Lahana where the men get accustomed to wearing their helmets in gas and experiencing the safety of them even in a very concentrated atmosphere of chlorine.[61]

As the quality of gas protection improved generally, so new designs were rolled out to the division. However, due to a shortage of the most recent models, it is obvious that the Salonika front was a low priority although equally this may have been due to an assessment of the risk of the enemy using gas in the theatre. Routine Orders of 12 March 1917 set out the procedure for the replacement of older models of gas helmet by the Small Box Respirator (SBR), which had been issued to men on the Western Front in late 1916. The seriousness with which gas was considered is shown by the instruction that:

> Directly after issue the men are to be trained in the use of the respirator (four drills of one hour should be sufficient). During the period of training small box

respirators must not be breathed through for more than 1½ hours. On conclusion an entry will be made on the last page of each man's pay book, recording:

The size of the small box respirator.

The words "Trained in use of small box respirator".[62]

Evidence that insufficient SBRs were available in the theatre for all personnel is found in Routine Orders of 21 March 1917, which repeats instructions from GHQ:

> In the case of the following units:- Artillery, Machine Gun teams, signallers, and Trench Mortar teams, all personnel will be issued with PHG Helmets in lieu of PH Helmet and goggles.
>
> In addition to the above, all officers and men who have occasion at any time to enter the zone of hostile shell fire, are to be provided with anti-gas protection. This applies equally to staffs of divisions, corps and General Headquarters. Normally it should be sufficient for all such officers and men to carry a PHG Helmet or PH Helmet and goggles. Demand for such small box respirators and helmets as may be necessary will be made in the usual manner.[63]

Even after the division's arrival in Egypt, shortages of the SBR, which by now was the standard issue British gas-mask, was still in evidence. The 29th Brigade war diary records:

> In the morning all men in the Bde not yet fitted with box respirators were tested with gas, but it was impossible to complete everyone as all the last drafts have been joining without box respirators and a sufficient supply was not available to fit out everyone. This fact has been brought to the notice of the division and efforts are being made to obtain a sufficient supply from ordnance to complete the issue.[64]

Anti-gas measures were not confined to the provision of gas masks. As Major-General Longley, GOC 10th (Irish) Division, informed his officers and men in accordance with Notes on Gas Defence dated February 1917, GHQ had approved 'the issue of two blankets per dug-out, in order to prevent any possible in-rush of gas'.[65]

The BEF was influenced not only by the changed nature of warfare but also by supply problems at home. When the army had introduced quick-firing artillery in 1908, the scale of artillery ammunition set after the Boer War remained unaltered as sufficient for six infantry divisions and a cavalry division for a South African sized conflict. The army had therefore entered the war with only 1,500 rounds per gun for its most common field piece the 18-pounder QL and a manufacturing capacity to produce only 30 rounds per month, all shrapnel. Table 8.1 shows the availability of ammunition for divisional artillery at the beginning of the war. Of the 1,500 rounds per gun of 18-pounder ammunition available, 1,000 went with the BEF to France leaving only 500 rounds per gun in England. It should be noted that no provision had been made in pre-war planning for the need to equip, supply and train either the Territorial Force artillery or the artillery of New Army divisions such as the 10th (Irish) Division then being raised. On 17 September 1914, Kitchener informed the House of Lords that 'our chief difficulty is one of matériel rather than of personnel'.[66]

	Ammunition Available			Estimated Manufacturing Capacity per Month	
	Rounds per Gun	Guns	Total Rounds	Total Rounds	Rounds per Gun
13-pdr.	1,900	30	57,000	10,000	333
18-pdr.	1,500	324	486,000	10,000	30
4.5 inch howitzer	1,200	108	129,600	10,000	92
60-pdr.	1,000	24	24,000	100	4

Table 8.1: Availability of ammunition for divisional artillery August 1914.[67]

Britain's lack of manufacturing capacity was not confined to artillery ammunition. Government armaments factories, including the Royal Small Arms Factory producing the army's SMLE rifle, were only manned to meet half the daily needs of a six division Expeditionary Force. Nor did the army possess sufficient reserves to equip the New Army battalions now forming or embodied Territorial Force battalions. As a result, a number of Territorial Force battalions, including the London Scottish, the first Territorial Force battalion to go overseas, did so with the older Lee-Metford rifle which tended to jam when using the army's standard Mark VII ammunition. Despite letting contracts to commercial firms, including some overseas, provision of a number of items continued to fall short of need throughout 1914 and 1915, as manufacturers needed time to increase their capacity to wartime requirements. Table 8.2 below shows the level of delivery of artillery shells to the BEF during December 1914 when the level of stocks of 18-pounder and 4.5 inch ammunition per gun in France was only 648 and 260 rounds each compared with their authorised establishment of 1,000 and 800 rounds respectively.[68]

	Daily requirement per gun		Average received per day December 1914	
	Shrapnel	High Explosive	Shrapnel	High Explosive
18-pdr.	25	25	5.76	0.24
4.5-inch how.	5	35	2.4	2.2
60-pdr.	10	15		
6-inch how.		25		4.6
4.7-inch gun	10	15	3.6	4.0
6-inch gun		25	5.9	0.4
9.2-inch how.		12		5.8

Table 8.2: Level of delivery of artillery shells per day compared with daily requirement December 1914.[69]

The delay in building up reserves of artillery ammunition had a serious impact not only on operations on the Western Front but also in other theatres such as Gallipoli. In mid-July Hamilton recorded in his diary that since 4 June there was not a single 18-pdr H.E. round on the peninsula and in a telegram to Kitchener stated his belief that 'each successive fight shows more clearly than the last how much may hang on the ample supply of ammunition, more especially high explosive howitzer ammunition'. In the same telegram Hamilton asked that in addition to the amount of ammunition accompanying the troops that Kitchener supply him by 1 August with '4.5-inch howitzer, 3,000 rounds; 5-inch howitzer, 7,000 rounds; 6-inch howitzer, 5,000, and 9.3-inch howitzer, 500 rounds, all high explosive'.[70] In addition to an increased supply of ammunition, Hamilton also requested additional ordnance including 'two batteries of 4.5-inch howitzers for each of the Xth and XIth Divisions (since 5-inch howitzers are found to be too inaccurate to bombard the enemy trenches even in close proximity to our own)'.[71] There is no indication that Hamilton received either the additional ammunition or ordnance requested. On 22 August the use of artillery at Helles was, with the exception of counter-battery fire and what were termed special shoots, restricted to 2 rounds per gun per day, a level of expenditure extended to the Anzac and Suvla sectors when the fighting there had died down.[72] Just as the Battle of Loos created a shortage of shells at Gallipoli in August/September 1915, so the Somme offensive had a similar impact in Salonika in September 1916 as the 10th Division's artillery were restricted to 24 rounds per day per 18-pdr battery and 12 for howitzer batteries, 'except in case of emergency'.[73]

Static warfare also led to developments in the use of artillery and methods to improve its effectiveness, while information on enemy defences could be obtained from aerial reconnaissance. Prior to the Battle of Neuve Chapelle in March 1915, Haig referred to 'the wonderful maps of the enemy's trenches which we now had as the result of the aeroplane reconnaissances [sic]' upon which they could 'make our plans very carefully beforehand and with full knowledge of how the enemy's trenches run'.[74] From the RFC's photographs, 1,000 to 1,500 maps were issued to each corps and artillery battery showing positions up to 1,500 yards behind the German frontline.[75] At this stage of the war RFC aircraft equipped with wireless were used as spotter planes for the artillery's heavy guns to facilitate predictive shooting from maps.[76] Predictive shooting as an off-shoot of indirect fire was part of the Royal Artillery's toolkit prior to the war but depended on accurate maps, to be successful. Maps of the necessary quality were unavailable for the continent and until they became available predictive fire could not be undertaken with any degree of accuracy. On 20 May 1915 the British used observation balloons on the Western Front for the first time.[77]

At Gallipoli the 10th Division had to rely heavily on the Royal Navy and a few antiquated mountain guns for the bulk of its artillery support particularly in the Suvla sector, neither of which provided an adequate answer to the division's needs. Accordingly it was not until the division disembarked at Salonika that it encountered many of the problems experienced by divisions on the Western Front. As the Royal Horse Artillery had at Néry in the opening encounters of the war, the division's artillery discovered the dangers of providing close support at Kosturino (Serbia) where the guns of two batteries of LXVII Brigade Royal Field Artillery (RFA) had to be abandoned when the trenches of the infantry they were supporting were overrun.[78] A contributing factor to the loss of the guns was that, due to the nature of the terrain, the guns had had to be manhandled to positions where they could provide direct fire support by line of sight and were therefore unable to be moved when the infantry was forced to withdraw.

During 1916 the division's artillery adopted many of the changes brought about by the BEF's experience in France and Flanders. In July the divisional artillery was reorganised to include a howitzer battery in each artillery brigade enabling the shelling of targets over intervening obstacles and the destruction of trenches by plunging fire.[79] A standard work on the use of field artillery published in 1914 contained no reference to the use of observers being used anywhere but in the vicinity of the guns and emphasised that guns should be deployed at a range of not much over 3,000 yards and with a clear field of fire. According to Bishop 'his (the battery commander's) sole idea is to get his first salvo within the field of his glasses'.[80] By 1916 the principle of Forward Observation Officers (FOOs) had been officially recognised on the Western Front, but it was not until August/September 1916 when the division moved to the Struma valley that the practice appears to have been adopted by the 10th

Division. On 3 September 1916, LXVII Brigade RFA recorded that 'we bombarded with all batteries the villages of Komartan, Gudeli and Dzamimah but with what results is not known as the amount of damage done is very difficult to observe owing to the flat nature of the country & the lack of really good observation stations'.[81] The difficulty of finding good observation points was partially resolved on 15 September when two FOOs and telephonists accompanied a company from the Royal Irish Rifles and Leinster Regiment on a large scale daylight raid on Bulgarian positions on the far bank of the Struma. Despite difficulties when telephone wires were severed, the artillery was able to provide sufficient effective support to enable the capture of 23 prisoners for the loss of only 2 killed, 1 wounded and 1 missing from the attacking force.[82] The success of this action led to FOOs being used in support of even smaller raids. On 30 September a FOO accompanied a party of 25 men of the 5th Royal Irish Fusiliers who, supported by A Battery, LXVII Brigade RFA, raided enemy positions at dawn and captured 16 Bulgarians.[83]

Like the Western Front, artillery observation was not confined to forward observers. As the war progressed, the division's artillery also made use of aircraft for observation, particularly after its move to Egypt and Palestine.[84] On the Western Front aircraft had assisted artillery in the delivery of predictive fire by spotting the fall of shot. There is no direct evidence to suggest that such support was given to the 10th Division's artillery, though ample evidence exists for the use of predictive fire using maps by the division and that artillery officers had begun to understand the scientific nature of this method of delivery. On 29 March 1917, LXVII Brigade RFA was issued maps and a series of range tables from each of its batteries to location of lines to be bombarded. A note accompanying the range tables states that 'fire will never be opened at less ranges than the measured gun range to the barrage lines after making due corrections for wind, temperature, barometer, 100 per-cent zones etc. but can be reduced later if accurate observation ensures that our own troops will not be endangered'.[85]

Prior to the Boer War the bombardment - preparatory fire before an assault - had been widely practiced by the Royal Artillery but had largely fallen out of favour because of the infantry's demand for close support during the war. The static nature of trench warfare, however, brought the bombardment once again to the fore. At this stage of the war the Royal Artillery lacked both the means and experience to do the latter effectively. A barrage by contrast supports the attacker during the assault phase of an operation. At Neuve Chapelle a barrage was fired behind the enemy frontline during the assault, literally creating a barrier to delay the arrival of reinforcements. Neuve Chapelle was only a partial success and had the effect of delaying any further offensive action on the front for a number of months because the British artillery had used practically all its ammunition in the three-day battle and its reserves were reduced to but a few dozen rounds per gun.[86]

In September 1915 during the Battle of Loos, the assault was supported by a lifting barrage during which artillery fire was concentrated on the enemy's frontline trenches until just before the arrival of the assaulting infantry when it would lift to the next line of trenches. The problem experienced by the British infantry with the lifting barrage at Loos was that in some cases the infantry was not sufficiently trained to keep close up to the barrage and that the timings between lifts were too short resulting in artillery fire falling beyond the line where it was needed.[87] The lifting barrage introduced at Loos was the forerunner of the creeping barrage used during the Somme offensive of 1916 with its associated images of lines of men going over the top. Whereas the lifting barrage moving from trench line to trench line would have failed to hit any enemy troops located between the lines of trenches, the creeping barrage was designed so that artillery fire advanced across the landscape, regardless of enemy positions, at a speed calculated to stay just ahead of the advancing infantry. Neither technique had brought great success and, looking back, Charteris, Haig's chief of intelligence, observed that 'we were learning our jobs by hard experience, and progress was on the whole rapid but costly' and that though tactically and strategically unsuccessful this could be justified by 'the lessons learnt and subsequently applied'.[88]

While both these techniques were developed after the 10th Division's period at Gallipoli, evidence suggests that they later became part of the division's repertoire. According to the war diary of LXVII Brigade RFA, following the bombardment of Komarjan at 15.40 'infantry advance commenced under artillery support' and at 16.00 'halted for guns to Lift, which was done, and the advance continued under slight opposition from the enemy'.[89] Following the division's transfer to Egypt, Drury recorded what he called 'a queer stunt, viz., practicing [sic] a creeping barrage with the gunners firing live shell. It's alright doing this in a real scrap, but it's a creepy thing as well as a dangerous one done in cold blood in the desert. I heard that a couple of men in the Connaughts got wounded through advancing too fast, and getting into the barrage'.[90]

The arrival of the Lewis gun has already been noted, as has the creation of specialist bombing sections, and in February 1917 GHQ in France published two training pamphlets that were to revolutionise the British infantry tactics. Pamphlet SS143 provided an outline for the training of specialist teams able to overcome any enemy resistance, such as that provided by pill-boxes, through fire and movement techniques rarely seen in the British army since 1914 while SS144 identified the platoon as the key building block of future tactics.[91] Building on the knowledge gained from 2½ years' experience, SS144 purported to provide junior officers with guidelines on how to deal with a range of situations from trench to trench attacks to open warfare. These pamphlets led to the reorganisation of the infantry platoon into a 5-man HQ and four 8-man sections, each with their own specialism of Lewis gun, bombing, rifle or rifle grenade.

During the winter of 1916-17 the German army withdrew to the Hindenburg Line, which not only shortened their defensive line but integrated into it a series of mutually supporting reinforced concrete pill-boxes to protect their machine gunners. This presented the allies with a tactical problem in as much as these pill-boxes, often constructed in the ruins of buildings or at key positions in the trench line, could put up a protracted resistance that would delay the attacking infantry while their supporting barrage moved on. In response to this problem the British infantry adopted what an anonymous British officer termed the leap-frog system.[92] The principle of this system was firmly rooted in the developments contained in SS143 and SS144. The leading troops would attack the first objective only and remained there to mop up any resistance, such as a pill-box, and prepare for a possible counter-attack while supporting troops passed through them to attack a second objective. The obvious advantages of this system were

1. The platoon commander had to concentrate his attention on a single objective and how to get there, capture it and consolidate the position, enabling him to brief each man in the platoon on their role and what is expected of them;

2. If some portions of the enemy front line held out the attack still went on to the new objective and the supporting barrage was not lost; and

3. The troops detailed to take the final objective have not been exhausted by having to fight all the way and are therefore relatively fresh.

There is insufficient evidence to suggest that leap-frog tactics were used by units of the 10th Division in either Salonika or Palestine. However, the 29th Brigade's war diary records that following their arrival in Egypt from Salonika, the Brigadier 'turned to the lessons learnt from recent tactical exercises which had been carried out and emphasised the differences between the open warfare which may be expected in this country and the normal trench to trench attack which had hitherto been practised'.[93] This, together with a training programme for January 1918 outlining the training of specialised platoon sections organised in accordance with SS143 and SS144, suggests that the infantry of the division may at this stage of the war have adopted these practices from the Western Front.[94]

Terraine's perceptive description of the Great War as 'the only war ever fought without voice control' bears repeating.[95] From the beginning communication between units often separated by distances greater than any previous battlefield proved difficult. In July 1915 GHQ in France officially recognised in one of its series of tactical notes the difficulties of communication particularly after units had advanced beyond their frontline trenches. This tactical note stated that:

> Beyond the 'departure' trench, it has been found possible to run out telephone lines. They are either taken forward with the first advancing troops, or are run out quickly during pauses in the enemy's fire; but they are liable to constant damage by hostile artillery.
>
> The telephone cannot, therefore, be relied on after the Infantry has advanced. It has, however, so many advantages over other means of communication that every effort should be made to lay the lines and keep them in repair.[96]

The tactical note recognised, however, the reality of trench warfare and suggested other methods of maintaining contact with advancing troops including the use of runners and visual signalling indicating that 'semaphore, Dietz discs, lamps, helio and flag have all been used at various times'.[97]

At Gallipoli communication had proved difficult for the 10th Division from the beginning. During the opening hours of the offensive communications took an inordinate amount of time to pass between Hammersley's headquarters and formations under his command. The Dardanelles Commission's report recorded that on the morning of 7 August that it had taken 45 minutes for a message to travel from Hammersley's command post at Lala Baba to Sitwell's located to the south of Hill 10, a distance of little over a mile.[98] A message sent by Sitwell to Hammersley at 06.30 apparently took more than 90 minutes to arrive.[99] Later in the day a telephone line was established between Hammersley's divisional and Sitwell's headquarters but in the period before its installation considerable confusion occurred, which undoubtedly caused substantial delay in the capture of key objectives. Telephone communication when established was still subject to maintenance problems in particular to lines being cut, either accidentally or by enemy action.[100]

Even when orders were received at divisional/brigade headquarters it took time to disseminate them to lower levels. At

08.40 on 15 August, Mahon's two brigades on Kiretch Tepe Sirt received preparatory orders for an attack at 13.00 and although the 6th Royal Irish Fusiliers received their orders at 09.00, Verschoyle, 5th Royal Inniskilling Fusiliers, claims that his battalion had only about fifteen minutes notice of the attack and as a result:

> We told the chaps nothing, 'Come on chaps we've got to go'. The only plan was that two companies went forward and two companies came up behind in support. We started off. There were no tactics other than advancing straight ahead. The thick scrub absolutely prohibited any sort of supporting fire because nobody could see what was happening on each side.[101]

In Salonika, where certain similarities existed with the permanent trench lines of the Western Front, Drury wrote in his diary in April 1916 that 'the signalling arrangements were very well done with laddering and alternative lines', much in the way described in the GHQ tactical note of 31 July 1915.[102] As on the Western Front, however, telephone cables accompanying advancing troops were still prone to be cut by enemy fire as experienced by a FOO of LXVII Brigade RFA who took 40 minutes to regain communication with his battery when both lines were cut.[103]

On 10 November 1917 following his battalion's transfer to Palestine where the warfare was more akin to that experienced by the BEF in 1914, Drury noted that:

> During the recent operations the signallers and arrangements for communications seemed to work well. The small signalling shutter which the men carry (a miniature contact aeroplane one) is a great success. It can be read in good light at one mile without using glasses and much more than this with glasses and a suitable background. In trenches or during an attack, the men hooked it on the muzzle of their rifles and holding the bundock upright, worked the shutter by the spring without exposing themselves.[104]

The increase in the number of aircraft even on a secondary front such as Palestine also played an increasing role in communications. Whereas earlier in the war aircraft had been used to spot for artillery batteries, by 1918, their use had been expanded to include a ground support role for the infantry. Drury noted in his diary for the week ending 26 January 1918, 'I got word that I was to go down to the 14th Squadron RAF [sic] near Junction Station for a course in contact patrol work (in which planes are allotted to the infantry in attack and receive messages from them and note their positions and carry information back to Bde or Div HQrs)'.[105]

A final aspect of the army's learning curve was training. A GHQ pamphlet of May 1916 expressed the view that 'officers and troops generally do not possess that military knowledge arising from a long and high state of training which enables them to act promptly on sound lines to unexpected situations'.[106] At the time this was written the majority of British formations in France were, like the 10th (Irish) Division, men of Kitchener's New Army sent to the front with little more than a year's basic training. In response to these deficiencies, the army in France from 1915 onward became a large-scale training provider with an increasing number of schools of instruction for all ranks. Due to the size of the BEF by December 1916, schools of instruction, depending on their nature, were operating at all levels from division up to GHQ.[107] The size of the armies on secondary fronts, however, reduced the number and level of schools of instruction that could be provided. Nevertheless there is strong evidence to suggest that the 10th Division took training very seriously, particularly in the development of specialists, although the basic skills of the infantryman were not neglected.

The experience of IX Corps on the Somme, not to be confused with Stopford's IX Corps at Gallipoli, led it to conclude at the end of July 1916 that 'the rifle has been neglected during trench warfare and that more musketry training is required'.[108] Perhaps recognising a similar deficiency in this area Drury noted in March 1916 that construction of a rifle range had begun and at the beginning of April 'our new rifle range has now been fixed up and we are having daily practice with good results'.[109] Specialist training was not neglected, and during March courses of instruction had also taken place for machine gun, signalling and bombing sections, as well as a scouting class for 21 men.[110]

Nor was training confined to what could be provided from within the unit's own resources. With the introduction of the Lewis gun in 1916, several officers and NCOs had been sent to Hortiack for a course of instruction in the new weapon and, on their return, they provided training classes to others in the battalion.[111] Drury's diary also makes reference to divisional signal and trench mortar schools, while passing mention is made to the return of Major John Luke from a senior officers' course.[112] War diaries also show that by March 1917 the division possessed a divisional gas school.[113]

Evidence therefore suggests that the 10th (Irish) Division was part of the learning organisation that the British army had become after the hard lessons of the first two years of the war. Although the division's experience may have differed considerably from the experience of divisions on the Western Front, its officers and men demonstrated their ability to assimilate and adapt the lessons learned through the experience of others to their own circumstances. Like the BEF in France and Flanders, the 10th Division was subject to a series of learning curves in technology and tactics which mirrored developments in the main theatre - albeit after a significant time delay reflecting the front's secondary status. The nature of the 10th Division's deployment to Salonika and Palestine, however, meant that some developments such as tanks had little relevance to the division while, unlike the BEF during the last 100 days of the war, it was given sufficient time to reacquaint itself with open warfare.

CHAPTER 9

Just Another Kitchener Division?

Throughout this book comparison has been made, where possible, between the 10th (Irish) and the 13th (Western) Divisions as the only two K1 divisions not to have served on the Western Front. While as yet no divisional history of the 13th (Western) Division in the Great War has been published, Cooper's partial history of the 10th (Irish) Division has been accepted as the standard work on the division's early history. Due to its significance in the historiography of the division, however, a number of the statements made by Cooper in the main text, and repeated by John Redmond in his introduction, have gained general acceptance and, ignoring the political and military context in which it was written, have remained unchallenged since its publication.

As argued in Chapters 2 and 3, there is no evidence to support Cooper's assertion that, excluding the 10th Hampshires 'in the Infantry of the Division 90 per cent of the officers and 70 per cent of the men were either Irish or of Irish extraction', or that a large proportion of the men joining from England were the sons or grandsons of Irishmen who had settled there.[1] The evidence suggests that rather than being of Irish descent the majority of men joining from England were in fact men who were surplus to requirements for the completion of other formations. Does this in any way negate the right of the 10th Division to bear the name Irish? From the beginning the division sought to establish an Irish ethos through regimental tradition, symbols and music, including the formation of regimental bands that played Irish tunes while on the march. The training of the division in Ireland also helped to imbue a sense of Irishness in officers and men, not least by their acceptance into a regimental family that provided them with comforts and support while they were overseas. That ethos is as important as ethnic origin to the establishment of group identity, is demonstrated in the composition of some formations that acquired an elite reputation during the war. In the 51st (Highland) Division, for example, less than 30% of its original strength came from above the Highland line, yet the ethos of the Highland Scot was stamped on the division.[2] Likewise perhaps the most effective British formation of the period was the Canadian Corps, some 42% of whose troops were British by birth, although in 1911 British-born Canadians only accounted for 11% of the Canadian population.[3] Fuller notes, regarding those of British birth in the Canadian Corps, that because they were the first to enlist they played a large part in establishing the original character of units.[4] While the 10th Division experienced initial recruiting difficulties all but three of its Irish battalions (the 6th and 7th Royal Munster Fusiliers for which data is incomplete, and the 6th Royal Inniskilling Fusiliers) had between 30-90% of their ranks already filled before any troops were transferred from England.[5] It was these early recruits that imbued the 10th Division with what many regard as distinctive Irish qualities, such as the stoicism, comradeship and sense of humour that carried it through numerous campaigns. That troops transferred from English regiments to units of the 10th (Irish) Division, however reluctantly, came to accept the situation is demonstrated by the fact there is no evidence of any sizable body of men returning to their former regiment despite assurances that they would be given the opportunity of transferring when opportunities arose.

Demographic reasons had resulted in the number of men of military age in Ireland falling over the previous half century, while the male population in Great Britain had almost doubled over the same period. Analysis shows that men enlisting in the 10th (Irish) Division tended to be older than those joining the 13th Division. Nevertheless, it is noteworthy that the pattern of recruitment to the Wiltshire Regiment, from an area dominated by Swindon's railway industry, resembles most closely that of the 6th Royal Irish Rifles recruited from industrial Belfast and surrounding areas.

The pre-war army had been largely dependent on unskilled labour for the majority of its recruits, and while Simkins suggests that the rapid expansion of the army had brought greater diversity of social background, the evidence suggests that unskilled labour was still the main source of recruits in K1 divisions. An exception to this is the 7th Royal Dublin Fusiliers of the 10th (Irish) Division, which with its 'Pals' company reflected more the mixed composition of later New Army divisions. That the evidence runs contrary to Fitzpatrick's analysis of collective sacrifice is perhaps a result of the more general nature of the source data used in his study and that in the intervening period more specific sources of data, such as service records, have become available which have enabled the examination of individual units rather than the blanket approach adopted by Fitzpatrick.[6] Evidence that the 10th (Irish) and 13th (Western) Divisions were still dependent on unskilled labour as their main source of recruits is consistent with Germains' observation that 'the men of the First New Army, generally speaking, were of the same class as the average run of Regular recruit'.[7]

Just as the pre-war army was largely dependent on recruits from the unskilled classes for its rank and file, so its officer corps was drawn from a narrow social background mainly the peerage, gentry, military families, the clergy and the professions, with a small minority from business, commercial and industrial families. Of those officers serving in pre-war Irish line battalions, the evidence suggests that almost three-quarters were from military families or the senior professions and that 60% had attended a public school. Analysis also suggests that only about a third of officers serving in Irish line battalions were either born or had a permanent address in Ireland.

Although both the 10th and 13th Divisions still depended on military families and the senior professions for the majority of their original officers, evidence suggests that the shortage of potential officer material led to a higher proportion of officers from less traditional sources. This was particularly the case for the 10th (Irish) Division where some 47% of officers were recruited from professionals (other than the law, the church or medicine), business, commerce or industry, and from other sources. The continued predominance of a public school background is apparent to a lesser extent among their New Army counterparts and differs greatly between the two divisions examined. Analysis of the educational background of officers of the 13th (Western) Division shows that some 82% were educated at a public school, almost on a par with a pre-war regular battalion.[8] By comparison only 42% of officers in the 10th (Irish) had been educated at a public school, which is significantly less than the 54% identified in pre-war Irish line regiments. This is probably symptomatic of the fact that the division had proportionately more Irish officers than were usually to be found in pre-war Irish regiments. While both divisions had approximately the same proportion of serving and former serving officers, the 13th Division was more dependent on university students to meet its officer requirements than the 10th Division in which a higher proportion of officers appear to have abandoned careers to answer Kitchener's call for volunteers. The implication is that the officer cadre of the 10th (Irish) Division may have been older than their English counterparts.

The rapid expansion of the British Army in the months following the declaration of war on Germany was beyond the capacity of the existing structures and facilities available. In the 13th Division's recruiting area, enlistment had to be suspended at the depot of the Wiltshire Regiment in early September because the number of men offering to enlist had so greatly exceeded the available accommodation that some men had been reduced to sleeping under hedges.[9] The lack of accommodation was not such a problem for the 10th (Irish) Division as the political history of Ireland had led to an initial surfeit of barrack accommodation to which could be added the accommodation vacated by the embarkation of regular battalions to join the BEF.

Although the 10th Division had adequate accommodation, both divisions suffered from delays in providing other essentials such as training facilities, uniforms, rifles, other equipment, and, most importantly, training staff. Improvisation appears to have become the watchword of the 10th (Irish) Division. Training staff were found amongst the ranks of old soldiers, some of whom had not served since the Boer War, and others, because of their civilian employment, from their own ranks. Temporary rifle ranges were constructed when obsolete rifles became available and grenades made from jam tins. Despite these difficulties, both divisions appear to have completed their training programme on schedule. However, it took years to inculcate the skills that the pre-war regular army possessed and the war for which these divisions were embarking had changed considerably since its beginning and had left them inadequately prepared.

If the New Army divisions were ill-prepared for what they were to face in combat, those that were to lead them, tactically and strategically, were equally ill equipped for the nature of war they now encountered. Although the pre-war army had shunned the adoption of any overarching doctrine, the majority of its officers, including Hamilton, thought that high morale would overcome the problems posed by increased firepower. This view was reinforced by a misunderstanding of the lessons of the Boer and Russo-Japanese wars where the increasing imbalance between offensive and defensive firepower was demonstrated, as was the power of modern artillery. Consequently, although in the years immediately before the outbreak of war the British army had been greatly modernised, little had been done to co-ordinate the use of its three core elements infantry, cavalry and artillery.

The size of Britain's pre-war professional army also influenced the rapid expansion that had brought New Army divisions such as the 10th (Irish) and 13th (Western) into being. The need for battalion officers has already been discussed but there was also a dearth of senior officers, particularly trained staff officers, to lead higher formations. Patronage was still a major factor in advancement in the pre-war army and selection for Staff College entry, and the size and role of that army, left little opportunity for promotion and the development of tactical skills.[10] The formation and staffing of the BEF sent the majority of the army's most senior officers and the small cadre of trained staff officers to France and Belgium, and so when the decision to open a campaign on another front was taken, the choice of commanders and their staff was severely limited.

Both the 10th and 13th Divisions were nominally part of Stopford's IX Corps, although for strategic reasons the 13th (Western) Division and the 29th Brigade of the 10th (Irish) Division found themselves detached from the corps during Stopford's tenure as corps commander. Although Stopford has been highly criticised for his lack of drive during and after the Suvla landings, the blame for its failure rests squarely with Hamilton and his staff who, in common with the majority of senior officers at this stage of the war, were unable to respond to the needs of a new type of warfare for which they were totally unequipped. While Hamilton was unquestionably physically brave, he had neither the moral courage to overrule his subordinates when necessary nor accept responsibility for the strategic failure of the Gallipoli campaign, particularly that of August 1915 for which he made every effort to shift the blame onto his subordinates.

In many ways Hamilton was a 'very model of a modern major general'. He knew the theory, but like the majority of his fellow senior officers at this stage of the war, he was at the bottom of a very unfamiliar learning curve. Full of self-confidence, he had assured Kitchener that 'we have done this sort of thing before', but technically and tactically the battlefield had changed greatly since Hamilton, or indeed Kitchener, had last commanded an army in the field, and Hamilton had never commanded a force even approaching the size of the one entrusted to him in August 1915. Hamilton's belief in moral superiority and the offensive spirit had been hardly dented by the time the 10th and 13th Divisions were committed to their first major engagements. Nevertheless, there are those, such as Liddell Hart, who praised Hamilton and blamed instead 'the defects of the military system under which he had to operate'. Liddell Hart identified the changed nature of warfare and leadership rather than Hamilton's ability to adapt. [11] John Lee, Hamilton's most recent biographer, supports Liddell Hart's analysis suggesting that 'we do not need to hunt out individuals to blame, but rather see a failure of the British political and military system to cope with the demands of mass, industrial warfare with which it was wholly unfamiliar'. [12] Perhaps Liddell Hart, however, was nearer the truth when he said of Hamilton:

If he was diffident, and in a sense, dilatory, in breaking through these barriers and establishing contact with leaders in the fighting line at the crucial time, when the opportunity of victory still existed, his reluctance to intervene may be explained by his natural kindliness. Intervention demanded a ruthlessness from which, despite high personal courage, he instinctively shrank.[13]

Notwithstanding the old military maxim, variously attributed to Sun Tzu, Clausewitz and Napoleon, which cautions against reinforcing failure, Hamilton's August offensive demonstrated little creative thinking. The main thrust of the attack, despite Hamilton's later claims to the contrary, was a breakout from the Anzac sector to capture an enemy position where all the advantages of terrain favoured the defenders, while diversionary attacks were to be undertaken at Suvla and on the Helles front. For the breakout from the Anzac sector the ANZAC divisions were reinforced by the 29th (Indian) Brigade, the 29th Brigade of the 10th (Irish) Division, and the 13th (Western) Division, the latter two formations detached from IX Corps which was to land at Suvla. Hamilton's plan therefore was to attack the enemy's strongest part of the line while allowing a nominal corps, composed of raw New Army divisions, less artillery and virtually half their infantry battalions, led by an inexperienced and untried corps commander, to land on a largely undefended beachhead.

The United States Marine Corps uses the term 'main effort' to define the focal point where the decisive thrust of an operation is to be applied in order to deliver a decisive outcome.[14] Such thinking is not new. Clausewitz in his *Principles of War* (1812), stated that even when the attacking force is stronger than the defender's 'we should still direct our main attack against one point only' and if weaker 'the fewer troops we should use to keep the enemy occupied at unimportant points, in order to be as strong as possible at the decisive point'.[15] On 7 August 1915 Hamilton spread his troops too thinly, having failed to designate either Suvla or the attack on Sari Bair as the decisive point of the operation. In the unlikely event of the British expelling the enemy from their positions on the crest of the Sari Bair range, the attacking force had no reserves with which to exploit their success as all Hamilton's reserves had already been deployed at Suvla.

Not only had Hamilton failed to concentrate sufficient force at Sari Bair to achieve a tactical superiority capable of pushing the enemy out of their prepared positions and capture the Narrows, but he neglected to ensure that the tasks assigned to Stopford's force landing at Suvla were both understood and delivered by those involved. It has been noted that, due to Hamilton's paranoia, the details of the Suvla operations were only disclosed to Stopford and his divisional commanders shortly prior to the landing. Consequently, some brigade commanders, most notably Hill (31st Brigade), received no orders before their arrival at Suvla Bay on the morning of the landing and thus the officers and men under their command were sent into action with only the barest idea of their objectives. To make matters worse, despite objections by Stopford and his staff, Hamilton's orders included an expectation of the achievement of a number of objectives beyond the capabilities and resources of the troops employed. Furthermore, throughout the first critical 36 hours of the Suvla offensive, Hamilton was so occupied with the outcome of events on the Anzac front that he totally neglected the debacle developing at Suvla. It should be stated that, even if Stopford's corps had managed to take Anafarta Ridge, it is unlikely given the supply problems at Suvla that they would have been able to hold it. Likewise, if Mahon's greatly reduced command had been able to take Kiretch Tepe Ridge, thus outflanking the Turkish army on the peninsula, it was still some distance from the campaign's strategic objective of capturing the Narrows.

Of the leadership at battalion level there was no lack of courage, indeed it was often a leadership by example which frequently ended in death or injury. During the nine weeks the division was in Gallipoli, its infantry battalions suffered 238 officer casualties, including eight battalion commanders killed or wounded, the equivalent to 63% of its original officer complement. While many of these officers had been retired prior to the war, for the majority of junior officers Gallipoli was their first experience of leadership under battlefield conditions and was largely uncoordinated. Following the failure of the Suvla landings, Guy Dawnay, a member of Hamilton's staff, blamed the lack of success of New Army divisions on the 'fact that their officers are insufficiently trained. It is no one's fault – but officers can't be made good company leaders even after a year'.[16]

It was apparent from the beginning that the 10th Division had disciplinary problems. During training, all the battalions of the division bar two had higher levels of indiscipline than battalions of the same regiment in the other two Irish divisions, and offences for the division as a whole were some 68% higher than that of the 13th Division. The first twelve months on active service continued to show a higher level of indiscipline in the 10th Division than for either the 36th (Ulster) and 16th (Irish) Divisions, although in the case of the latter the difference narrowed to about 10%, while incidence of indiscipline compared to the 13th (Western) Division remained high. The 10th Division continued to have higher levels of indiscipline than the other two Irish divisions until its 'Indianisation' at the end of April 1918. However, indiscipline does not appear to have been viewed as either a matter of concern or as an indicator of a morale problem.

In common with all the other K1 divisions raised in August 1914, the 10th (Irish) Division's first experience of battle came at a time when the British army, its commanders, and the British war effort as whole, were at the lowest point of a cycle of experience that would develop over the course of the war. At Gallipoli, the division's leaders from Hamilton downwards, were encountering a new form of warfare that was totally beyond their experience. Over time tactics and weapons developed on the Western Front filtered down to other theatres and a greater emphasis was placed on training at all levels. This led to a greater understanding and co-operation between the three arms and, as the war progressed, all became more technically proficient. Only in the latter stages of its existence, however, did the division receive all the material resources it required, reflecting the secondary status of the theatres in which it operated. Nevertheless, by the time the 10th (Irish) Division was broken up to provide reinforcements for the Western Front, it had shown itself to be an organisation which had greatly developed its skills and ability since its first unfortunate experiences on the Gallipoli peninsula.

To conclude, the 10th (Irish) Division was a solid if unspectacular K1 division. In common with the early divisions of Kitchener's New Army, it was sent into battle for the first time with insufficient training, inexperienced officers and men, and ill-equipped to fight the novel kind of warfare to which it was committed. Its initial deployment to Gallipoli gave it no opportunity, unlike later New Army units, to acclimatise to battlefield conditions before being committed to battle under the strategic command of a senior officer who was unable to recognise or adapt to the changed nature of warfare and to a campaign that was under-resourced from the beginning. When first committed to battle the 10th (Irish) Division, like its contemporaries, found itself at the bottom of a steep learning curve. Nevertheless, it adapted well and demonstrated a capacity to adopt tactical, structural and technical developments. Finally, there is no evidence to support claims that the division was largely composed of officers and men either born in Ireland or of Irish descent. However, what the evidence suggests is that the division fully deserves its Irish title, not because of its ethnic composition, but rather for its ethos and character. Indeed, not unlike the three trajectories offered by Malvolio in *Twelfth Night*, the 10th (Division) was not only born Irish and had (by the likes of Redmond and Cooper among others) Irishness thrust upon it, but throughout its existence it developed the traditional fighting spirit expected of Irish regiments.

Annex 1

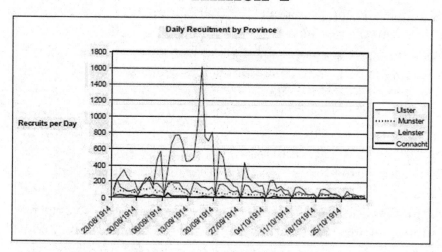

Figure 2.1: Daily recruitment by Province 23 August to 31 October 1914.[1]

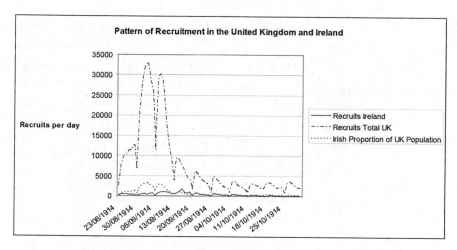

Figure 2.2: Daily recruitment in the United Kingdom and Ireland 23 August to 31 October 1914.[2]

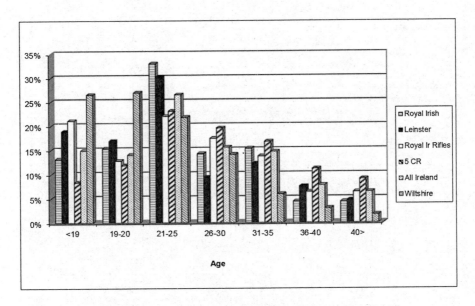

Figure 2.3: Distribution of enlistments by age group.[3]

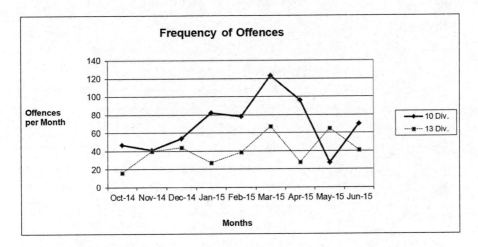

Figure 7.1: Frequency of courts martial offences during training.[4]

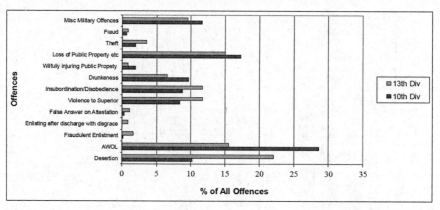

Figure 7.2: Distribution of offences tried by courts martial in the 10th (Irish) and 13th (Western) Divisions between 1 October 1914 and 30 June 1915.[5]

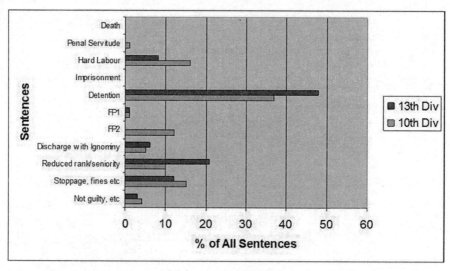

Figure 7.4: Distribution of sentences passed by courts martial in the 10th (Irish) and 13th (Western) Divisions between 1 October 1914 and 30 June 1915.[6]

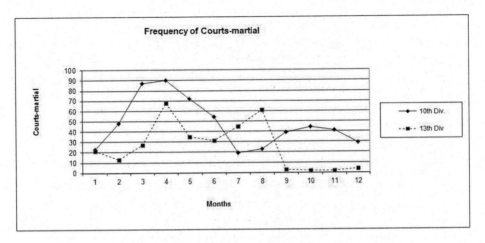

Figure 7.5: The courts martial held by the 10th (Irish) and 13th (Western) Divisions during their first 12 months of active service.[4]

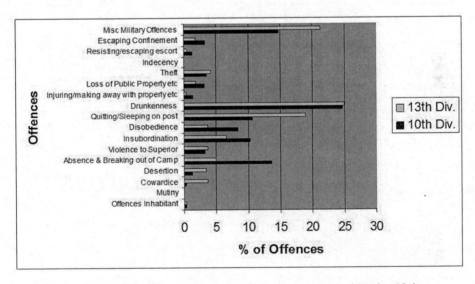

Figure 7.6: Distribution of offences tried by courts martial in the 10th (Irish) and 13th (Western) Divisions during their first 12 months of active service.[5]

Annex 2

	Ireland			Scotland
	Inspected	Rejected	%	Inspected
Agricultural Labourers	10,736	2,677	25	4,049
Other unskilled workers	12,417	3,534	28	13,761
Total Unskilled	**23,153**	**6,211**	**27**	**17,810**
Skilled Labourer	6,075	1,635	27	13,435
Other occupations	8,962	2,414	27	7,668
Professionals, Students etc.	431	91	21	203
Boys under 17	1,389	114	8	828
	40,010	10,465	26	39,944

Table 2.1: Inspection and rejection rates for the British regular army 1903–1913.[1]

Rejected	%	E&W			%	Total			%
		Inspected	Rejected	%		Inspected	Rejected	%	
822	20	40,506	9,905	24		55,291	13,404	24	
3,845	28	140,588	43,690	31		166,766	51,069	31	
4,667	**26**	**181,094**	**53,595**	**30**		**222,057**	**64,473**	**29**	
3,455	26	91,238	26,077	29		110,748	31,167	28	
2,105	27	101,406	30,402	30		118,036	34,921	30	
49	24	3,142	666	21		3,776	806	21	
107	13	16,380	2,182	13		18,597	2,403	13	
10,383	26	393,260	112,922	29		473,214	133,770	28	

	Officers	Warrant Officers	Sergeants	
5th Royal Irish Regiment	15	1	27	
6th Royal Irish Rifles	14		47	
5th Connaught Rangers	16		42	
6th Leinster Regiment	13		43	
6th Royal Munster Fusiliers	13		18	
7th Royal Munster Fusiliers	10	1	77	
6th Royal Dublin Fusiliers	10		36	
7th Royal Dublin Fusiliers	10		19	
5th Royal Inniskilling Fusiliers	10	1	23	
6th Royal Inniskilling Fusiliers	9	1	29	
5th Royal Irish Fusiliers	9	1	32	
6th Royal Irish Fusiliers	8	1	23	

Table 2.5: Battalion strengths at 19 September 1914.[2]

Rank and File (R&F)

Trained	Sick	Recruits	Total R &F
256	7	1023	1286
183	24	842	1049
600	3	754	1357
258	18	813	1089
145	23	1054	1222
84		926	1010
243	26	888	1157
204		1001	1205
65	6	1126	1197
58	47	987	1192
	20	1582	1602
156	18	1009	1183

Offence	5RI	5RInnsF	5RIF	5CR	6RInnF	
Mutiny	0	0	0	0	0	
Desertion	0	1	1	5	0	
Absence	5	0	7	15	8	
Striking or Violence	3	5	3	7	2	
Insubordination	4	1	3	8	0	
Disobedience	0	0	0	0	0	
Quitting post	0	0	1	0	0	
Drunkenness	2	1	12	6	7	
Injury to property	1	1	1	2	0	
Loss of property	1	0	5	9	6	
Theft	4	0	0	0	1	
Indecency	0	0	0	0	0	
Resisting escort	0	0	0	0	0	
Escaping Confinement	0	0	0	0	0	
Miscellaneous and multiple military offences	4	1	7	16	4	
Miscellaneous civil offences	0	0	0	0	0	
Self-inflicted wound	0	0	0	0	0	
Fraudulent enlistment	0	0	0	1	0	
Enlisting after discharge	0	0	0	0	0	
False answer on attestation	0	0	1	0	0	
Neglect	0	0	0	0	0	
Fraud	0	0	0	2	0	
Totals	**24**	**10**	**41**	**71**	**28**	

Table 7.1: Offences for which men serving in the Service battalions of the 10th (Irish) Division were tried, while in training in the United Kingdom.

6RIRifs	6RIF	6RMF	6 Leins	6RDF	7RMF	7RDF	10 Hamps
0	0	0	0	0	0	0	0
14	7		14	12	2	3	2
20	3	11	7	89	20	5	2
9	4	2	7	3	6	2	0
7	2	5	4	6	15	2	0
0	0	0	0	0	0	0	0
0	0	0	0	0	0	0	0
15	4	1	8	6	1	2	0
1	0	0	4	0	1	1	0
31	10	3	13	26	1	0	1
3	3	0	0	0	1	0	
0	0	0	0	0	0	0	0
0	0	0	0	0	0	0	0
0	0	0	0	0	0	0	0
7	5	2	8	8	9	3	1
0	0	0	1	0	0	0	0
0	0	0	0	0	0	0	0
0	0	0	0	0	0	0	0
0	0	0	0	0	0	0	0
0	1	0	0	0	0	0	0
0	0	0	0	0	0	0	0
0	0	0	0	0	1	0	0
107	**39**	**24**	**66**	**150**	**57**	**18**	**6**

Offences	10th Division				
	5RInnsF	6RInnF	6RIRifs	5CR	6RDF
Mutiny	O	O	O	O	O
Desertion	1	O	14	5	12
Absence	O	8	20	15	89
Striking or Violence	5	2	9	7	3
Insubordination/ Disobedience	1	O	7	8	6
Quitting/ sleeping at post	O	O	O	O	O
Drunkenness	1	7	15	6	6
Injury to property	1	O	1	2	O
Loss of property	O	6	31	9	26
Theft	O	1	3	O	O
Indecency	O	O	O	O	O
Resisting escort	O	O	O	O	O
Escaping confinement	O	O	O	O	O
Miscellaneous and multiple military offences	1	4	7	16	8
Miscellaneous civil offences	O	O	O	O	O
Self-inflicted wound	O	O	O	O	O
Fraudulent enlistment	O	O	O	1	O
Enlisting after discharge	O	O	O	O	O
False answer on attestation	O	O	O	O	O
Neglect	O	O	O	O	O
Fraud	O	O	O	2	O
Totals	**10**	**28**	**107**	**71**	**150**

Table 7.2: Offences for which men serving in sample Irish Service battalions were tried, while serving in the United Kingdom.[4]

	16th Division			36th Division		
7RDF	8RInnF	6CR	8RDF	10RInnsF	9RIRifs	13RIRifs
0	7	0	0	0	0	0
3	1	1	6	0	12	0
5	2	0	1	1	8	1
2	6	3	0	1	1	0
2	2	2	0	3	1	0
0	0	0	0	0	0	0
2	1	2	0	1	2	0
1	0	0	0	0	0	0
0	0	0	0	0	0	0
0	0	2	0	1	1	1
0	0	0	0	0	0	0
0	0	0	0	0	0	0
0	0	0	0	0	1	0
3	31	33	0	11	21	3
0	0	0	9	0	0	4
0	0	0	0	0	0	0
0	0	0	0	0	0	0
0	0	1	0	0	0	0
0	0	0	1	0	0	0
0	0	0	0	0	0	0
0	0	0	0	0	0	0
18	50	44	17	18	47	9

Sentence	5RI	5RInnsF	5RIF	5CR	6RInnF	6RIRifs	
Death	0	0	0	0	0	0	
Penal Servitude	0	0	0	0	0	0	
Hard Labour	9	3	4	5	1	9	
Imprisonment	0	0	0	0	0	0	
Detention	5	4	7	19	11	32	
FP1	0	0	3	0	0	0	
FP2	0	0	1	7	1	14	
Discharge with Ignominy	6	0	3	0	0	0	
Reduced rank or seniority	3	0	3	11	5	4	
Stoppage, fines etc	0	0	11	14	7	22	
Not guilty, etc	0	0	1	4	2	7	
Totals	**23**	**7**	**33**	**60**	**27**	**88**	

Table 7.3: Sentences passed by courts martial, for offences for which men serving in Service battalions of the 10th (Irish) Division were tried, while training in the United Kingdom[5]

		10th Division				
	5RInnsF	6RInnF	6RIRifs	5CR	6RDF	
Death	0	0	0	0	0	
Penal Servitude	0	0	0	0	0	
Hard Labour	3	1	9	5	29	
Imprisonment	0	0	0	0	1	
Detention	4	11	32	19	68	
FP1	0	0	0	0	0	
FP2	0	1	14	7	11	
Discharge with Ignominy	0	0	0	0	9	
Reduced rank or seniority	0	5	4	11	4	
Stoppage, fines etc	0	7	22	14	10	
Not guilty, etc	0	2	7	4	1	
Total	**7**	**27**	**88**	**60**	**133**	
% awarded Hard Labour, Imprisonment or Detention	100	44	47	40	74	

Table 7.4: Sentences passed by courts martial, relating to sample Irish Service battalions while training in the United Kingdom.[6]

6RIF	6RMF	6 Leins	6RDF	7RMF	7RDF	10 Hamps
0	0	0	0	0	0	0
0	0	0	0	1	0	0
11	4	5	29	6	4	1
0	0	0	1	0	0	0
7	7	14	68	26	5	2
0	0	0	0	0	0	0
3	7	8	11	11	1	1
5	1	1	9	1	4	0
3	3	13	4	7	1	1
6	0	14	10	0	0	2
2	0	4	1	1	0	0
37	**22**	**59**	**133**	**53**	**15**	**7**

	16th Division			36th Division		
7RDF	8RInnF	6CR	8RDF	10RInnsF	9RIRifs	13RIRifs
0	0	0	0	0	0	0
0	0	0	0	0	0	0
4	21	5	1	1	2	0
0	0	2	0	0	0	0
5	23	30	10	6	32	4
0	2	0	0	0	0	0
1	0	2	5	1	0	1
4	0	0	0	0	0	0
1	1	0	0	0	10	0
0	1	0	0	0	1	0
0	1	3	0	2	1	4
15	**49**	**44**	**16**	**11**	**46**	**9**
60	90	84	69	64	74	44

Unit	1915			1916		
	Oct	Nov	Dec	Jan	Feb	
36th Division						
107 Brigade	13	13	19	14	13	
108 Brigade	4	10	2	2	1	
109 Brigade	2	8	13	9	6	
Divisional Pioneers	1	0	1	1	0	
	20	31	35	26	20	
16th Division						
47 Brigade	-	-	0	12	13	
48 Brigade	-	-	0	26	17	
49 Brigade[2]	-	-	-	-	0	
Divisional Pioneers	-	-	0	0	0	
	-	-	0	38	30	

Table 7.5: The number of men (at brigade level) tried by courts martial in the 16th (Irish) and 36th (Ulster) Divisions while serving on the Western Front during the period 1 October 1915 to 30 September 1916.[7]

	Mar	Apr	May	Jun	Jul	Aug	Sep	Total
	5	10	9	7	2	12	5	122
	6	2	4	3	1	3	3	41
	5	13	7	2	3	5	11	84
	0	0	0	2	0	1	1	7
	16	25	20	14	6	21	20	254
	16	19	6	12	18	12	4	112
	16	5	13	17	12	11	6	123
	28	18	27	27	14	27	6	147
	0	0	0	0	0	0	0	0
	60	42	46	56	44	50	16	382

	1915					
	Aug	**Sep**	**Oct**	**Nov**	**Dec**	
29 Brigade						
10 Hamps			3			
6RIRifs	4	3	25	25	7	
5CR	1		14	10	4	
6 Leins	3	6	10	8	26	
	8	9	52	43	37	
30 Brigade						
6RMF	4	9	4	3	2	
7RMF	2	3	5	8	4	
6RDF	1	4	9	5	1	
7RDF		1	3	2	1	
	7	17	21	18	8	
31 Brigade						
5RInnsF	1			1	1	
6RInnF		10	6	5	6	
5RIF		9	2	3	11	
6RIF			3	7	8	
	1	19	11	16	26	
5 RI (Divisional Pioneers)	7	3	3	13	1	
Divisional Total	**23**	**48**	**87**	**90**	**72**	

Table 7.6: The number of men tried by courts martial while serving in the 10th (Irish) Division, 1 August 1915 to 31 July 1916.[8]

| 1916 | | | | | | | |
Jan	Feb	Mar	Apr	May	Jun	Jul	Total
		2	2	3		2	12
1	1	4	3	7	7	1	88
18	3	4	10	7	13	8	92
	4	1	4	3	2	2	69
19	8	11	19	20	22	13	261
3			2	2	1	3	33
4	1	3	1	4	3	2	40
5	1	5	1	1	5	3	41
3	1	1	7	8	5		32
15	3	9	11	15	14	7	146
	1						4
5	2		1	1	1	1	38
5	3	2	2	5	3	3	48
5		1	4			6	34
15	6	3	7	6	4	9	124
5	2		2	3	1		41
54	19	23	39	44	41	29	572

	5RI	5RInnsF	5RIF	5CR	6RInnF	
Offences against Inhabitant	0	0	0	0	0	
Mutiny	0	0	0	0	0	
Cowardice	0	0	0	0	1	
Desertion	1	0	1	5	0	
Absence & Breaking out of Camp	8	2	7	16	8	
Violence to Superior	5	0	1	5	0	
Insubordination	2	0	4	5	4	
Disobedience	4	0	2	9	9	
Quitting/Sleeping on post	6	0	8	1	8	
Drunkenness	22	1	13	39	8	
Injuring/ making away with property etc	2	0	3	3	0	
Loss of Public Property etc	2	1	2	4	2	
Theft	1	0	3	4	0	
Indecency	0	0	0	1	0	
Resisting/escaping escort	0	0	1	3	0	
Escaping Confinement	1	1	2	4	0	
Misc Offences	7	0	9	27	5	
Totals	**61**	**5**	**56**	**126**	**45**	

Table 7.7: Offences for which men serving in Service battalions of the 10th (Irish) Division were tried, during its first 12 months of active service.[9]

6RIRifs	6RIF	6RMF	6 Leins.	6RDF	7RMF	7RDF	10 Hamps
1	0	0	1	0	0	0	0
0	0	0	0	0	0	0	0
0	0	0	1	0	0	0	0
1	1	1	0	1	2	0	0
19	7	2	3	18	4	10	2
5	2	1	4	1	2	0	0
17	5	2	18	2	8	3	4
9	5	2	13	1	5	3	1
9	8	14	1	5	7	1	2
36	7	11	17	18	9	15	3
2	1	0	0	0	0	1	0
5	4	1	0	3	0	1	0
3	2	2	7	2	2	0	0
0	0	0	0	0	0	0	0
2	2	0	1	1	1	0	0
6	2	0	2	0	1	7	0
26	2	4	14	8	8	10	2
141	**48**	**40**	**82**	**60**	**49**	**51**	**14**

Sentence	5RI	5RInnsF	5RIF	5CR	6RInnF	
Death	1	1	0	1	0	
Penal Servitude	5	0	11	7	13	
Hard Labour	16	1	5	31	13	
Imprisonment	0	0	0	2	0	
Detention	1	0	0	4	0	
FP1	8	1	18	28	9	
FP2	3	0	3	6	0	
Discharge with Ignominy	0	0	1	0	0	
Reduced rank or seniority	1	2	7	12	1	
Stoppage, fines etc	8	0	7	7	4	
Not guilty, etc	3	0	2	2	1	
Totals	**46**	**5**	**54**	**100**	**41**	

Table 7.8: Sentences passed by courts martial in the 10th (Irish) Division during the first 12 months of active service.[10]

6RIRifs	6RIF	6RMF	6 Leins	6RDF	7RMF	7RDF	10 Hamps
4	1	2	4	2	2	0	0
5	5	3	6	1	9	0	0
27	3	14	15	16	6	6	2
2	0	1	0	0	0	0	0
0	1	0	0	0	1	0	0
30	18	5	23	11	14	21	3
14	2	3	10	4	2	2	2
0	1	0	1	0	0	0	0
5	1	2	6	5	1	3	3
6	5	1	1	5	3	3	0
2	2	2	5	2	5	0	2
95	**39**	**33**	**71**	**46**	**43**	**35**	**12**

	1916								
	Oct	Nov	Dec	Jan	Feb	Mar	Apr	May	
29 Brigade									
1 Leins		2		3	1	3			
10 Hamps	2	1							
6RIRifs	5	2		1	1	1	1	3	
5CR	2	5	7	2	1	4	4	3	
6 Leins	4			1		1	1	2	
	13	10	7	7	3	9	6	8	
30 Brigade									
1RI		4	2	5	1		3	2	
6RMF	2	4	3	2	2	2	10	4	
7RMF	4			1	3				
6RDF	6		4	3	5		6		
7RDF		6		1	1	9	2	3	
	12	14	9	12	12	11	21	9	
31 Brigade									
2RIF			2	1		5	2		
5RInnsF		1	1			1	3		
6RInnF	2		1		1	3	3	2	
5RIF			6	1	1	9		2	
6RIF				1	1			1	
	2	1	10	3	3	18	8	5	
5RI Divisional Pioneers	3							1	
Divisional Total	30	25	26	22	18	38	35	23	

Table 7.9: The number of men tried by courts martial while serving in the 10th (Irish) Division, 1 October 1916 to 28 February 1918.[11]

| 1917 | | | | | | | 1918 | | Total |
un	Jul	Aug	Sep	Oct	Nov	Dec	Jan	Feb	
3	4		1	8	2	2	10	12	**51**
									3
1	4	3	1		3	2	7	5	**40**
1	1	2	2	6	2	2	12	8	**64**
3	3		7	2	2	3	6	5	**40**
8	12	5	11	16	9	9	35	30	**198**
1	1	1	2	4	3	3	13	5	**50**
3	1	3	2	5	4	3	3	8	**61**
									8
1	1			6	3	4	12	4	**55**
1	2	1	4	1	5	1	5		**42**
6	5	5	8	16	15	11	33	17	**216**
4	1		1	5	3	1	4	1	**30**
1			1	5	3	2	1		**19**
2	2			2	1	1	2	3	**25**
2	2		2	3	3			2	**33**
				1	1	1	1		**7**
9	5	0	4	16	11	5	8	6	**114**
		1		1		2	3	3	**14**
23	22	11	23	49	35	27	79	56	**542**

Offences	1RI	1 Leins	2RIF	5RI	5RInnsF	5/6RIF	
Offences against an inhabitant	0	1	0	0	0	1	
Mutiny	0	0	0	0	0	0	
Cowardice	0	2	0	0	0	0	
Desertion	3	2	1	0	2	1	
Absence & Breaking out of Camp	7	4	8	0	3	4	
Violence to Superior	5	2	3	1	0	5	
Insubordination	8	2	3	2	1	4	
Disobedience	7	3	5	1	1	4	
Quitting/Sleeping on post	6	1	0	0	0	0	
Drunkenness	16	22	9	6	9	22	
Injuring/ making away with property etc	0	0	0	0	0	0	
Loss of Public Property etc	0	0	2	0	3	1	
Theft	2	6	3	2	3	2	
Indecency	0	0	0	1	0	0	
Resisting/escaping escort	1	3	2	1	2	5	
Escaping Confinement	1	3	0	1	4	1	
Misc Offences	12	15	4	2	3	5	
Totals	**68**	**66**	**40**	**17**	**31**	**55**	

Table 7.10: Offences for which men serving in Service battalions of the 10th (Irish) Division were tried by courts martial between 1 October 1916 and 28 February 1918.[12]

5CR	6RInnF	6RIRifs	6/7 RMF	6 Leins	6RDF	7RDF	10 Hamps
0	0	2	1	0	0	0	0
0	0	0	0	0	0	0	0
0	0	0	5	0	0	1	0
1	3	4	4	1	1	3	1
9	5	13	5	6	7	5	0
0	0	2	3	2	1	0	0
7	3	0	7	2	13	3	0
1	5	1	6	1	7	3	0
3	0	1	11	1	3	4	0
30	9	17	28	21	16	20	1
0	0	0	1	1	1	0	0
5	0	4	6	6	3	1	0
15	0	3	2	8	3	11	0
1	0	1	0	0	0	0	0
2	1	3	2	0	2	3	0
0	5	1	3	2	2	3	0
17	5	8	18	6	8	7	1
91	**36**	**60**	**102**	**57**	**67**	**64**	**3**

Offence	10th Division						
	5RInnsF	6RInnF	6RIRifs	5CR	6RDF	7RDF	
Offences Inhabitant	0	0	2	0	0	0	
Mutiny	0	0	0	0	0	0	
Cowardice	0	0	0	0	0	1	
Desertion	2	3	4	1	1	3	
Absence & Breaking out of Camp	3	5	13	9	7	5	
Violence to Superior	0	0	2	0	1	0	
Insubordination	1	3	0	7	13	3	
Disobedience	1	5	1	1	7	3	
Quitting/ Sleeping on post	0	0	1	3	3	4	
Drunkenness	9	9	17	30	16	20	
Injuring/ making away with property etc	0	0	0	0	0	0	
Loss of Public Property etc	3	0	4	5	3	1	
Theft	3	0	3	15	3	11	
Indecency	0	0	1	1	0	0	
Resisting/ escaping escort	2	1	3	2	0	3	
Escaping Confinement	4	5	1	0	2	3	
Misc Offences	3	5	8	17	8	7	
Totals	**31**	**36**	**60**	**91**	**67**	**64**	

Table 7.11 Offences for which men serving in sample of Irish battalions were tried during the period from 1 October 1916 to 28 February 1918.[13]

16th Division				36th Division			
8RInnF	**6CR**	**2RDF**	**8RDF**	**1RInnsF**	**10RInnsF**	**9RIRifs**	**14RIRifs**
O	O	O	1	O	1	O	O
O	1	O	O	O	O	O	1
O	1	O	O	O	O	O	1
5	O	11	4	12	4	2	
O	O	O	O	O	O	O	O
1	O	1	O	O	O	O	O
3	1	2	1	O	O	1	1
3	3	9	1	4	O	O	3
O	3	O	O	O	O	1	3
3	12	19	4	15	4	7	12
O	1	O	O	O	O	O	1
O	O	O	O	O	O	O	O
O	2	2	2	1	O	O	2
O	O	O	O	O	O	O	O
O	O	O	O	O	O	O	O
1	O	O	O	O	O	O	O
12	36	49	30	31	15	7	36
28	**60**	**93**	**43**	**63**	**24**	**18**	**60**

Sentence	1RI	1 Leins	2RIF	5RI	5RInnsF	5/6RIF	
Death	0	0	1	0	0	0	
Penal Servitude	4	4	2	1	2	5	
Imprisonment	0	1	0	0	0	0	
Hard Labour	13	18	9	3	9	12	
Detention	0	0	0	0	1	0	
FP1	20	13	11	4	4	10	
FP2	1	4	0	0	1	4	
Discharged with Ignominy	0	0	0	0	0	0	
Reduced rank or seniority	11	3	4	4	1	11	
Stoppage, fines etc	1	5	4	0	5	0	
Not guilty, etc	2	7	3	3	0	1	
Totals	**52**	**55**	**34**	**15**	**23**	**43**	

Table 7.12: Sentences passed by courts martial in the 10th (Irish) Division between 1 October 1916 and 28 February 1918.[14]

	5CR	6RInnF	6RIRifs	6/7 RMF	6 Leins	6RDF	7RDF	10 Hamps
	0	0	2	5	0	2	5	0
	3	3	3	9	1	11	3	1
	0	1	0	0	0	1	0	0
	25	8	10	16	15	17	15	0
	0	0	0	0	0	0	0	0
	19	7	13	17	13	7	7	1
	6	1	4	4	4	4	3	0
	0	0	0	0	0	0	0	0
	8	6	9	9	5	8	5	0
	7	0	7	11	10	2	8	0
	4	0	2	8	3	5	3	1
	71	**26**	**50**	**79**	**51**	**57**	**49**	**3**

Endnotes

INTRODUCTION

1   Cooper, Bryan, *The Tenth (Irish) Division in Gallipoli* (London, 1918) p. 256.

2   *Belfast News-Letter*, 9 Aug. 1919; *The Times*, 11 Aug. 1919; *Freeman's Journal*, 30 July 1919

3   *Freeman's Journal*, 15 Aug. 1919.

4   Spiers, Edward M., 'The regular army in 1914' in Beckett and Simpson (eds.) *A nation in arms*, pp 49-55.

5   Denman, Terence, *Ireland's Unknown Soldiers*; Alexander, Jack, *McCrae's Battalion, the Story of the 16th Royal Scots*. Both these examples provide details of the backgrounds of a number of officers but their coverage is neither inclusive nor systematic.

CHAPTER 1 - A COUNTRY DIVIDED

1   McManus, Ruth, 'Blue collars, "red forts," and green fields: working-class housing in Ireland in the twentieth century' in *International labor and working-class history*, No. 64, Workers, suburbs, and labor geography (Fall, 2003), pp 38-39; *Census of Ireland for the year 1911- Preliminary report with abstract of enumerator's summaries* [Cd. 5691] H.C. 1911, p.1.

2   Craft, Maurice, 'The development of Dublin: background to the housing problem' in *Studies: An Irish Quarterly Review*, Vol. 59, No. 235 (Autumn, 1970), p. 308.

3   Mitchell, B. R., *British historical statistics*, p.13.

4   Bielenberg, Andrew, 'What happened to Irish industry after the British industrial revolution? Some evidence from the first UK census of production in 1907' in *The Economic History Review*, New Series, Vol. 61, 4 (Nov. 2008) p. 828.

5   *Board of Trade Journal*, 26 Jan. 1928.

6   Gribbon, H. B., 'Economic and social history' in *A new history of Ireland*, VI, p. 307.

7   Oldham, C. H., 'The history of Belfast shipbuilding' in *Journal of the Statistical and Social Inquiry Society of Ireland*, xii, part 91 (Dec. 1911), p. 431.

8   Ibid., p. 429; Harland and Wolff managing directors minutes 1907- 1912 (PRONI, D.2805/MIN/A/1); Moss, Michael and Hume, J. R., *Shipbuilders to the world*, p. 133.

9   Shaw, C., 'The largest manufacturing employers of 1907' in *Business History*, 25, 1 (1983) pp 52-53; Grew, J. A., 'The Derry shirt making industry', p. 253.

10 McManus, 'Blue collars, "red forts," and green fields', p. 39.

11 *Royal commission on the poor laws*, appendix vol. xi, [Cd. 5072] H.C. 1910, p. 60.

12 Humphreys, A.J., *New Dubliners: Urbanisation and the Irish Family*, pp 47-48.

13 'Unskilled labour in Dublin: its housing and living conditions' a paper delivered to the Royal Irish Academy by D. A. Chart, M.I.R.A., 6 Mar. 1914; Coyle, Eugene A., 'Larkinism and the 1913 County Dublin Farm Labourer's Dispute' in *Dublin Historical Record*, Vol. 58, No. 2 (Autumn, 2005), pp 176-177.

14 Murray Frazer, *John Bull's other homes*, p. 64.

15 *Freeman's Journal*, 23 Jan. 1901; Armstrong, D.L., 'Social and economic conditions in the Belfast linen industry, 1850-1900' in *Irish Historical Studies*, vii, 28 (Sept. 1951) p. 264; Riordan, Edward J., *Modern Irish trade and industry*, p. 109.

16 *Standard time rates of wages in the United Kingdom ... October 1910*, [Cd. 5459] H.C. 1910.

17 Thompson, William J., 'The Census of Ireland, 1911' in *Journal of the Royal Statistical Society*, Vol. 76, No. 7 (June 1913), p. 640.

18 Chart D. A., 'Unskilled labour in Dublin – its housing and living conditions' in *Journal of the Statistical and Social Inquiry Society of Ireland*, xiii, part 94 (Mar. 1914) p. 162.

19 *Report of the departmental committee appointed ... to inquire into the housing conditions of the working classes in the city of Dublin*, [Cd. 7273] H.C. 1914, p. 2.

20 Ibid., p. 3.

21 Quoted in Gribbon, H. D., 'Economic and social history', p. 336.

22 *Report of the departmental committee appointed ... to inquire into the housing conditions of the working classes in the city of Dublin*, p. 4.

23 O'Brien, J. V., *'Dear, dirty Dublin'*, pp 126-158.

24 Gribbon, H. D., 'Economic and social history' p. 336.

25 McCarthy, John Paul, and O'Riordan, Tomás, 'Dublin 1913 – strike and lockout' in Ó Corráin and O'Riordan (eds), *Ireland 1870 – 1918*, pp 168, 171.

26 *Royal commission on the poor laws*, appendix vol. xi, 61 [Cd. 5072] H.C. 1910.

27 For a fuller account of the Home Rule crisis see A.T.Q. Stewart, *The Ulster Crisis* (London 1967).

28 Oldham, C.H., 'The public finances of Ireland' in *Journal of the Institute of Bankers of Ireland*, xiii (1911), p. 286.

29 *Seventeenth abstract of labour statistics for the United Kingdom*, [Cd. 7733] H.C. 1914, p. 185. The cost of paying the first full year of pension in Ireland was £2,321,729.

30 Jalland, Patricia, 'Irish home-rule finance: a neglected dimension of the Irish question, 1910-14' in *Irish Historical Studies*, Vol. 23, No. 91 (May, 1983), p. 233.

31 Digby Hussey de Burg, *Irish Times*, 28 Feb. 1912.

32 *Nation*, 7 Dec. 1912

33 Stewart, *The Ulster Crisis*, p. 128; Lists of commanding officers and unit strengths, Public Records Office of Northern Ireland (PRONI), D.1327/4/20.

34 Holmes, Richard, *The Little Field Marshal: A Life of Sir John French*, p .386.

35 Ibid., pp183-184; *Correspondence relating to recent events in the Irish command*, [Cd. 7318] H.C. 1914, p 4.

36 Stewart, *The Ulster Crisis*, p. 178; Spender to McNeill, not dated, PRONI, MIC 103; 'Landing the cargo', *The Times*, 27 Apr. 1914; Col. T.V.P. McCammon 'Report on the operations at Bangor, 24/25 Apr. 1914', PRONI, D.1327/3/8.

37 Ó Snodaigh, A., 'The Irish Volunteers founded', *An Phoblacht/Republican News*, 26 Nov. 1998.

38 'Fight with Volunteers for rifles', *The Times*, 27 July 1914.

39 'The Dublin inquest', *The Times*, 31 July 1914 and 1 Aug. 1914.

40 Ellis, P. B., *Eyewitness to Irish history*, p. 207

CHAPTER 2 - FILLING THE RANKS

1 H.J. Hanham, 'Religion and nationality in the mid-Victorian army' in M.R.D. Foot, (ed.), *War and Society* (London, 1973), p. 178; Analysis of figures contained in the *General annual report on the British army for the year ending 30 September 1913, with the annual report of recruiting, prepared by command of the Army council for 1912-13*, [Cd 7252], H.C. 1914.

2 Memorandum Adjutant General's Department to Prime Minister, 25 Mar. 1916 (TNA, WO 162/18); *Statistics of the military effort of the British empire*, p. 749 gives the strength of the British army on 4 Aug. 1914 as 733,514.

3 According to W.V. Germains (*The Kitchener armies* (London, 1930), p. 56) these units were the Northumberland Yeomanry, the Dorset Fortress Coy. R.E. and the 6th East Surrey and 7th & 8th Middlesex Regiments.

4 *Statistics of the military effort of the British empire*, pp. 163-66.

5 John Terraine, *Mons: the retreat to victory* (paperback ed., Barnsley, 1991); A.G. Wauchope (ed.), *A history of the Black Watch in the Great War* (London, 1925).i, 1; F.E. Whitton, *The history of the Prince of Wales's Leinster Regiment* (2 vols. Aldershot, 1926)., ii, 4.

6 J. A. Hammerton, *A popular history of the Great War* (6 vols, London, nd.), i, 77-78.

7 Memorandum by the military members of the army council on the situation in Ireland, 4 July, 1914 (TNA, CAB 37/120).

8 Allan Mallinson, *1914 Fight the Good Fight* (London, 2013) pp. 227 and 475.

9 Hansard 5 (Commons), lxv [col. 2082, 1914-15]; *The Times*, 7 Aug. 1914.

10 Minutes of the proceedings of the Army Council, 11 Aug. 1914 (TNA, WO 163/21); *Army Order 324 of 1914*(London, 21 Aug. 1914).

11 Minutes of meeting of the Military Members of the Army Council, 29 Aug. 1914 (TNA, WO 163/44).

12 Tom Johnstone, *Orange, Green and Khaki* (Dublin, 1992) pp. 89-90.

13 Augustine Birrell to John Redmond quoted in Denis Gwynn, *The life of John Redmond*, (London, 1932), p. 368.

14 Denman, *Ireland's unknown soldiers,*p. 24.

15 *Irish Times*, 26 Aug. 1914.

16 R. Stevenson to Carson, 18 Aug. 1914 (quoted in Ian Colvin, *The life of Lord Carson*, iii, 30).

17   Frank Fox, *The Royal Inniskilling Fusiliers in the World War* (London, 1928), p. 56.

18   Irish Times, 28 *Aug. 1914*.

19   Ibid., 22 Aug 1914; Daily recruiting returns 23 Aug. to 31 Oct. 1914 (TNA, NATS 1/394).

20   See annex 1.

21   Minute from the Adjutant General's Office to General Maxwell, 3 Sept. 1914 (TNA, WO 162/4).

22   Statistical abstract on information regarding the armies at home and abroad, p. 365 (TNA, WO 394/20).

23   Minute from the Adjutant General's Office to General Maxwell, 29 Aug. 1914 (TNA, WO 162/4).

24   Minute to General Maxwell, 5 Sept. 1914 (TNA, WO 162/4).

25   Contained on undated strength returns (TNA, WO 162/4).

26   Ibid.

27   W.E. Vaughan. & A.J. Fitzpatrick (eds), *Irish historical statistics – population 1821 – 1971* (Dublin, 1978), pp 82-86.

28   New armies, establishments and strengths (TNA, WO 162/4).

29   Ibid.

30   Memorandum on recruiting, 29 Aug. 1914 (TNA, Kitchener papers, WO162/20).

31   Ibid.

32   New armies, establishments and strengths (TNA, WO 162/4).

33   Ibid.

34   Wiltshire Gazette, *27, Aug. 1914.*35 Memo A.G.10, 8 Sept. 1914 (TNA, WO 162/40).

36   Cooper, *The Tenth (Irish) Division*, p. xi.

37   New Armies, Establishments and Strengths (TNA. WO 162/4).

38   Cooper, *The Tenth (Irish) Division*, pp 12-13.

39   New Armies, Establishments and Strengths (TNA. WO 162/4).

40   Charles Drage, *Chindwin to Criccieth - The life of Godfrey Drage* (Caernarvon, 1956), p. 101.

41   Wiltshire Gazette, *17 Sept. 1914.*

42   Ibid.

43   Ibid., 24 Sept. 1914.

44   Information supplied by Graham Croad Private Croad's grandson.

46   Ibid.

45   Hughes 'The forgotten army' (IWM, Hughes papers, D. 4432).

47   Cooper, *The Tenth (Irish) Division* p. 13; Nicholas Perry, 'Nationality in the Irish regiments' in *War and Society*, 12 (1994), p. 78.

48   Ibid.

49   This is based on a sample 223, of which 97 were born in Ireland.

50   Of the 126 rank and file identified from census records as non-Irish by birth, only 3 had a parent born in Ireland.

51 H.F.N. Jourdain, *History of the Connaught Rangers* (3 vols, London,1928), iii, 3.

52 Whitten, *TheLeinster Regiment*, ii, p. 97.

53 Battersby manuscript Leeds University Library, Liddle Collection, [Liddle/ WW1/Gall (Rec.)/146/Battersby].

54 Verschoyle, Personal reminiscences Leeds University Library, Liddle Collection[Liddle/WW1/GS/1654/Verschoyle].

55 Ibid.

56 *Weekly return of the British army at home - January - March 1915* (TNA, WO 114/26).

57 Minutes of the meeting of the military members of the Army Council, 29 Aug. 1914 (TNA, WO 162/4).

58 Telegram from Irish Command to War Office, 31 Aug. 1914 (TNA,WO 162/24).

59 Army Order 382 of 1914 (London, 11 Sept. 1914).

60 Peter Simkins, *Kitchener's army: the raising of the New Armies, 1914-16*(Manchester, 1988), p. 96; *The Times*, 5 Sept. 1914; Monthly recruiting figures for cities and regimental districts for September 1914 (TNA, WO 1/85).

61 Daily recruiting returns (TNA, NATS 1/394).

62 Richardson to Lord Midleton, 13 Apr. 1915 (TNA, PRO 30/67/29).

63 Army Order 383 of 1914; *Freeman's Journal*, 21 Sept 1914.

64 Keith Jeffery, *Ireland and the Great War* (Cambridge, 2000), p. 13; Daily recruiting returns 23 Aug. to 31 Oct. 1914 (TNA, NATS 1/394).

65 *Irish Times*, 11 Jan. 1915.

66 Ian F.W. Beckett, 'The nation in arms' in Beckett and Simpson (eds), *A nation in arms*, p. 7.

67 See Annex 1.

68 *Irish Times*, 9 Jan. 1915.

69 *Census of Ireland*, 1871 (1876, C1377); 1911 (1913, Cd 6663); *Census of England and Wales*, 1861, (1863, C3221); 1911 (1912, Cd 6258).

70 *Irish Times*, 11 Jan. 1915.

71 Minutes of meeting of the Military Members of the Army Council, 27 Aug. 1914 (TNA, WO 163/44); *The Times*, 28 Aug. 1914.

72 *Census of Ireland*, 1871 (1876, C1377); 1911 (1913, Cd 6663).

73 *Belfast Evening Telegraph*, 14 Aug. 1914.

74 Ibid., 13 Aug. 1914.

75 Jonathan Bardon, *A history of Ulster* (Belfast, 1992), p. 456.

76 *Belfast Evening Telegraph*, 5 Aug. 1914.

77 Hansard 5 (Commons), lxi [cols. 841-2, 1914-15].

78 Gwynn, *The life of John Redmond*, pp 435-7.

79 Ibid.

80 Colin Cousins, *Armagh and the Great War* (Dublin, 2011), p. 123.

81 Ibid., p. 105.

82 Hansard 5 (Commons), lxv, 1829.

83 *Irish Times*, 14 Nov. 1914.

84 Callan,'Voluntary recruiting for the British army in Ireland during the First World War' (Ph.D. thesis, University College Dublin, 1984), p. 39.

85 For a fuller explanation of how this under estimation occurred see Stephen Sandford, 'The 10th (Irish) division in the Great War - the experience of Ireland's first New Army division' (Ph.D. thesis, Queen's University Belfast, 2012), p. 25 and Annex 3.

86 See Annex 2.

87 David Fitzpatrick, 'Militarism in Ireland, 1900-1922' in Bartlett and Jeffery (eds), *A military history of Ireland* (Cambridge, 1996), p. 381.

88 Entry for 29 Aug. 1915 (Bean papers AWM 38 3DRL 606, item 10).

89 C.E.W. Bean, *The official history of Australia in the war of 1914 – 1918 the story of Anzac: from 4 May 1915 to the evacuation* (2 vols, Sydney, 1924), ii, 4-5.

90 *Alpine Observer*, 28 Jan., 4 Feb. 1916 (quoted in John McQuilton, *Rural Australia and the Great War*, p. 45).

91 http://mappingouranzacs.naa.gov.au/ (last accessed 3 Sept. 2010)

92 Annex 2.

93 Cooper,*The Tenth (Irish) Division*,p. 11.

94 *Soldiers died in the Great War* (CD-ROM, London: Naval & Military Press, 1999).

95 Hanna, *The pals at Suvla*, p. 190.

96 Note by Brigadier-General F.A. Greer, 5 April, 1951 contained in papers relating to the service of the 6th Battalion, Royal Irish Fusiliers in the Great War (Greer papers, Royal Irish Fusiliers Museum).

97 Minutes of meeting of the military members of the Army Council, 27 Aug. 1914 (TNA, WO 163/44).

98 George O'Brien, http://www.cwgc.org/debt_of_honour.asp (last accessed 30 July 2014)

99 Ivor Evans, First World War casualty portraits classified collection (IWM, HU 93410).

100 David Martin (ed.), *The Fifth Scottish Rifles 1914 – 1919*, (Glasgow, 1936),p. 3; Jill Knight, *The Civil Service Rifles in the Great War* (Barnsley, 2004),p. 31

101 K.W. Mitchinson, *Officers and gentlemen* (London, 1995), p. 30

102 *Ballymena Observer*, 3 Sept. 1915.

103 Campbell, Leeds University Library, Liddle Collection [Liddle/WW1/ GS/0261/Campbell], p. 2.

104 Owen Farrelly (TNA, WO 363) ; Michael Flynn, (TNA, WO 329/2818).

105 Own Farrelly, www.ancestry.co.uk (last accessed 30 July 2014)

106 Michael Flynn, www.ancestry.co.uk (last accessed 30 July 2014)

107 Germains *The Kitchener armies*, p. 52.

108 Richard van Emden, *Boy soldiers of the Great War* (London, 2008).

109 Callan, 'Recruiting for the British army' in *Irish Sword*, 66, 1987, p.49.

110 Annex 1. The age of recruits was obtained from census records, enlistment papers (TNA, WO 363 and 364), officers' service records (TNA, WO 339 and 374), obituaries and the CWGC's Debt of Honour database. Analysis was

based on data of 683 enlisted men from the 5th Royal Irish Regiment (91), 6th Royal Irish Rifles (109), 5th Connaught Rangers (143), 6th Leinster Regiment (106) and 5th Wiltshire Regiment (234).

111 The approximate population of Wiltshire in 1911 was 286,800, while that of Antrim and Down, including Belfast, was 785,100.

112 Irish born enlistments in 6th Royal Irish Rifles compared with 5th Wiltshires.

113 George O'Brien and James Quinn, http://www.cwgc.org/debt_of_honour. asp (last accessed 30 July 2014)

114 Drury war diary, 11 March 1916 (NAM, Drury papers, 7607-69) ii, p. 119.

115 Fitzpatrick, 'The logic of collective sacrifice: Ireland and the British army' in *Historical Journal*, 8, 4 (1995), pp 1017-30.

116 Peter Karsten, 'Irish Soldiers in the British Army, 1792-1922: Suborned or Subordinate?' in *Journal of SocialHistory*, 17, 1 (1983), p. 35.

117 *Irish Times*, 24/11/1914.

118 Grayson, *Belfast boys – how unionists and nationalists fought and died together in the First World War* (London, 2009), pp 50 – 62. I wish to thank Professor Grayson for access to his unpublished data.

119 Ruvigny's *Roll of honour*, i, II. After a time in the ranks Currie was commissioned in January 1915 and served at Gallipoli where he was killed on 10 August 1915.

120 Spiers, 'The regular army in 1914' in *A nation in arms*, p. 44.

121 *Report of the Health of the Army for the year 1909*, Cd 5477, 1911, XLVII, p. 2.

122 Fitzpatrick, 'Militarism in Ireland', p. 381.

123 Data extracted from the *General annual report on the British army*, for the years ending 30 September 1904 to 30 September 1913.

124 Ibid.

125 John M. Bourne, *Britain and the Great War 1914 -1918* (London, 1989), p. 217.

126 Simkins, *Kitchener's army*, p. 207.

127 Germains *The Kitchener armies*, p. 66.

128 Previous employment data was obtained from census records, enlistment papers (TNA, WO 363 and 364), officers' service records (TNA, WO 339 and 374) and obituaries. In the case of occupations declared on census records for 1911, it was assumed that lack of social mobility would mean that the majority would be still employed in the same occupational grouping when they enlisted in 1914. Analysis was based on data of 326 enlisted men, born in Ireland, from the 5th Royal Irish Regiment (9), 6th Royal Irish Rifles (69), 5th Connaught Rangers (41), 6th Leinster Regiment (10) and 7th Royal Dublin Fusiliers (197).

129 Hervey de Montmorency, *Sword and Stirrup - memories of an adventurous life* (London, 1936),p. 245. Despite an extensive search of personnel records it has not been possible to identify any of the men described above by Montmorency and therefore they could not be included in the employment statistics for the battalion.

130 Previous employment data was obtained from census records, enlistment papers (TNA, WO 363 and 364), officers' service records (TNA, WO 339 and 374) and obituaries. Analysis was based on data of 326 enlisted men, born in Ireland, from the 5th Royal Irish Regiment (9), 6th Royal Irish Rifles (69), 5th

Connaught Rangers (41), 6th Leinster Regiment (10) and 7th Royal Dublin Fusiliers (197).

131 T.P. O'Connor to Lloyd George, 29 Sept 1914, Lloyd George papers, Parliamentary Archives C/6/10/4.

132 Fitzpatrick, 'Home front and everyday life', p. 135; Fitzpatrick, 'Militarism in Ireland', p. 389; Callan, 'Recruiting for the British army' in *Irish Sword*, 66 p. 54.

133 Patrick Callan, 'Recruiting for the British Army in Ireland during the First World War' in *Irish Sword*, 66, (1987-8), p.54.

134 Michael MacDonagh, *The Irish at the front* (London, 1916),p. 74.

135 Data was obtained from census records, enlistment papers (TNA, WO 363 and 364), obituaries and in respect of the men of D Company Royal Dublin Fusiliers, *The Pals at Suvla*. Analysis was based on data of 313 enlisted men, born in Ireland, from the 5th Royal Irish Regiment (12), 6th Royal Irish Rifles (80), 5th Connaught Rangers (46), 6th Leinster Regiment (12) and 7th Royal Dublin Fusiliers (162).

136 *Irish Independent*, 21 Sept 1915.

137 10th (Irish) Division religious census Nov. 1915 (PRONI, D627/429/8).

CHAPTER 3 - OFFICERS AND GENTLEMEN

1 Cooper, *The Tenth (Irish) Division*, p. 13.

2 *Statistics of the military effort of the British Empire*, pp 234-5; *the annual return of the Territorial Force for the year 1913*, [Cd 7254], H.C. 1914, lii, 5 and 125.

3 Parl. Deb. Fifth Ser., 63, 25 May 1914, col. 37; *Statistics of the military effort of the British empire*, p. 364.

4 Ronald Clifford, 'What is a battalion?' in *Stand to!* no. 30 (Winter 1990), pp 17–19; 22.

5 Instructions of the Secretary of State for War, 6 Sept. 1914; Memorandum - How to carry out Secretary of State's instructions, 6 Sept 1914 (TNA, WO 162/24).

6 Simpson, 'The officers', p. 64.

7 Richard Holmes, *The little field marshal – the life of Sir John French* (2nd ed., London, 2004), pp 19-20.

8 Cooper, *The Tenth (Irish) Division*, p. 4.

9 Major-General Sir Henry Seymour Rawlinson Bt. (1914), son of Sir Henry Creswicke Rawlinson, first baronet; Brigadier-General Hubert de la Poer Gough (1914), son of General Sir Charles John Stanley Gough GCB, VC.

10 John Baynes, *Morale: A study of men and courage* (London, 1982), p. 125.

11 Simpson,'The officers', p. 65.

12 Spiers, 'The regular army in 1914', p.39.

13 C.F. Oterly, 'Origins and recruitment of the British Army elite' (Ph.D. thesis, University of Hull, 1965),p.14.

14 Analysis based on biographies contained in *Bond of sacrifice* (Naval and Military Press ed., 2 vols, Dallington, 1992)i.

15 Ibid.

16 Ibid., *Bond of sacrifice* provides educational details for 71 of the 88 officers killed in 1914.

17 Joseph Whitaker, *Whitaker's almanack* (London, 1912)., pp 311-8. For the purposes of this and later analysis, a public school is one that was a member of the Headmaster's Conference.

18 Based on a population of 73 officers (source: *Bond of sacrifice*).

19 Cooper, *The Tenth Irish Division*, p. 13.

20 de Ruvigny, *The roll of honour: a biographical record of all members of His Majesty's naval and military forces who have fallen in the war* (5 vols, London, 1916).

21 Simpson,'The officers', p. 66.

22 Gordon Corrigan, *Sepoys in the trenches: the Indian corps on the Western Front* (Staplehurst, 1999),p. 31.

23 Ibid., p. 14.

24 Cooper, *The Tenth (Irish) Division*, p. 8.

25 Ibid.

26 Corrigan, *Sepoys in the trenches*, pp 9-12.

27 Ibid., p. 13.

28 War Office, *Manual of military law*, pp 197 – 8. Category 'A' meant compulsory service for those who retired as Captains and Lieutenants up to the age of 50, Colonels, Lieutenant-Colonels, Majors and Quarter-Masters up to 55 and more senior ranks up to 67. Category 'B' contained those eligible for voluntary commissions in the Reserve of Officers, these included retired regulars (not category 'A'), Special Reserve officers and those with Officer Training Corps (OTC) experience.

29 Cooper, *The Tenth (Irish) Division*, p. 8.

30 Kirkpatrick papers(IWM, 79/50/1) p. 4.

31 Drury war diary, nd c Oct. 1914 (NAM, Drury papers, 7607-69),i, p. 14.

32 Personal reminiscences of T.T.H. Verschoyle, Leeds University Library, Liddle Collection[Liddle/WW1/GS/1654/Verschoyle].

33 Battersby, unpublished account of war experiences Leeds University Library, Liddle Collection, [Liddle/WW1/Gall (Rec.)/146/Battersby].

34 Of these three, Lieutenant-Colonel M.J.W. Pike, 5th Royal Irish Fusiliers had the most extensive experience having served with the 1899 Nile expedition, and in South Africa, Burma, India and the East Indies.

35 Cooper, *The 10th (Irish) Division*, p. 9.

36 Campbell, Leeds University Library, Liddle Collection [Liddle/WW1/ GS/0261/Campbell], p. 2.

37 Ibid., p. 3.

38 Analysis based on information extracted from the service records/ biographical details in the Marquis de Ruvigny's *Roll of Honour* of 121 officers.

39 J.E.G. O'Bryne (TNA, WO 339/32877).

40 I.A. Millar (TNA, WO 339/3201).

41 R.A. Rutherford (TNA, WO 339/1279).

42 R.N. Bellairs (TNA, WO 339/20469); R.G. Livens (TNA, WO 339/1039).

43 Based on the service records of 134 officers (TNA, WO 339 and WO 374).

44 After the war Slim transferred to the Indian army. On the outbreak of the Second World War he commanded the 10th Brigade of the Indian 5th Infantry Division took part in the East African campaign to liberate Ethiopia from the Italians. In May 1941 he was appointed Brigadier-General Staff to the commander of operations in Iraq but within days of his arrival in the theatre was promoted to the rank of acting Major-General and given command of the 10th (Indian) Division which he led during the Anglo-Iraq war, the Syria-Lebanon campaign and the invasion of Persian. In March 1942 he was given command of the Burma Division and was given the rank of acting Lieutenant-General in May 1942. Following the retreat to India Slim took command of XV Corps and following the dismissal of the commanding officer of the Eastern Army was promoted and given command of the newly created Fourteenth Army which ultimately drove the Japanese out of Burma. On 1 July 1945 Slim was promoted to the rank of General and Field Marshal in 1949.

45 Simpson 'The officers', p. 65.

46 J.W. Elliot, (TNA, WO 339/13244).

47 Excludes Campbell College, Belfast, which was a member of the Headmaster's Conference and therefore classed as a public school.

48 Based on the service records of 119 officers (TNA, WO 339 and WO 374).

49 Cooper, *The Tenth (Irish) Division*, p. 10.

50 Campbell, Leeds University Library, Liddle Collection [Liddle/WW1/GS/0261/Campbell], p. 2.

51 Based on the service records of 228 officers of the 10th (Irish) Division and 180 from the 13th (Western Division (TNA, WO 339 and WO 374; BL, L/MIL/14).

52 J. Daly (TNA, WO 339/39510); F.C. Clements (TNA, WO 339/37523).

53 Otley, 'Origins and recruitment of the British Army elite', p 85.

54 Including a former officer of an Irish militia battalion who was commissioned into a battalion of his old regiment.

55 Based on the service records of 48 officers (TNA, WO 339).

56 R.H. Scott, 6th Royal Inniskilling Fusiliers(TNA, WO 339/20766).

57 Letter from John Newell Jordan, His Majesty's Minister to China (TNA, WO 339/20710).

58 Cooper, *The 10th (Irish) in Gallipoli*, p. ix.

59 De Ruvigny, ii, III:(TNA, WO 339/8072).

60 H.G. Montagu (TNA, WO 339/8072).

61 CWGC Debt of Honour (http://www.cwgc.org/debt_of_honour.asp) (10 June 2007); *Soldiers died in the Great War* – Part 47 (London, 1921).

62 Montagu (TNA, WO 339/8072).

63 Based on the service records of 209 officers of the 10th (Irish) Division and 192 from the 13th (Western Division (TNA, WO 339 and WO 374; BL, L/MIL/14).

64 Cooper,*The 10th (Irish) in Gallipoli*, p.13.

65 Based on a sample of 227 officers whose place of birth could be identified from

census, service records and obituaries, 168 were found to have been either born, educated or have a permanent home in Ireland.

66 Based on the data extracted from service records, obituaries, school records and CWGC Debt of Honour database.

67 C.L. Mere (TNA, WO 339/12276).

68 C.H.C. de Fallott (TNA, WO 339/14440).

CHAPTER 4 - PREPARING FOR BATTLE

1 20/Gen.No./3593 (A.G.1) 3 Dec. 1914 (TNA, WO 162/3).

2 K.W. Mitchinson, *Pioneer Battalions in the Great War*, x-xi.

3 Jourdain, *The Connaught Rangers*, iii, 3-7; Whitton, *The Leinster Regiment*, ii, 97-98 and 178.

4 *Army Order 324 of 1914*(London, 21 Aug. 1914).

5 Jourdain, *5th (Service) Battalion, The Connaught Rangers*, p. 9.

6 Whitten, *The Leinster Regiment*, ii, p. 99.

7 Verschoyle, Leeds University Library, Liddle Collection [Liddle/WW1/GS/1654/Verschoyle], p.1

8 Daniel McKeown, Pension records, (TNA, WO 364).

9 Drury war diary, Sept/Oct. 1914 (NAM, Drury papers 7607-69), i, p. 11.

10 Battersby, unpublished account of war experiences Leeds University Library, Liddle Collection, [Liddle/WW1/Gall (Rec.)/146/Battersby].

11 Ibid.

12 Ibid.

13 Hanna, *The pals at Suvla*, p. 18.

14 H.F.N. Jourdain, *Ranging memories* (Oxford, 1934), p. 162.

15 Clive Hughes, 'The new armies'in Beckett and Simpson (eds), A nation in arms, p. 109; R*udyard Kipling, New army training* (London, 1915), p. 5.

16 Battersby, unpublished account of war experiences Leeds University Library, Liddle Collection, [Liddle/WW1/Gall (Rec.)/146/Battersby].

17 Ibid.

18 Hanna, *The pals at Suvla*, p.18; Whitten, *The Leinster Regiment*, ii, p. 97.

19 Drage, Chindwin *to Criccieth, p. 101.22* Campbell, Leeds University Library, Liddle Collection[Liddle/WW1/GS/0261/Campbell], p. 1.

20 Campbell, Leeds University Library, Liddle Collection [Liddle/WW1/GS/0261/Campbell], p. 2.

21 Letter from Hill to Aspinall-Oglander 5 Mar. 1931 (TNA, CAB 45/242).

22 Campbell,Leeds University Library, Liddle Collection[Liddle/WW1/GS/0261/Campbell], p. 1.

23 Ibid., p. 2.

24 Ibid., p. 4.

25   G.F. MacNie (TNA, WO 339/16433).

26   Cooper, *The Tenth (Irish) Division*, p. 20.

27   Hill to Aspinall-Oglander, 5 Mar. 1931 (TNA, CAB 45/242).

28   Cooper, *The Tenth (Irish) Division*, p. 17; Battersby, (Liddle Collection Gall(Rec.) 146).

29   Ibid., p. 19.

30   Hanna, *The pals at Suvla*, pp 19 – 20.

31   Cooper, *The Tenth (Irish) Division*, pp 20 – 21.

32   Drage, *Chindwin to Criccieth*, p. 102. Captain Alexander accompanied 30 Brigade to Gallipoli but due to illness was unable to take part in the Suvla landings being left at Mudros.

33   Drury war diary, nd c Jan. 1915 (NAM, Drury papers, 7607-69), i, p. 20. 34 Verschoyle, Leeds University Library, Liddle Collection[Liddle/WW1/GS/1654/Verschoyle], p. 2.

35   Hanna, *The pals at Suvla*, p. 20.

36   Letter from J.H.H. Pollock to Mr W Charles Pollock, 27 Mar. 1915 (PRONI, D1581/2/1).

37   Drury war diary, nd pre-Apr. 1915 (NAM, Drury papers, 7607-69), i, pp 18 – 19; 27.

38   Ibid., p. 31.

39   Ibid., p. 33.

40   Campbell, Leeds University Library, Liddle Collection [Liddle/WW1/GS/0261/Campbell], pp 5-6.

41   Cooper, The Tenth (Irish) *Division*, pp 24-25.

42   Ibid., pp 23-24.

43   Drage, *Chindwin to Criccieth, p. 103.*

44   Cooper, *The Tenth (Irish) Division*, p. 22.

45   Ibid., p. 22; Jourdain, *The Connaught Rangers*, iii, p. 12.

46   Letter from J.H.H. Pollock to Mr W Charles Pollock, 13 June 1915 (PRONI, D1581/2/1).

47   Letter from Tenant to Redmond, 17 June 1915 (quoted in Denis Gwynn, *The Life of John Redmond*, pp 434-35).

48   Ibid., p. 435.

49   Cooper, *The Tenth (Irish) Division*, p. 32 gives the date of receipt of this order as 27 June but the War Diary of the 5th Royal Inniskilling Fusiliers gives the date as 28 June (TNA, WO 95/4296).

50   Letter from J.H.H. Pollock to Mr W Charles Pollock, 6 July 1915 (PRONI, D1581/2/1).

51   Hargrave, *The Suvla Bay landing* (London, 1964), pp 59-60.

CHAPTER 5 -GALLIPOLI AND AFTER

1   Aspinall-Oglander, C.F., *Military Operations - Gallipoli*, i, p. 57.

2   Hankey to Balfour, 10 Feb. 1915 (BL, Balfour papers, Ms 49703).

3   Hamilton to Kitchener, 19 Mar. 1915 (LHCMA, Hamilton papers 7/1/16).

4   Braithwaite to Stopford, 22 July 1915, para. 2 (TNA, CAB 19/28).

5   Ibid.,para. 6.

6   Braithwaite to Stopford, 29 July 1915, para.3 (TNA, CAB 19/28); Hamilton, *Gallipoli diary*, ii, p. 315; to GHQ, 31 July 1915; and Operational Order No. 1, 3 Aug. 1915 (TNA, WO 138/40).

7   Hammersley to Stopford, 19 Aug. 1915 (TNA, CAB 19/29).

8   Ibid.

9   Poett, nd(TNA, CAB 45/244),p. 11; Memorandum by Lieutenant-General Sir F.W. Stopford submitted to the Dardanelles Commission, 18 Aug. 1915 (TNA, CAB 19/29).

10 Ibid.

11 Report by Brigadier-General F.F. Hill Commanding 31st Infantry Brigade of 10th Division and attached troops at SuvlaBay, n.d. (TNA, CAB 45/242).

12 Statement by Brigadier-General F.F. Hill to the Dardanelles Commission, n.d. (TNA, CAB 19/29).

13 Hammersley to Stopford, 19 Aug. 1915, (TNA, CAB 19/29).

14 31 Brigade War Diary, 7 Aug. 1915 (TNA, WO 95/4296).

15 Malcolm, pp 15–16 (TNA, CAB 95/4297).

16 C.F. Aspinall-Oglander, *The history of the Great War: military operations Gallipoli* (2 vols, London, 1932), ii, 258.

17 Drage,*Chindwin to Criccieth*, p. 106.

18 30 Brigade War Diary (TNA, WO 95/4296).

19 Goodland to Aspinall-Oglander, 26 Mar. 1931 (TNA, CAB 45/242).

20 McCance, Munster Fusiliers, ii, p. 178. Cooper, *The 10th (Irish) Division in Gallipoli*, p. 86. also records this action as taking place on 8 August but the action described actually took place on 9 August; Aspinall-Oglander, *Military Operations*, ii, p. 268.

21 Nicol to Aspinall-Oglander, 21 Jan. 1931 (TNA, CAB 45/243).

22 Drage to Aspinall-Oglander, 28 Jan. 1931 (TNA, WO 95/4296).

23 Ibid.

24 Drage, *Chindwin to Criccieth*, p. 107

25 30 Brigade War Diary (TNA, WO 95/4296).

26 Aspinall-Oglander, *Military Operations*, ii, p. 291.

27 Drury war diary, 9 Aug. 1915 (NAM, Drury papers, 7607-69) i, p. 89; Aspinall-Oglander, Military Operations, ii, p. 291.

28 Drury, p. 91.

29 Goodland to Aspinall-Oglander, 26 Mar. 1931 (TNA, CAB 45/242).

30 Ibid.

31 Brighten to Aspinall-Oglander, 28 Jan. 1931 (TNA, CAB 45/241).

32 Telegram B234, CGS to Mahon, 15 Aug. 1915 (TNA, WO 138/63)

33 Telegram G159, Mahon to CGS, 15 Aug. 1915 (TNA, WO 138/63); Telegram B237, CGS to Headquarters IXth Corps, 15, Aug. 1915 (TNA, WO 138/63).

34 Aspinall-Oglander, *Military Operations,* ii, p. 324.

35 Cooper, *The 10th (Irish) Division,* p. 52.

36 War Diary of 6th Leinster Regiment (TNA, WO 95/4296).

37 Aspinall-Oglander, Military Ope*rations, ii, p. 306.*

38 Bean, *The Story of Anzac,* ii, p. 701;War Diary of 6th Leinster Regiment (TNA, WO 95/4296).

39 Cooper, *The 10th (Irish) Division in Gallipoli,* pp 58–9.

40 Campbell, Leeds University Library, Liddle Collection [Liddle/WW1/ GS/0261/Campbell], p. 18.

41 Bean, *The Story of Anzac,* ii, p. 711; 29 Brigade War Diary,10 Aug. 1915 (TNA, WO 95/4296).

42 Bean, The Story of Anzac, *ii, pp 711–12.*

43 Cooper, *The 10th (Irish) Division in Gallipoli,* p. 105.

44 War Diary 5th Connaught Rangers (TNA, WO 95/4296).

45 29 Brigade War Diary, 10 Aug. 1915 (TNA, WO 95/4296).

46 Ibid.

47 Morley, L.C., in Cowlands (ed.) *The 10th and 12th Hampshires,* p. 17.

48 Ibid.

49 Aspinall-Oglander, *Military Operations: Gallipoli,* ii, p. 358.

50 Cooper, *The 10th (Irish) Division,* pp 255; 259-62.

51 Falls, Cyril,*The history of the Great War: military operations Macedonia* (2 vols, London, 1933), i, 51.

52 Ibid., p. 50.

53 30 Brigade War Diary (TNA, WO 95/4836).

54 MacPherson, William Grant , *History of the Great War: medical services* (4 vols, London 1921-24), ii, 486 – 7.

55 Message from J.E. King King to 10th Division, n.d. (TNA, WO 95/4836).

56 Report on operations in Serbia between 4th and 11th December 1915, 24 Dec. 1915 (TNA, WO 95/4836).

57 10th Hampshire Regiment War Diary, 28-31 Dec. 1915 (TNA, WO 95/4836).

58 Falls, *Military operations: Macedonia,* i, 144, fn 2.

59 6th Royal Dublin Fusiliers War Diary, 30 Sept. 1916 (TNA, WO 95/4836).

60 Ibid., 3 Oct, 1916 (TNA, WO 95/4836).

61 Ibid., 4 Oct, 1916 (TNA, WO 95/4836).

62 Archibald P. Wavell, *The Palestine campaigns* (1941), pp 112, 203.

63 For a fuller account of the Australian Light Horse's charge at Beersheba see

Gullett, Henry S.,*Official history of Australia in the war of 1914-1918*, vii, pp 384-404.

64 Falls, Cyril, *Military Operations –Egypt and Palestine*, ii, part 1, pp282-6.

65 Ibid., pp 284-6.

66 Ibid., p. 288.

67 Ibid., pp 310-26.

CHAPTER 6 - GALLIPOLI: THE LEADERSHIP DEFICIT

1 Gary Sheffield, *Leadership in the trenches: officer-man relations, morale and discipline in the British army in the era of the First World War* (London, 2000), p. 42.

2 Ibid.

3 This is a paraphrase of the definition for senior leadership found in *Field manual 22-100: Leadership and command at senior levels*, HQ, Department of the Army, Washington, D.C., June 1987, p. 3.

4 Archibald P. Wavell, *Generals and generalship* (New York, 1942), p.17.

5 Bernard L. Montgomery, quoted in P.A. Pedersen, *Monash as military commander* (paper back ed. Melbourne, 1992) p. 25.

6 The Times, 1 Apr. 1916.

7 Address given by Bach published in the *Daily Times Herald* (Waco, Texas, 27 Jan. 1918) and reprinted in *Stand To!* Apr. 2006, p. 24.

8 Basil H. Liddell Hart, *The war in outline 1914-1918* (London, 1936), p. xii.

9 Hugh Strachan, 'The real war: Liddell Hart, Crutwell, and Falls' in Brian Bond (ed.) *The First World War and British history*, p. 49.

10 Edmonds to Spenser Wilkinson, 15 Mar. 1916, Edmonds papers, II/1/133a. According to the Oxford Dictionary of Quotations (7th edn, 2009) the statement is usually ascribed to the Duke of Wellington, letter, 29 Aug 1810 in 'Supplementary Despatches ...' (1860) vi.

11 Liddell Hart. *Through the fog of war* (London, 1938), p. 104.

12 Terraine, 'British military leadership in the First World War' 1914-1918 Essays on leadership and War, Ann Clayton (ed) p. 51.

13 Terraine, '"Wully" Field Marshal Sir William Robertson Bart.; GCB, KCVO, DSO,' 1914-1918 Essays on leadership and War, Clayton (ed) p. 73.

14 Hussey, 'The deaths of qualified staff officers in the Great War', in *JSAHR*, lxxv, (1997) pp 246-59.

15 Spiers, *The regular army*, p. 44.

16 *Report of a conference of staff officers at the Royal Military College, 12th to 15th January, 1914*, p. 8 (TNA, WO279/495).

17 Hussey, 'Staff officers in the Great War', *JSAHR*, lxxv, p. 250.

18 Baynes, Morale, p. 124.

19 Bean, The story of Anzac, ii, 711-12.

20 Ibid., p. 699.

21   Hamilton to Churchill, 12 Mar. 1915 (quoted in Jenny Macleod, *Reconsidering Gallipoli*, p. 193).

22   Ian S.M. Hamilton, *Gallipoli diary* (2 vols, London, 1920-22), i, 161 and 287.

23   John Lee, *A soldier's life: General Sir Ian Hamilton 1853-1947* (paperback ed., London, 2000), p. 165.

24   Hamilton (LHMRC, Hamilton papers, 7/10/3), p. 192

25   Aspinall-Oglander, *Military operations: Gallipoli*, i, 205 fn2.

26   Travers, *British army command and leadership styles*, p. 416.

27   Aspinall-Oglander, *Military operations: Gallipoli*, I, 205.

28   Hamilton, *Gallipoli diary*, i, 181.

29   Ibid. p. 3.

30   Hamilton to Kitchener, 27 Apr. 1915 (LHCMA, Hamilton Papers, 7/1/21); Hamilton, *Gallipoli diary*, i, 163

31   Hunter-Weston to his wife, 27 Apr. 1915 (BL, Hunter-Weston papers, Add 48355 - 48368).

32   Hamilton to War Office (MF 313), 10 May 1915 (LHCMA, Hamilton papers 7/2/3).

33   Hamilton to Kitchener, (MF 381) 28 June 1915 (LHCMA, Hamilton papers 7/2/3).

34   George H. Cassar, *Asquith as war leader* (London, 1994), p. 128.

35   Cassar, 'Hamilton, Sir Ian Standish Monteith (1853–1947)', *Oxford Dictionary of National Biography*.

36   Stopford to GHQ, 31 July 1915; and Operational Order No. 1, 3 Aug. 1915 (TN°A, WO 138/40).

37   Travers, *Gallipoli 1915* (Stroud, 2004), p. 142.

38   Hamilton, *Gallipoli diary*, ii, 36; L.A. Carlyon, *Gallipoli* (Bantam ed., London, 2003), p. 452.

39   Aspinall-Oglander, *Military operations: Gallipoli*, ii, 149.

40   Ibid.

41   Hamilton, *Compulsory service: a study of the question in the light of experience* (1911), pp 121-2.

42   Travers, *British army command and leadership styles*, p. 411.

43   Hamilton, Gallipoli di*ary*, *i, 363-4.*

44   Ibid., p. 229.

45   *Dardanelles Commission*, para. 78, p. 35.

46   Robin Prior and Trevor Wilson, *Command on the Western Front: the military career of Sir Henry Rawlinson* (paperback ed., Barnsley, 2004), p. 85 states that the number of guns firing on the German front line fell from 1/30 yards at Neuve Chapelle (10 Mar. 1915) to 1/50 yards at Aubers Ridge (8 May 1915).

47   Major A Murray, A short account of the landing at Suvla Bay, Gallipoli in Aug. 1915, 29 July, 1929 (TNA, CAB 45/233).

48   Reed to Hill, 7 Aug. 1915 (TNA, CAB 19/29).

49   S. McCance, *The history of the Royal Munster Fusiliers* (Aldershot, 1927), ii, 178:

Cooper, *The 10th (Irish) Division*, p. 86 records this action as taking place on 8 August but the action described actually took place on 9 August; Aspinall-Oglander, *Military operations: Gallipoli*, ii, 268.

50 Stopford, Operations from 6th to 15th Aug. 1915, 26 Oct. 1915 (TNA, WO 106/707).

51 Robin Prior, *Gallipoli, the end of the myth* (New Haven, 2009), p. 245; Orlo Williams, 15 Aug. 1915 (Williams papers, IWM, 69/78/1).

52 Roberts to the Secretary of State for War, 9 July 1900 (TNA, WO32/7989).

53 Kitchener to Hamilton (No. 5708, cipher) 23 June 1915 (LHCMA, Hamilton papers 7/2/3).

54 Statement by Mahon to the Dardanelles Commission, nd. (TNA, CAB 19/30).

55 Ibid.

56 King-King to Aspinall-Oglander, 5 Feb. 1931 (TNA, CAB45/243).

57 Williams, 21 July 1915 (IWM, Williams papers, 69/78/1).

58 Third supplement, *London Gazette*, 10 Apr. 1916.

59 Hamilton to Kitchener, 21 Sept. 1915 (LHCMA, Hamilton papers 7/1).

60 Braithwaite to Stopford, 22 July 1915, para 2 (TNA, CAB 19/28)

61 Travers, 'Command and leadership', p. 418.

62 Braithwaite to Stopford, 29 July 1915, para. 3 (TNA, CAB 19/28); Hamilton, *Gallipoli diary, ii, p. 315*.

63 Dawnay to his wife, 9 Aug. 1915 (IWM, Dawnay Papers, 69/21/1).

64 Statement by Lieut.-General The Hon. Sir F Stopford respecting the operations of the 9th Army Corps at Suvla Bay, Aug. 6th to 15th 1915, 31 July 1915 (TNA, CAB 19/31).

65 Major-General J.H. Poett, an account of his time at Gallipoli, nd. p. 3 (TNA, CAB 45/244).

66 Hamilton to Vice Admiral commanding, Eastern Mediterranean Squadron, 4 July 1915 (TNA, WO 15/888).

67 Poett, pp 11-12 (TNA, CAB 45/244).

68 Braithwaite to Stopford, 22 July 1915 (TNA, CAB 19/28) Hamilton, *Gallipoli diary*, ii, 310.

69 Report by Brigadier-General F.F. Hill Commanding 31st Infantry Brigade of 10th division and attached troops at Suvla Bay, nd, p.1 (TNA, CAB 45/242).

70 Ibid., p. 2.

71 Lieutenant-Colonel F.W. Greer, 5 Apr. 1951 (PRONI, D3574/E/6/6).

72 Goodland to Oglander, 26 Mar. 1931 (TNA, CAB 45/242).

73 Samuel Roskill, *Hankey: man of secrets* (3 vols, London, 1970-72), i, 213.

74 Terraine, *British military leadership in the First World War*, WFA Website, 8 Jul. 2008.

75 Hamilton, *Gallipoli diary*, i, 169-170.

76 Stopford to GHQ, 31 July 1915; and Operational Order No. 1, 3 Aug. 1915 (TNA, WO 138/40).

77 Stopford to GHQ, 31 July 1915 para. 10 (TNA, WO 138/40).

78 Aspinall-Oglander, *Military operations: Gallipoli*, ii, 276-7.

79 Ibid. 279.

80 Ibid. 282.

81 Limon von Sanders, *Fünf Jahre Türkei*, pp 114-15 (as quoted in Aspinall-Oglander, *Military operations: Gallipoli*, ii, 282-3).

82 Travers, *Gallipoli 1915*, p. 140.

83 Hamilton to Kitchener, 11 Aug 1915 (LHCMA, Hamilton papers, 7/1); Braithwaite to Hamilton, 25 Aug. 1915 (LHCMA, Hamilton papers 17/4/1/15).

84 As quoted by Travers, *Gallipoli 1915*, pp 140-141.

85 Stopford, 18 Aug. 1915, (TNA, CAB 19/29).

86 30 Brigade War Diary (TNA, WO 95/4296).

87 De Lisle, Memo on trench warfare, 10 July 1915 (TNA, WO95/4264).

88 Nicol to Aspinall-Oglander, 21 Jan. 1931 (TNA, CAB 45/243).

89 Ibid.

90 King-King to Aspinall-Oglander 5 Feb. 1931 (TNA, CAB45/243).

91 Hamilton, Dardanelles Commission, Jan, 1917 (TNA, CAB 19/33).

92 Hamilton, *Gallipoli diary*, ii, 75.

93 Martin Samuels, *Command or control? Command, training and tactics in the British and German armies, 1888-1918* (London, 1995), p. 49.

94 Ibid.

95 Anthony Farrar-Hockley (ed.), *Sir Ian Hamilton, The Commander* (London, 1957), pp 52-3.

96 Hamilton, *Gallipoli diary*, i, 132-33.

97 Ibid. 147.

98 Travers, *British army command and leadership styles*, p. 414.

99 Samuels, *Command or control*, p. 50.

100 War Office to GOC MEF (No. 5250, cipher), 9 June 1915 (LHCMA, Hamilton papers 7/2/3);Hamilton to War Office (MF 313), 10 June 1915 (LHCMA, Hamilton papers 7/2/3).

101 Hamilton to Kitchener (MF 334), 15 June 1915 (as recorded in Hamilton, *Gallipoli diaries*, i, 302).

102 Kitchener to Hamilton (No. 5501, cipher), 15 June 1915 (LHCMA, Hamilton papers 7/2/3).

103 Hamilton, *Gallipoli diary*, i, 307.

104 Roberts to the Secretary of State for War, 9 July 1900 (TNA, WO32/7989).

105 Kitchener to Roberts, 21 March 1900; French to Roberts, 20 Nov. 1900 (TNA, WO 105/16).

106 Statement by Mahon to the Dardanelles Commission, nd (TNA, CAB 19/30).

107 Ibid.

108 Aspinall-Oglander, *Military operations: Gallipoli*, ii, 268.

109 Braithwaite to Hamilton 25 Aug, 1916 (LHCMA, Hamilton papers, 17/4/1/15).

110 Dawnay to his wife, 9 Aug. 1915 (IWM, Dawnay papers, 69/21/1).

111 Ibid. 12 Aug. 1915.

112 Ibid. 24 Aug. 1915.

113 Beecroft to Aspinall-Oglander, 9 Feb. 1931 (TNA, CAB 45/241).

114 Temperley to Aspinall-Oglander, 10 Oct. 1930 (TNA, CAB 45/244).

115 Williams, 12 Aug. 1914 (IWM, Williams papers, 69/78/1).

116 Ibid. 14 Aug. 1914.

117 Ibid. 23 Aug. 1914.

118 Hill to Aspinall-Oglander, nd but c. 1930 (TNA, CAB 45/242).

119 Beecroft to Aspinall-Oglander, 9 Feb. 1931 (TNA, CAB 45/241).

120 Verschoyle (IWM Sound Archive, AC 8185)

121 The final report of the Dardanelles Commission [Cmd 341], H.C. 1919, para. 144, p. 64.

122 Letter from Lord Granard to his wife, 15 Aug. 1915 (PRONI, T/3765/K/12/2).

123 Dardanelles Commission, para. 78, p. 35.

124 Braithwaite to Stopford, 22 July 1915, para. 8 and Table (TNA, CAB 19/28).

125 31st Brigade War Diary, 7 Aug. 1915 (TNA, WO 95/4296).

126 Dardanelles Commission, p. 95.

127 Lord Granard to his wife, 10 Aug. 1915 (PRONI, T/3765/K/12/2).

128 Ibid. 15 Aug., 1915.

129 Hamilton to Kitchener 16 Aug. 1915 (MF 560) (LHCMA, Hamilton Papers, 7/2/28).

130 Anonymous enclosure in a letter from E to Hankey, 13 Sept. 1915 (TNA, CAB17/124).

131 Dawnay to his wife, 19 Oct. 1915 (IWM, Dawney papers, 69/21/1)

132 Travers, British army command and leadership styles, p. 428-9.

133 Hamilton to Kitchener, 2 July 1915 (LHCMA, Hamilton papers, 7/1).

134 Quoted in Travers, Gallipoli 1915, pp 109-110.

135 Williams, 8 May 1915 (IWM, Williams papers, 69/78/1).

136 K. Fewster (ed.), Gallipoli Correspondent: the frontline diary of CEW Bean (Sydney, 1983), pp 169-70.

137 Ibid., p. 170.

138 Hamilton, Gallipoli diary, 26 April, i, 147.

139 Report of a conference of staff officers at the Royal Military College, 12th to 15th January, 1914, p. 5 (TNA, WO279/495.

140 G H. Cassar, 'Sir Ian Standish Monteith Hamilton (1853–1947)', Oxford Dictionary of National Biography, Oxford University Press, Sept 2004; online edn, Jan 2008.

141 Williams, 2 June 1915 (IWM, Williams papers, 69/78/1).

142 Ibid.

143 Hamilton to Wolf-Murray, 1/7/1915 (LHCMA, Hamilton papers, 7/1).

144 DCIGS, Landing at Suvla Bay, 20 Sept. 1915 (TNA, WO106/707).145 Hamilton, Gallipoli diary, ii, 101-2.

146 Ibid. 101.

147 Ibid. 105.

148 Mahon to Hamilton, 15 Aug. 1915 (TNA138/63).

149 Nicol to Aspinall-Oglander, 21 Jan. 1931 (TNA, CAB 45/243).

150 Prior, *Gallipoli*, p. 245.

151 Mahon to Braithwaite, 15 Aug. 1915 (TNA, WO WO138/63); Birdwood to his wife, Aug. 1915 (AWM, 3DRL3373).

152 Hamilton to Kitchener, 16 Aug. 1915 (TNA, WO138/63).

153 Hamilton. *Gallipoli diary*, ii, 109.

154 Williams, 15 Aug. 1915 (Williams papers, IWM, 69/78/1).

155 Hamilton to Roberts, 24 Aug. 1900 (TNA, WO 105/16).

156 Hamilton, *Gallipoli diary*, ii, 76-77; Hamilton to Kitchener, 16 Aug. 1915 (TNA, WO138/63).

157 Monro's first despatch, third supplement, *London Gazette*, 10 April 1916

CHAPTER 7 - MORALE AND DISCIPLINE

1 Travers, *The killing ground*, pp 42-4.

2 Hamilton, *Compulsory service*, pp 121-2.

3 Jean de Bloch, *Is war now impossible?*(London, 1899), pp xiii – xxxviii.

4 Creagh, 'The army in India', *Army Review*, 4 (Jan. 1913), p. 36.

5 *Infantry Training 1902*, pp 146- 47, 194, 201, 234; *Field Service Regulations 1909*, pp 11, 114; *Training and Manoeuvre Regulations1909*, pp 1- 5.

6 Travers, 'Technology, tactics and morale: Jean de Bloch, the Boer War, and British military theory, 1900-1914' in *Journal of Modern History*, ci, no. 2 (June 1979), p. 277.

7 Charles M.W. Moran, *The anatomy of courage* (1966), pp 16 and 81.

8 Baynes, Morale, p. *108.*

9 Ibid.

10 Timothy Bowman, *Irish regiments in the Great War: discipline and morale* (Manchester, 2003), p. 10.

11 Ibid.

12 Ian Beckett, *The Great War* (2nd ed., London, 2007), pp 102-3.

13 See Annex 2.

14 Drage, *Chindwin to Criccieth*, p. 100; Verschoyle, Leeds University Library, Liddle Collection[Liddle/WW1/GS/1654/Verschoyle].

15 Nugent to his wife, 26 Oct. 1915, Farren Connell papers (PRONI, D.3835/E/2/5/20A).

16 F.P. Crozier, *A brass hat in no man's land* (Reprint ed., Norfolk, 1989), pp 77-8.

17 Ibid., p. 78.

18 Cooper, *The 10th (Irish) Division*, p. 14.

19 See Annex 2.

20   Bowman, *Irish regiments in the Great War*, p. 86.

21   Montmorency to John Redmond, 24 Jan. 1915 (NLI, Redmond Papers, Ms. 15261(2)).

22   Anon. 'Service with the 14th Battalion, Royal Irish Rifles (Young Citizen Volunteers), 1914-18', p. 61 (Royal Ulster Rifles Museum).

23   Manual of military law (London, 1914), p. 15.

24   WO 86/63; Staniforth, Letter to his parents, 1 Nov. 1914 (IWM, 67/41/1).

25   Ibid., 25 Dec. 1914 (IWM, 67/41/1).

26   See Annex 1.

27   Roger Swift, 'Crime and the Irish in Nineteenth Century Britain', in Roger Swift and Sheridan Gilley (eds), *The Irish in Britain 1815-1939*, p. 167.

28   Joseph V. O'Brien *'Dear Dirty Dublin' a city in distress, 1899-1916* (Berkeley, 1982), pp 184-6.

29   Simpson, 'The officers', p. 73.

30   See Annex 1.

31   Courts-martial Records (TNA, WO86/63).

32   See Annex 2.

33   Field Punishment was introduced in 1881 as a replacement for flogging. Field Punishment No.1 (FP1) consisted of the convicted man being placed in fetters, handcuffs or similar restraints and attached to a fixed object for up to two hours per day. The lesser punishment of Field Punishment No.2 (FP2) was similar to FP1 except that the prisoner was not attached to a fixed object.

34   See Annex 2.

35   Gerald Oram, *Worthless men: eugenics and the death penalty in the British army during the First World War* (London, 1998), pp 42, 59 and 119.

36   Annex 1.

37   Bowman, *Irish regiments in the Great War*, pp 11 and 87.

38   R.A.F. Gill (TNA, WO 339/18329).

39   H.G. Montagu (TNA, WO 339/8072).

40   Drury war diary, nd. but probably end of May/beginning of June 1915 (NAM, Drury papers, 7607-69) i, p. 34.

41   Liddell Hart, *A history of the world war 1914-1918* (London, 1934), p. 177.

42   Crozier, *A brass hat in no man's land*, p. 61.

43   Drury war diary, nd Spring 1915 (NAM, Drury papers, 7607-69) i,p. 17.

44   Ibid., 1 Jul. and 17 Jul. 1915, pp 52 and 59.

45   Cooper,*The 10th (Irish) Division*, p. 25.

46   Drury war diary, 17 Mar. 1915 (NAM, Drury papers, 7607-69) i, p. 22.

47   Ibid., 30 Apr. 1915, p. 28.

48   Ibid., 30 Apr. 1915, pp 28-9.

49   Cooper, *The 10th (Irish) Division*, p. 32.

50   Dart, unpublished recollections, Leeds University Library, Liddle Collection[Liddle/WW1/Gal/025/Dart].

51   Drury war diary, 17 Mar. 1915 (NAM, Drury papers, 7607-69) i, pp 22-3.

52   Hanna, *The pals at Suvla*, p.21.

53   Ibid., p. 46.

54   Cooper,*The 10th (Irish) Division*, p. 25.

55   *Soldiers' and Sailors' Families Association, annual report, 1914-1915*, pp 26-32.

56   Irish Times, 14 Nov. 1914.

57   Ibid., 1 Jan. 1915.

58   Letter from Broun to his family, 2 Dec. 1915 Leeds University Library, Liddle Collection[Liddle/WW1/GS/0206/Broun].

59   Cooper, *The 10th (Irish)* Division, p. 35.

60   Annex 2; Bowman, *Irish regiments in the Great War*, pp 113 & 120.

61   Annex 2; Bowman, *Irish regiments in the Great War*, p. 113.

62   Ibid., p. 120.

63   Annex 1; 10th Division 1 Aug. 1915 to 31 July 1916; 13th Division 1 July 1915 to 30 June 1916.

64   Drury war diary, 28 Nov. 1915 (NAM, Drury papers, 7607-69) ii, p. 63.

65   Cooper, *The 10th (Irish) Division*, pp 142-5.

66   6th Royal Irish Rifles, A narrative of events 5 – 19 August 1915 (TNA, WO95/4296).

67   30 Brigade War Diary, (TNA, WO95/4296); McCance, *The history of the Royal Munster Fusiliers*, ii, 180, 193.

68   Sheffield, *Leadership in the trenches*, p. 155; .John F. Tucker, *Johnny get your gun: a personal narrative of Somme, Ypres and Arras* (London, 1978), p. 110.

69   Drury war diary, c 8 Oct. 1915 (NAM, Drury papers,7607-69). ii p.18.

70   Ibid., p. 20.

71   Drury, 10 Dec. 1915 (NAM, Drury papers, 7607-69) ii, p. 85).

72   War Diaries. The 6th Connaught Rangers were still receiving men from their regimental depot on 14 Sept. 1916 when 74 men arrived from the 3rd and 4th battalions, while the 5th Royal Irish Rifles received a draft of 32 other ranks 'from home' on 8 December 1916 (TNA, WO95/4835).

73   Sheffield, *Leadership in the trenches*, p. 155.

74   Memoir of G. Nicholson, (Royal Hampshire Regimental Museum, 10th Hampshires Scrapbook).

75   29 Brigade War Diary (TNA, WO95/4835).

76   Diary of C.Q.M.S. John McIlwain (IWM, 96/29/1).

77   Wakefield and Moody, *Under the Devil's eye*, p. 238.

78   Courts-martial Records (TNA, WO213/7).

79   Diary of C.Q.M.S. John McIlwain (IWM, 96/29/1).

80   Beckett, *The Great War*, p. 314.

81   Court-martial record of Private P. J. Downey (TNA,WO71/441).

82   Myles Dungan, *They shall grow not old - Irish soldiers and the Great War* (Blackrock, 1997), p. 92.

83   Jourdain, *The Connaught Rangers*,iii, 384.

84 *Form for assembly and proceedings of field general court martial on active service*, 1 Dec. 1915 (TNA, WO71/441).

85 The instruction was issued by the Adjutant-General after Private Joseph Byers pleaded guilty to desertion and had been executed on 1 July 1915.

86 Courts-martial records (TNA, WO 213/6).

87 Courts-martial records (TNA, WO 213/4-10).

88 Stephen Walker, *Forgotten Soldiers – the Irishmen shot at dawn* (Dublin, 2007),pp 157-160.

89 Court-martial record of Private G. Hanna (TNA,WO71/611).

90 Fuller, *Troop morale and popular,*pp 85-113.

91 Fuller, *Troop morale and popular culture*, p. 186.

92 Wakefield and Moody, *Under the Devil's eye*, p. 156; Melville J. Rattray, *Three years in the Balkans - further recollections of 107th Field Coy, R.E.* (Darlington, 1920), p. 125.

93 War diary 6th Leinster Regt. 13 Nov. 1917 (TNA, WO95/4573).

94 Bowman, *Irish regiments in the Great War*, p. 157.

95 Diary of CQMS John McIlwain, 6 Dec. 1915 (IWM, 96/29/1).

96 Fuller, *Troop morale and popular culture*, p. 73.

97 Englander and Osborne, 'Jack, Tommy and Henry Dubb', in *Historical Journal*, xxi, (1978) p. 601.

98 Malcolm Brown, *Tommy goes to war* (London, 1978), pp 232-3.

99 Falls, *Military operations, Macedonia*, i, 258.

100 Ibid., ii, 34.

101 6th R.D.F. War Diary, 17 Jan. 1917 (TNA, WO95/4836).

102 G.R.O. No. 969, 5 April 1917 (TNA, WO95/4289).

103 Rattray, Three years in *the Balkans*, pp 219-20.

104 Analysis of leave due by Lt.-Col. H.F. Watson, 6th Royal Inniskilling Fusiliers, nd., (TNA, WO95/4296).

105 Simkins, *Kitchener's army: the raising of the New Armies, 1914-16* (Manchester, 1988), p. 182.

106 Cockburn, Diary and recollections (IWM, P. 258).

107 Ibid.

108 Ms letter by the Rev. John Crozier nd. (IWM, P346).

109 Diary of CQMS John McIlwain, (IWM, 96/29/1).

110 Wakefield and Moody, *Under the Devil's eye*, p. 5.

111 Surfleet, 'Blue chevrons: an infantry private's Great War diary', unpublished account based on author's diaries for 1916 and 1917 c. 1962 (IWM, P.126).

112 Phillips, H.C. Deb., 2I March 1917 (XCI), col. 1961-2.

113 'First to land in Salonika' in *The Mosquito*, Dec. 1934, p. 81.

114 Drury war diary, 20 Oct. 1915 (NAM, Drury papers, 7607-69) ii, p. 19.

115 Cooper, *The 10th (Irish) Division*, p. 41.

116 Beecroft, Signal Officer, 11th Division to Aspinall-Oglander,9 Feb. 1931 (TNA,

CAB45/241)

117 Cooper, *The 10th (Irish) Division*, pp 92-3.

118 WD 6th Leinster Regiment (TNA, WO95/4296).

119 Falls, *Military operations: Macedonia*, i, 64.

120 Ts. Diary of William Knott, 28 Nov. 1915 (IWM, P305).

121 *The Sprig*, x, p. 318.

122 Falls, *Military operations: Macedonia*, i, 65.

123 War diary of the 10th Hampshire Regiment, 21 Aug. 1916 (TNA, WO95/4835).

124 T.J. Mitchell and G.M. Smith, *Medical services: casualties and medical statistics of the Great War* (London, 1933), pp 187, 194.

125 G.M. Willoughby and Louis Cassidy, *Anti-malaria work in Macedonia among British troops* (London, 1918),p. 58.

126 *British Medical Journal*, i, p. 346.

127 Memoir G. Nicholson, (Royal Hampshire Regimental Museum).

128 C.H. Tredgold, 'The prophylactic use of quinine in malaria: with special reference to experiences in Macedonia', *BMJ*, 1918, i, pp 525-9; A. Cecil Alport, *Malaria and its treatment: in the line and at the base* (London, 1919), pp 17-22, 25; H.R. Whiteside, *Report on the incidence of malaria*, 20 Nov. 1916 (TNA, WO32/5112).

129 Beckett, *The Great War*, p. 303.

130 W.B. Spender, Ms history of the U.V.F. and 36th (Ulster) Division, p. 29 (PRONI, D.1295/2/1A-9); Falls, *The history of the 36th Ulster Division* (Belfast, 1922), p. 16.

131 Cooper, The 10th *(Irish) Division, p. 48.*

132 Drury war dairy, 26 Sept. 1915 (NAM, Drury papers, 7607-69) i, pp 141-2.

133 William Lucas, *Life and letters of Norman Carey Lucas* (Melbourne, 1920), p. 23.

134 Ibid., p. 228.

135 Ibid., p. 243.

136 Drury war diary, 9 Dec 1917 (NAM, Drury papers, 7607-69) iii, p. 102.

137 W. Turner, 'The record book of Mr Thomas Glover', in *Stand to!* Summer 1989, 26, pp 6-8.

138 Drury war diary, 15 Aug 1915 (NAM, Drury papers, 7607-69) i, p. 101.

139 Drury war diary, 9 Dec. 1915 (NAM, Drury papers, 7607-69) ii, p. 83.

140 Ibid., 22 Aug. 1915 ii, p. 137.

141 A postcard in the possession of Andrew Brook quoted in *Stand To!* Jan. 2007, 78, p.31.

142 Drury war diary, 27 Apr. 1916 (NAM, Drury papers, 7607-69-2) ii, p. 130.

143 Recruitment statistics 4 Aug. 1914 - 31 July 1916 (TNA, NATS 1/399).

144 'Minutes of the proceedings of, and précis prepared for the Army council for the years 1915 and 1916, p. 55 (TNA, WO163/21).

145 Adjutant-General's war diary, 26 Oct. 1916 (TNA, WO95/26).

146 Bowman, *Irish regiments in the Great War*, p. 156

147 Annex 2.

148 Bowman, *Irish regiments in the Great War*, p. 156

149 See Annex 2.

150 David Englander, 'Discipline and morale in the British army 1917-1918' in John Horne (ed.), *State, society and mobilisation in Europe during the First World War*, p. 139.

151 See Annex 2.

152 Bowman, *Irish regiments in the Great War*, pp 156-7.

153 Jourdain diary, 13 Mar. 1917 (NAM, 5603-12-1).

154 Mitchell and Smith, Medical services: *casualties and medical statistics Table II*, p. 279

155 Private P Moore, 6th Leinster Rgt., 17 Feb. 1916 (TNA, WO 213/7); Private D Bill, 6th Royal Irish Rifles, 12 Apr. 1918 (TNA, WO 213/20); Private P Hunt, 6th Leinster Rgt., 21 Apr. 1918 (TNA, WO 213/21).

156 Courts-martial records May 1915 to May 1917 (TNA, WO213/4-14).

157 War Diary, 5th Connaught Rangers 29 Dec. 1915 (TNA, WO 95/4835). The only member of the battalion to die during December 1916 was Private Michael Shortt from Enniskerry Co. Wicklow who died of wounds on 30 Dec. 1916. The CWGC website incorrectly gives the date of death as 30 Dec. 1915.

158 War Diary, 67 Brigade, RFA, 14 Oct. 1916 (TNA, WO 95/4831). The only artilleryman from the battery to die on 14 Oct. 1916 is Gunner Joseph Hughes who is buried in Struma Military Cemetery, Greece.

159 Jasper Thomas Brett, (TNA, WO 339/46640).

CHAPTER 8 - FROM THE CURRAGH TO THE JUDEAN HILLS – THE LESSONS LEARNED

1 TTH Travers, *The killing ground – the British army, the Western Front and the emergence of modern warfare 1900-1918* (Barnsley, 2003); Paddy Griffith, *Battle tactics of the Western Front* (New Haven, CT, 1994).

2 *Field Service Regulations 1909* (quoted in Shelford Bidwell and Dominick Graham, *Fire-power: British army weapons and theories of war, 1904-45* (paperback ed., London, 2004), p. 51).

3 Bidwell and Graham, *Fire-Power*, pp 9 – 10.

4 Staff conference 1910 (quoted in Bidwell and Graham, *Fire-Power*, p. 52).

5 See Sir Charles Oman, *Wellington's Army 1809-1814* (London, 1913) pp 61-93 for an assessment of Wellington's infantry tactics.

6 *Infantry Training 1914* (London, 1914).

7 *Field Service Regulations 1909*, p. 135.

8 John French, *1914* (London, 1919) p. 144.

9 Stephen Badsey, The Boer War (1899-1902) and British cavalry doctrine: a re-evaluation in *The Journal of Military History*, 71, Jan. 2007, p. 76.

10 Erskine Childers, *War and the Arme Blanche* (London, 1910), p. 105; *Elgin Commission Report*, ii, Cd. 1791, p. 403.

11 Edmonds, *The history of the Great War: military operations, France and Belgium, 1914*, i, 10.

12 Keith Simpson, *The old contemptibles* (London, 1981), p. 43; John Keegan, *The First World War* (New York, 1998), p. 102.

13 *Field Artillery Training 1914* (here after *FAT 1914*), p. 175; C.E.D Budworth, Artillery in Co-operation with Infantry, in *Journal of the Royal Artillery*, 37:1 (1910) pp 2, 9; Shelford Bidwell, *Gunners at war: a tactical study of the Royal Artillery in the twentieth century* (Revised ed., London, 1972). pp 17-19.

14 Jac Weller, *Wellington at Waterloo* (London, 1992) p. 25.

15 Edmonds, *The history of the Great War: military operations, France and Belgium, 1915* (2 vols, London, 1928), ii, 82.

16 Edmonds, *Military operations: France and Belgium, 1915*, ii, 240.17 Travers, *British army command and leadership styles*, p. 428.

18 Drury war diary, 23 Dec. 1915 (NAM, Drury papers, 7607-69) ii, p. 97.

19 See Waldron, *Elements of Trench Warfare*, pp 1-4 for a description of the normal organisation of a trench line.

20 Drury war diary, 5 Nov. 1915 (NAM, Drury papers, 7607-69) ii, p. 33.

21 Ibid., 6 Nov. 1915 (NAM, Drury papers, 7607-69) ii, p. 34.

22 Ibid., 9 Nov. 1915 pp 36-37.

23 War Diary 1st Battalion Irish Guards, 28 Sept. 1914 (TNA, WO95/1342).

24 Kipling, *The Irish Guards in the Great War – the first battalion* (Tonbridge, 1997) p. 47.

25 Drury war diary, 23 Nov. 1915 (NAM, Drury papers, 7607-69), ii, p. 55

26 Ibid., 8 Jan. 1916, p. 104.

27 Waldron, *Elements of Trench Warfare*, pp 4-5.

28 Drury war diary, 14 Jan. 1916 (NAM, Drury papers, 7607-69) ii, p. 106.

29 For fuller coverage of the debate see Tim Travers *The killing ground – the British army, the Western Front and the emergence of modern warfare 1900-1918* (Barnsley, 2003), pp 62-70.

30 Unsigned minute, 24 Nov. 1914 (TNA, WO 32/11324).

31 Ibid.; Drury war diary, 25 Nov. 1915 (NAM, Drury papers, 7607-69) ii, p. 57.

32 Notes on the employment of machine guns, (GHQ) July 1915 (TNA, WO 33/718).

33 30th Machine Gun Company War Diary (TNA, WO 95/4837).

34 30th Machine Gun Company War Diary, October 1916 (TNA, WO 95/4837).

35 Cornish, The Machine Gun in the Great War, HBSA Lecture, IWM, 20 July 2011.

36 29th Machine Gun Company War Diary (TNA, WO 95/4835); 30th Machine Gun Company War Diary (TNA, WO 95/4837).

37 Graham Seton Hutchinson, *Machine guns, their history and tactical employment : (being also a history of the Machine Gun Corps, 1916-1922)* (London, 1938), p. 194.

38 Edmonds, *Military operations: France and Belgium, 1914*, ii, 381.

39 Eliot A. Cohen and John Gooch, *Military misfortunes: the anatomy of failure in war* (New York, 1990), p. 136.

40 Bean, *The story of Anzac*, ii, 62, 75 and 288.

41 Ibid., ii, 289-90.

42   Ibid., ii, 233 and 252.

43   Nicol to Aspinall-Oglander, 21 Jan. 1931 (CAB 45/243).

44   Drury war diary, 8 Jan. 1916 (NAM, Drury papers, 7607-69) i, p. 104.

45   10th Division General Staff War Diary, 14 Aug. 1915 (TNA, WO 95/4294).

46   10th Division CRE War Diary, 28 Aug. 1915 (TNA, WO 95/4294).

47   Ibid; 10th Division General Staff War Diary, 22 Sept. 1915 (TNA, WO 95/4294).

48   10th Division CRE War Diary, 31 Aug. 1915 (TNA, WO 95/4294); Drury war diary, 16 Sept. 1915 (NAM, Drury papers, 7607-69), i, p. 133.

49   Ibid., 1 Feb 1916, ii, p. 109.

50   Ibid., 22 Jan and 12 Feb. 1916 ii, pp 107 & 115.

51   Ibid., 3 Mar. 1916 ii, p. 118.

52   Ibid., 1 Apr. 1916 ii, p. 125; War Diary, 8th Stokes Trench Mortar Battery, 28 Sept. 1916 (TNA, WO 95/4837).

53   War Diary, 8th Stokes Trench Mortar Battery, 28 Sept. 1916 (TNA, WO 95/4837).

54   *Offensive chemical warfare prior to the formation of the Scientific Advisory Committee in 23rd June 1915*, pp 47-48 (TNA, WO 142/240).

55   Martin Gilbert, *Winston S. Churchill, the challenge of war: 1914-1916*, (London, 1990), iii, 889.

56   Hamilton to Kitchener, MF 240, 18 May 1915 (TNA, WO 33/731); De Robeck to Churchill, 19 May 1915 (TNA, ADM 137/154)

57   Admiralty to War Office, 24 May 1915; War Office to Admiralty, May 1915 (TNA, WO 32/5117). At this stage of the war, a respirator was little more than a cotton pad impregnated with a chemical solution and worn over mouth and nose, while a gas helmet was a flannel bag, with a celluloid window to allow vision, which was treated with chemicals, worn over the head and tucked into the wearer's collar.

58   Kitchener to Hamilton, no. 6743, 3 Aug, 1915; Hamilton to Kitchener, 4 Aug. 1915 (TNA, WO 31/731).

59   Reed to 10th Division, GS 111, 4 Aug. 1915 (TNA, WO 95/4294).

60   Juvenis, *Suvla Bay and after*, p. 6.

61   Drury war diary, 29 June 1916 (NAM, Drury papers, 7607-69) ii, p. 157.

62   War Diary A & Q Branch, routine orders 10th (Irish) Division, 12 Mar. 1917 (TNA, WO 95/4289).

63   Ibid., 21 Mar. 1917 (TNA, WO 95/4289).

64   29 Brigade War Diary, 14 Nov. 1917 (TNA, WO 95/4579).

65   War Diary A & Q Branch, routine orders 10th (Irish) Division, 28 Mar. 1917 (TNA, WO 95/4289).

66   *Hansard 5 (Lords)*, xvii, 738.

67   Edmonds, *Military operations: France and Belgium, 1914*, ii, 13.

68   Ibid., ii, 16.

69   Edmonds, *Military operations: France and Belgium, 1914*, ii, 16.

70   Hamilton, *Gallipoli diary*, ii, 9-10.

71   Ibid., ii, 11.

72 Aspinall-Oglander, *Military operations: Gallipoli*, ii, 392.

73 War Diary, 67 Brigade, RFA, 7 Sept. 1916 (TNA, WO 95/4831).

74 Douglas Haig's diary, 22 Feb. 1915 (NLS, Haig papers, MSS.28001).

75 23 Brigade War Diary, Nov. 1914 – May 1915 (TNA, WO 95/708).

76 Prior and Wilson, *Command on the western front*, p. 33.

77 Edmonds, *Military operations: France and Belgium, 1914*, ii, 303.

78 War Diary, 67 Brigade, RFA, 3 Dec. 1915 (TNA, WO 95/4831).

79 Ibid., 23 July 1916 (TNA, WO 95/4831).

80 Harry G. Bishop, 'Elements of modern field artillery, U.S. Service' in Prentice G. Morgan, The forward observer, in *Military Affairs*, 23, 4 (Winter, 1959 -60), p. 211.

81 War Diary, 67 Brigade, RFA, 3 Sept. 1916 (TNA, WO 95/4831).

82 Ibid., 15 Sept. 1916 (TNA, WO 95/4831).

83 Ibid., 30 Sept. 1916 (TNA, WO 95/4831).

84 Ibid., 28 Apr. 1918 (TNA, WO 95/4573).

85 Ibid., 29 Mar. 1917 (TNA, WO 95/4573).

86 Prior and Wilson, *Command on the western front*, p. 81.

87 A.F. Becke, 'The coming of the creeping barrage', in *Journal of the Royal Artillery'*, lviii, p. 23.

88 Brigadier-General John Charteris to Edmonds, 24 Feb. 1927 (TNA, CAB 45/120).

89 War Diary 67 Brigade RFA, 15 Sept. 1916 (TNA, WO 95/4831).

90 Drury war diary, 24 Oct 1917 (NAM, Drury papers, 7607-69) iii, p. 57.

91 SS143, Instructions for the training of platoons for offensive action, Feb. 1917 (IWM, SS/CDS Pamphlet Collection).

92 Anon., 'Infantry tactics 1914-1918' in *RUSI Journal*, 64 (1919), p. 466.

93 29th Brigade War Diary, 23 Oct. 1917 (TNA, WO 95/4578).

94 War Diary 6th Leinster Regiment, Jan. 1918 (TNA, WO95/ 4573).

95 Terraine, *British military leadership in the First World War*, WFA Website, 8 Jul. 2008.

96 Tactical Notes, para 2, 31 July 1915 (CDS 50, IWM SS/CDS Pamphlet Collection).

97 Ibid., para 3.

98 *The Final Report of the Dardanelles Commission* [Cmd 341], H.C. 1919, para. 84.

99 Ibid., para 81.

100 Drury war diary, 16 Aug. 1915 (NAM, Drury papers, 7607-69) ii, p. 104.

101 Verschoyle, (IWM Sound Archive, AC 8185).

102 Drury war diary, 15 Apr 1916 (NAM, Drury papers, 7607-69) ii, p. 127.

103 67 Brigade RFA War Diary, 15 Sept. 1916 (TNA, WO 95/4831).

104 Ibid., iii, p. 79. Drury war diary, 11 Nov 1917 (NAM, Drury papers, 7607-69) iii, p. 79.

105 Drury war diary, 26 Jan 1918 (NAM, Drury papers, 7607-69) iii, p. 129.

106 SS109, *Training of Divisions for Offensive Action*, 8 May 1916 (IWM, SS/CDS Pamphlet Collection).

107 Robbins, *British generalship on the Western Front 1914-18*, pp 90-91.

108 IXth Corps Notes on information collected from various sources including troops who have been engaged in the recent fighting, 31 July 1916 (LHCMA, Montgomery-Massingberd papers 47).

109 Drury war diary, 25 Mar and 1 Apr 1916 (NAM, Drury papers, 7607-69), ii, pp 123 & 125.

110 Ibid., 3 Mar and 22 Mar 1916 (NAM, Drury papers, 7607-69) ii, pp 118 & 122.

111 Ibid., 1 Apr 1916 (NAM, Drury papers, 7607-69) ii, p. 124.

112 Ibid., 1 Apr 1916, 28 Nov 1917 and 30 Jan 1918 (NAM, Drury papers, 7607-69) ii, p 125; iii, pp 91 & 133.

113 Routine orders, Major-General J.R. Longley, Commanding 10th (Irish) Division, 21 Mar. 1917 in war diary of 30 Brigade (TNA, WO 95/4289).

CHAPTER 9 - JUST ANOTHER KITCHENER DIVISION?

1   Cooper, *The Tenth (Irish) Division*, p. 13.

2   See Hugh Trevor-Roper, 'The invention of tradition', pp 25, 30 – 31.

3   Fuller, *Troop morale and popular culture*, pp 163 & 171.

4   Ibid., p. 172.

5   New armies, establishments and strengths (TNA, WO 162/4).

6   Fitzpatrick, 'The logic of collective sacrifice', pp 1017-30.

7   Germains, *The Kitchener armies*, p. 66.

8   See Table 2.5 'The educational background of the officers of the 1st Battalion, Black Watch, in August 1914', p. 54.

9   Hughes 'The forgotten army' (IWM, Hughes papers, D. 4432.).

10 See Travers, *The killing ground*, pp 3-36 for an assessment of the pre-war officer system.

11 Liddell Hart, *The war in outline*, p. xii.

12 Lee, *A soldier's life*, p.269.

13 Ibid., pp 268 – 69.

14 *Warfighting* (USMC, Washington, 1997), pp 90-1.

15 Carl von Clausewitz, http://www.clausewitz.com/readings/Principles/Clausewitz-PrinciplesOfWar-ClausewitzCom.pdf (last accessed 30 July 2014)

16 Dawnay to his wife, 9 Aug. 1915 (IWM, Dawnay papers, 69/21/1).

Annex 1

1   Source: (TNA, NATS 1/398).

2   Ibid.

3   The age of recruits was obtained from census records, enlistment papers (TNA, WO 363 and 364), officers' service records (TNA, WO 339 and 374), obituaries

and the CWGC's Debt of Honour database.

4   Courts martial Records (TNA, WO86/63).

5   Courts martial Records (TNA, WO86/63).

6   Courts martial Records (TNA, WO86/63).

7   10th Division 1 Aug. 1915 to 31 July 1916; 13th Division 1 July 1915 to 30 June 1916.

8   Courts martial Records (TNA, WO213/4-10).

Annex 2

1   The above statistics are based on data contained in Appendix F of the *General annual report on the British army* for each of the years 1903/04 to 1912/13.

2   *Weekly return of the British army at home - September - December 1914* (TNA, WO 114/25).

3   Courts martial Records, (TNA, WO86/63).

4   Courts martial Records (TNA, WO86/63); Bowman, *Irish regiments in the Great War*, p. 87.

5   Courts martial Records (TNA, WO86/63)

6   Courts martial Records (TNA, WO86/63); Bowman, *Irish regiments in the Great War*, p. 88.

7   The 49th Brigade did not arrive in France until February 1916.

8   Courts martial Records (TNA, WO213/4-10).

9   Courts martial Records (TNA, WO213/4-10).

10   Courts martial Records (TNA, WO213/4-10).

11   Courts martial Records (TNA, WO213/11-19).

12   Courts martial Records (TNA, WO213/11-19).

13   Courts martial Records (TNA, WO213/11-19).

14   Courts martial Records (TNA, WO213/11-19).

Sources & Bibliography

Archive Material

Australian War Memorial, Canberra:
Charles E.W. Bean papers AWM38, 3DRL606.
William R. Birdwood papers 3DRL3373.

British Library, London:
Balfour papers Ms 49703
Hunter-Weston papers Add 48355 - 48368
   Oriental and Indian Office Collections
   India Office: Military Department records 1708 – 1959 – Officers'
   service records L/MIL/14.

Contemporary Medical Archives Collection, Wellcome Institute for the History of Medicine, London:
Anon.   *Memorandum on anti-malarial discipline, 1944,* (RAMC 1900/14/5,
     CMAC).
Ernest Clovell *Malaria in the Sicilian campaign 9 July – 10 September 1943* (RAMC
     466/33, CMAC).

Imperial War Museum, London:
Department of Documents
   C.J.L. Allanson papers DS/Misc/69.
   J.A. Armstrong papers P405.
   Reginald Cockburn papers P258.
   John Crozier papers P346.
   Guy Dawnay papers 69/21/1.
   J.E. Dowling papers 02/4/1.
   F.G.J. Ford papers 97/16/1.
   Christopher S. Hughes papers D
   Ivone Kirkpatrick papers 79/50/1.
   John McIlwain papers 96/29/1.
   J.H.M. Staniforth papers 67/41/1.
   Archibald Surfleet papers P.126.
   A.C. Temperley papers 95/16/1.
   Orlo Williams papers 69/78/1.

   SS/CDS Pamphlet Collection
CDS 50, Tactical Notes (July 1915).

SS 109, Training of Divisions for Offensive Action (May 1916)
SS 143, Instructions for the training of platoons for offensive action (Feb. 1917).

Sound Archive
T.T.H. Verschoyle, AC8185.

Liddle Collection, Brotherton Library, University of Leeds:
F.W. Battersby papers Gall (Rec.) 146.
R.C. Broun papers GS 0206
David Campbell papers GS 0261
J.C. Dart papers Gal 025
T.T.H. Verschoyle papers GS1654.

Liddell Hart Centre for Military Archives, King's College, London:
James A. Edmonds papers.
Ian Hamilton papers.
Archibald A. Montgomery-Massingberd papers.

National Army Museum, London:
Noel E. Drury papers 7607-69-1
H.F.N. Jourdain papers 9306-150

National Library of Ireland, Dublin:
Redmond papers MS15261 – MS15262.

National Library of Scotland, Edinburgh:
Douglas Haig papers MSS.28001.

Parliamentary Archives, London:
Lloyd George papers, LG/C.

Public Record Office for Northern Ireland, Belfast:
Lists of commanding officers and unit strengths, D.1327/4/20.
Harland and Wolff managing directors minutes 1907- 1912 D.2805/MIN/A/1
Farren Connell papers D.3835/E/2/5/20A
W.B. Spender, Ms history of the U.V.F. and 36th (Ulster) Division D.1295/2/1A-9
Papers relating to the wartime service of the Earl of Granard and his command of the 5th Royal Irish Regiment T.3765/K/12

Royal Irish Fusiliers Museum, Armagh:
Material from Brigadier-General F.A. Greer relating to the service of the 6th Battalion, Royal Irish Fusiliers in the Great War D.3574/E/6/6

Royal Ulster Rifles Museum, Belfast:
Anon.   'Service with the 14th Battalion, Royal Irish Rifles (Young Citizen Volunteers), 1914-18'.

The National Archives, Kew:

ADM 137/154	Dardanelles Telegrams, IV.
CAB17/124	Committee of Imperial Defence: miscellaneous correspondence and memoranda - Dardanelles
CAB 19/28-31	Dardanelles Commission - statements and documents produced by witnesses before giving evidence.
CAB 45/120	Committee of Imperial Defence, Historical Branch and Cabinet Office, Historical Section: Official War Histories Correspondence and Papers Loos: Authors A-M.
CAB 45/233	Australian and New Zealand Army Corps (ANZAC): composition of corps and reports on campaign, including one by Lt.Gen. W.R. Birdwood, commanding ANZAC
CAB 45/241-45	Official War History Correspondence and Papers (Gallipoli) - Original letters, comments and personal accounts.
HO 184/46	Service Records of R.I.C. Officers
NATS 1/398	Statistical tables showing numbers of recruits accepted for the Army and the Navy.
PRO 30/57/63	Horatio Herbert Kitchener, 1st Earl Kitchener of Khartoum: Papers
PRO 30/67/29	Midleton papers: Home Rule
WO 45/888	War Diaries of the XI Corps
WO 31/731	Office of the Commander in Chief: memoranda and papers
WO 32/7989	Report by Brigadier General B Mahon on the relief of Mafeking by his flying column.
WO 32/11324	Accounts and accounting: General (Code 12(A)): Investigation of War Office claims system by Treasury committee on accounting methods of Government Departments.
WO 33/718	Notes on the employment of machine guns and training machine gunners
WO 71/441	Court-martial record of Private P. J. Downey
WO 79/41	Services of the 5th (Service) Battalion, The Connaught Rangers
WO 79/49	Material collected by Colonel H.F.N. Jourdain for his history of the Connaught Rangers
WO 86/63	Judge Advocate General's office: district courts-martial registers, home and abroad: Home 6 Oct 1914 – 20 Feb 1915.
WO 95	War Diaries:
WO 95/708	4 Corps – General Staff March – April 1915.
WO 95/1342	1st Battalion Irish Guards
WO 95/4264-5	GHQ Mediterranean Expeditionary Force
WO 95/4289	Australian and New Zealand Army Corps: Gallipoli.
WO 95/4294	General Staff 10th Division July - Oct 1915. A&Q 10th Division July - Sept 1915. Commander Royal Engineers July – Sept. 1915.
WO 95/4295	5th Royal Irish Regiment; July - September 1915
WO 95/4296	29 Brigade; August - September 1915 31 Brigade; 10 July - 15 August 1915 5th Royal Inniskilling Fusiliers; August - September 1915 5th Royal Irish Fusiliers; 23 - September 1915 6th Royal Irish Fusiliers; July - September 1915 5th Connaught Rangers; July - September 1915

	7th Royal Dublin Fusiliers: August 1915
	6th Leinster Regiment; August - September 1915
WO 95/4573	10th (Irish) Division – Divisional Troops Egypt, Palestine and Syria.
	LXVII Brigade R.F.A. Egypt, Palestine and Syria.
WO 95/4579	10th (Irish) Division – 29 Brigade, Egypt, Palestine and Syria.
WO 95/4635	54th (East Anglian) Division – General Staff, Oct. 1917 – March 1918.
WO 95/4831	10th (Irish) Division – Divisional Troops Salonika
	10th (Irish) Division – LXVII Brigade R.F.A. Salonika
WO 95/4835	10th (Irish) Division – 29 Brigade Salonika
	10th (Irish) Division – 29th Machine Gun Company Salonika
WO 95/4836	10th (Irish) Division – 30 Brigade Salonika
	10th (Irish) Division – 30th Machine Gun Company Salonika
WO 95/4837	8th Stokes Trench Mortar Battery, Nov. 1916 – Aug. 1917.
WO 105/16	Telegraphs and reports between Lord Roberts and officials in South Africa.
WO 106/707	Correspondence and papers – Dardanelles.
WO 114/25	Battalion strength returns - September - December 1914
WO 114/26	Battalion strength returns - January - December 1915
WO 138/37	Service record of General Sir Bryan Mahon
WO 138/40	Lieut-General Sir F.W. Stopford.
WO 138/63	General Sir Bryan T. Mahon KCVO, KCB, DSO
WO 142/240	Ministry of Munitions, Trench Warfare and Chemical Warfare Departments, and War Office, Chemical Warfare Research Department and Chemical Defence Experimental Stations (later Establishments), Porton: Reports and Papers.
WO 161/22	New Armies 1914-1915: arms and ammunition
WO 162/03	New Armies: organisation 1914-15
WO 162/04	New Armies: establishment and recruitment 1914-15
WO 162/18	Mobilisation and recruiting: miscellaneous papers
WO 162/20	Adjutant General's papers relating to recruitment for K2
WO 162/24	New Armies: recruiting officers and other ranks; statistical returns 1914-15
WO 162/40	Mobilisation: miscellaneous correspondence
WO 163/21	Army Council minutes: 11 Aug. 1914 – 27 Dec. 1916.
WO 163/44	Meetings of Military Members of the Army Council 3 Aug – 16 Oct. 1914.
WO 213/4-19	Field general courts martial 4 -19: May 1915 – 4 March 1918.
WO 279/495	Report of a conference of staff officers at the Royal Military College under the direction of the Chief of the Imperial General Staff 1914.
WO 329/2667	1914-15 Stars - Royal Irish Regiment (Other Ranks) Vol. 1.
WO 329/2668	1914-15 Stars - Royal Irish Regiment (Other Ranks) Vol. 2.
WO 329/2811	1914-15 Stars - Connaught Rangers (Other Ranks)
WO 329/2815	1914-15 Stars - Leinster Regiment (Other Ranks)
WO 329/2818	1914-15 Stars - Royal Dublin Fusiliers (Other Ranks) Vol. 1.
WO 329/2819	1914-15 Stars - Royal Dublin Fusiliers (Other Ranks) Vol. 2.
WO 329/2948	1914-15 Stars - Lincoln Regiment to Cheshire Regiment (Officers).

WO 329/2949	1914-15 Stars - Leinster Regiment (Officers).
WO 329/2952	1914-15 Stars - Seaforth to Cambridgeshire Regiment (Officers).
WO 329/2956	1914-15 Stars - Colonials & Misc.
WO 339	Officers' service records
WO 363	Service records - other ranks.
WO 364	
WO 374	Officers' service records, First World War (alphabetical).
WO 394/20	Summary of statistics 1914 – 1920.

Official Publications

Aspinall
-Oglander, C.F.,   *The history of the Great War: military operations Gallipoli* (London, ii, 1932).

Bean, C.E.W.,   *The official history of Australia in the war of 1914 – 1918 the story of Anzac: from 4 May 1915 to the evacuation* (Sydney, ii, 1924).

Edmonds, James, *The history of the Great War: military operations, France and Belgium, 1914,* (London, i, 1922).

The history of the Great War: military operations, France and Belgium, 1915, (London, ii, 1928).

Falls, Cyril   *The history of the Great War: military operations Egypt & Palestine: From June 1917 to the end of the war* (London, ii, part 1, 1930).

The history of the Great War: military operations Macedonia (London, i, 1933).

Gullett,
Henry S.,   *Official history of Australia in the war of 1914-1918* (Sydney, vii, 1941).

House of
Commons   *Annual report of the Inspector-General of recruiting for the British army and the annual report on recruiting for the year ending 30 September 1904,* [Cd 2265], H.C. 1905.

Annual report of the Inspector-General of recruiting for the British army and the annual report on recruiting for the year ending 30 September 1905, [Cd 2693], H.C. 1906.

Correspondence relating to recent events in the Irish command, [Cd. 7318] H.C. 1914

General annual report on the British army for the year ending 30 September 1906, [Cd 3365], H.C. 1907.

General annual report on the British army for the year ending 30 September 1907, [Cd 3798], H.C. 1908.

General annual report on the British army for the year ending 30 September 1908, [Cd 4493], H.C. 1909.

General annual report on the British army for the year ending 30 September 1909, [Cd 5016], H.C. 1910.

General annual report on the British army for the year ending 30 September 1910, [Cd 5481], H.C. 1911.

General annual report on the British army for the year ending 30 September 1911 with the annual report of recruiting, prepared by command of the Army council for 1911, [Cd 6065], H.C. 1912-13.

General annual report on the British army for the year ending 30 September 1912, with the annual report of recruiting, prepared by command of the Army council for 1911-12,[Cd 6656], H.C. 1912-13.
General annual report on the British army for the year ending 30 September 1913, with the annual report of recruiting, prepared by command of the Army council for 1912-13, [Cd 7252], H.C. 1914
Report of the War Office (reconstitution) committee, [Cd 1943], H.L. 1904.
Report of the departmental committee appointed … to inquire into the housing conditions of the working classes in the city of Dublin, [Cd. 7273] H.C. 1914.
Royal commission on the poor laws and the relief of distress, appendix vol. xi, [Cd. 5072] H.C. 1910.
Seventeenth abstract of labour statistics for the United Kingdom, [Cd. 7733] H.C. 1914.
Standard time rates of wages in the United Kingdom at 1st October 1910, [Cd. 5459] H.C. 1910.
The annual return of the Territorial Force for the year 1913, [Cd. 7254], H.C. 1914.
The final report of the Dardanelles commission [Cmd 341], H.C. 1919.

War Office — Field Service Regulations 1909 (London, 1909).
Infantry Training Manual 1902 (London, 1902).
Infantry Training Manual 1909 (London, 1909).
Infantry Training 1914, (London, 1914).
Manual of Military Law1914 (London, 1914).
Officers Died in the Great War, (London 1919).
Soldiers Died in the Great War (London, 1919).
Statistics of the military effort of the British Empire during the Great War 1914-1920 (London, 1922).
Training and Manoeuvre Regulations 1909 (London, 1909).

Web and Electronic Based Primary Source Collections

Census records (England and Wales) 1911 (Household returns) http://www.1911census.co.uk/
Census records (Ireland) 1901/1911 (Household returns) – National Archives, Ireland:
http://www.census.nationalarchives.ie/
Commonwealth Wargraves Commission - Debt of Honour: (http://www.cwgc.org/debt_of_honour.asp
Dictionary of Irish biography (DIB) – Royal Irish Academy and Cambridge University Press: http://dib.cambridge.org/
Hansard, 1803-2005 – Millbank Systems: http://hansard.millbanksystems.com/
Oxford dictionary of national biography – Oxford University Press: http://www.oxforddnb.org/
Mapping our ANZACs – National Archives, Australia. http://mappingouranzacs.naa.gov.au/
Soldiers Died in the Great War (CD-ROM, London: Naval & Military Press, 1999)

Newspapers & periodicals

An Phoblacht/Republican News
Ballymena Observer
Belfast Evening Telegraph
Belfast Newsletter
Freeman's Journal
Irish Independent
Irish Times
London Gazette
The Times
Wiltshire Gazette

Other Publications and Articles

Anon.	*A short record of the services and experiences of the Fifth Battalion Royal Irish Fusiliers in the Great War* (Dublin, 1919).
	'First to land in Salonika' in *The Mosquito*, Dec. 1934 p. 81.
	Grand lodge of free and accepted masons of Ireland roll of honour – the Great War 1914-1919 (Dublin, n.d.).
	'Infantry tactics 1914-1918' in *RUSI Journal*, 64 (1919) pp 460 - 469.
	Roll of employees who served in His Majesty's naval, military, and air forces, 1914-1918 – Arthur Guinness, Son & Co Ltd (Dublin, 1920).
Alport, A. Cecil,	*Malaria and its treatment: in the line and at the base* (London, 1919).
Armstrong, D.L.,	'Social and economic conditions in the Belfast linen industry, 1850-1900' in *Irish Historical Studies*, vii, 28 (Sept. 1951) p. 225-234.
Badsey, Stephen,	The Boer War (1899-1902) and British cavalry doctrine: a re-evaluation in *The Journal of Military History*, no. 71, Jan. 2007, pp 75-97.
Baynes, John,	*Morale: A study of men and courage* (London, 1982).
Becke, A.F.,	'The coming of the creeping barrage', in *Journal of the Royal Artillery'*, lviii, 1931, pp 19 – 42.
Beckett, Ian F.W.,	*The Great War* (2nd ed., London, 2007*).*
	'The nation in arms' in Beckett and Simpson (eds), *A nation in arms*, pp 1-35.
Beckett, Ian F.W. and Simpson, Keith, (eds)	*A nation in arms: a social study of the British army in the First World War* (London, 1985).

Bidwell, Shelford,   *Gunners at War*

Bidwell, Shelford,

and Graham, Dominick,   *Fire-power: British army weapons and theories of war, 1904-45* (paperback ed., London, 2004).

Bielenberg, Andrew,   'What happened to Irish industry after the British industrial revolution? Some evidence from the first UK census of production in 1907' in *The Economic History Review*, New Series, Vol. 61, 4 (Nov. 2008), pp 820-841.

Bishop, Harry G.,   Elements of modern field artillery, U.S. Service (Menasha, Wisc., 1914).

Bond, Brian, (ed.)   *The First World War and British history* (Oxford, 1991).

Bourne, John M.,   *Britain and the Great War 1914 -1918* (London, 1989).

Bowman, Timothy,   *Irish regiments in the Great War: discipline and morale* (Manchester, 2003).

Brown, Michael,   *Tommy goes to war* (London, 1978).

Budworth, C.E.D.   Artillery in Co-operation with Infantry, in *Journal of the Royal Artillery*, 37:1 (1910) pp 1-14.

Callan, Patrick,   'Recruiting for the British Army in Ireland during the First World War' in *Irish Sword*, 66, (1987-8) pp 42-56.

Carlyon, L.A.   *Gallipoli* (Bantam ed., London, 2003).

Cassar, George H.,   *Asquith as war leader* (London, 1994).

Chart D. A.,   Chart D. A., 'Unskilled labour in Dublin – its housing and living conditions' in *Journal of the Statistical and Social Inquiry Society of Ireland*, xiii, part 94 (Mar. 1914) pp 160-175.

Childers, Erskine,   *War and the Arme Blanche* (London, 1910).

Clifford, Ronald,   'What is a Battalion?' in *Stand To!* no. 30 (Winter 1990) pp. 17 – 19; 22.

Cohen, Eliot A.

and Gooch, John,   *Military misfortunes: the anatomy of failure in war* (New York, 1990).

Colvin, Ian,   *The life of Lord Carson* (London, iii, 1936).

Cooper, Bryan,   *The Tenth Irish Division in Gallipoli* (London, 1918).

Corrigan, Gordon,   *Sepoys in the trenches: the Indian corps on the Western Front* (Staplehurst, 1999).

Cousins, Colin,   *Armagh and the Great War* (Dublin, 2001).

Cowlands, W.S. (ed.),   *Some Account of the 10th and 12th Battalions the Hampshire Regiment* (Winchester, 1930).

Coyle, Eugene A.,   'Larkinism and the 1913 County Dublin Farm Labourer's Dispute' in *Dublin Historical Record*, Vol. 58, No. 2 (Autumn, 2005), pp 176-190.

Craft, Maurice,   'The development of Dublin: background to the housing problem' in *Studies: An Irish Quarterly Review*, Vol. 59, No. 235 (Autumn, 1970), pp 301-313.

Creagh,
Gerald O'Moore,
The army in India', in the *Army Review*, 4 (Jan. 1913).

Crozier, F.P.,
A brass hat in no man's land (Reprint ed., Norfolk, 1989).

Curtayne, Alice,
Francis Ledwidge: a life of the poet 1887-1917 (London, 1972).

D.J.H.,
The Reminiscences of Capt. D.J. Bell of Ballynahinch (Newcastle, 1962).

de Bloch, Jean.,
Is war now impossible? (London, 1899).

de Ruvigny,
The Marquis,
The roll of honour: a biographical record of all members of His Majesty's naval and military forces who have fallen in the war (London, 1916).

Denman, Terence
A lonely grave: the life and death of William Redmond (Blackrock, 1995).

Ireland's unknown soldiers, the 16th (Irish) Division in the Great war, 1914-1918 (Dublin, 1992).

'The Catholic Irish soldier in the Great War: the racial environment' in *Irish Historical Studies*, xxvii, no. 108 (1991) pp 352-65.

'The 10th (Irish) Division 1914-15:.a study in military and political interaction' in *Irish Sword*, 67, (1987-8), pp 16-25.

Drage, Charles,
Chindwin to Criccieth - The life of Godfrey Drage (Caernarvon, 1956).

Dungan, Myles,
Irish voices from the Great War (Blackrock, 1995).

They shall grow not old - Irish soldiers and the Great War (Blackrock, 1997).

Ellis, P. B.,
Eyewitness to Irish history (Hoboken, New Jersey, 2004).

Englander, David,
'Discipline and morale in the British army 1917-1918' in John Horne (ed.), *State, society and mobilisation in Europe during the First World War*, pp 125-43.

Englander, David,
& Osborne, James,
'Jack, Tommy and Henry Dubb: the armed forces and the working class', in *Historical Journal*, xxi, 3 (Sept. 1978) pp 593-62.

Ewing, John,
The history of the 9th (Scottish) Division 1914-1919 (London, 1921).

Falls, Cyril,
The history of the 36th Ulster Division (Belfast, 1922).

The history of the first seven battalions, the Royal Irish Rifles, now the Royal Ulster Rifles, in the Great War (Aldershot, 1925).

Farrar-Hockley,
Anthony,
Sir Ian Hamilton, The Commander (London, 1957).

Fitzpatrick, David,
'Home Front and everyday life' in John Horne (ed) *Our war - Ireland and the Great War* (Dublin, 2008).

'The logic of collective sacrifice: Ireland and the British army' in *Historical Journal*, 8, 4 (1995), pp 1017-30.

Revolution? Ireland 1917-1923 (Dublin, 1990).

Fox, Frank,   *The Royal Inniskilling Fusiliers in the World War* (London, 1928).

French, John,   *1914* (London, 1919).

Frewster, K., (ed.)   *Gallipoli Correspondent: the frontline diary of CEW Bean* (Sydney, 1983).

Fuller, J.C.,   *Troop morale and popular culture in the British and Dominion armies 1914-1918* (Oxford, 1990).

Geoghegan, S.,   *Campaigns and History of the Royal Irish Regiment* (Edinburgh, i, 1927).

Germains, W.V.,   *The Kitchener armies*, (London, 1930).

Gilbert, Martin,   *Winston S. Churchill, the challenge of war:, 1914-1916,* (London, 1990) ii

Grayson, Richard S.   *Belfast boys – how unionists and nationalists fought and died together on the First World War* (London, 2009).

Gregory, Adrian and Pašeta, Senia, (eds)   *Ireland in the Great War – 'a war to unite us all'?* (Manchester, 2002).

Gribbon, H. B.,   'Economic and social history' in *A new history of Ireland*, pp 260-356.

Griffith, Paddy,   *Battle tactics of the Western Front: the British army's art of attack* (New Haven, CT, 1994).

Gwynn, Denis,   *The life of John Redmond* (London, 1932).

Hamilton, I.S.M.,   *Compulsory service: a study of the question in the light of experience* (1911).

Gallipoli diary (2 vols, London, 1920-22).

Hammerton, J.A.,   *A popular history of the Great War* (London, i, n.d.).

Hanhan, H.J.,   'Religion and nationality in the mid-Victorian army' in M.R.D. Foot, (ed.), *War and Society* (London, 1973).

Hanna, Henry,   *The pals at Suvla: D company, the 7th Royal Dublin Fusiliers* (Dublin, 1916).

Hargrave, John,   *At Suvla Bay* (London, 1916).

The Suvla Bay landing (London, 1964).

Haywood, A. and Clarke, F.A.S.,   *The history of the Royal West African Frontier Force* (Aldershot, 1964).

Hennessy, T.F.,   *The Great War 1914 - 1918 Bank of Ireland staff record* (Dublin, 1920).

Hobsbawn, Eric, & Ranger, Terence, (eds)   *The invention of tradition* (Cambridge, 1983).

Holmes, Richard,   *The little field marshal – the life of Sir John French* (2nd ed., London, 2004).

Horne, John, (ed.)   *Our war - Ireland and the Great War* (Dublin, 2008).

State, society and mobilisation in Europe during the First World War (Cambridge, 1998).

Hughes, C.,   'The new armies', in Beckett and Simpson (eds), *A nation in arms*, pp 99-125.

Humphreys, A.J.,   *New Dubliners: Urbanisation and the Irish Family* (London, 1996).

Hussey, John,   'The deaths of qualified staff officers in the Great War', in *Journal of the Society for Army Historical Research*, lxxv, (1997) pp 246-59.

Jalland, Patricia,   'Irish home-rule finance: a neglected dimension of the Irish question, 1910-14' in *Irish Historical Studies*, Vol. 23, No. 91 (May, 1983), pp 233-253.

James, Robert Rhodes,   *Gallipoli* (Pimlico ed., London, 1999).

Jeffery, Keith,   'Ireland and Gallipoli', in Jenny Macleod (ed.), *Gallipoli: making history* (London, 2004) pp 98-109.

Ireland and the Great War (Cambridge, 2000).

Johnstone, Tom,   *Orange, green and khaki* (Dublin, 1992).

Jourdain, H.F.N.,   *History of the Connaught Rangers* (London, iii, 1928).

Ranging Memories (Oxford, 1934).

Record of the 5th (S) Battalion the Connaught Rangers (Oxford, 1916).

Keegan, John,   *The Mask of Command* (London, 1987).

Kipling, Rudyard,   *New army training* (London, 1915).

The Irish Guards in the Great War – the first battalion (Spellmount ed., Staplehurst, 1997).

Knight, Jill,   *The Civil Service Rifles in the Great War* (Barnsley, 2004).

Juvenis   *At Suvla Bay and after* (London, 1916).

Lavery, Felix., (ed.)   *Great Irishmen in war and politics* (London, 1928).

Lee, John,   *A soldier's life: General Sir Ian Hamilton 1853-1947* (paperback ed., London, 2000).

Leonard, Jane,   'Getting them at last: the IRA and ex-servicemen' in David Fitzpatrick, *Revolution? Ireland 1917-1923*, pp 118-29.

Liddell Hart, Basil H.,   *A history of the world war 1914-1918* (London, 1934)

The war in outline 1914-1918 (London, 1936).

Lucas, William,   *Life and letters of Norman Carey Lucas* (Melbourne, 1920).

MacDonagh, Michael,   *The Irish at the front* (London, 1916).

Macleod, Jenny, (ed.)   *Gallipoli: making history* (London, 2004).

Macleod, Jenny,	*Reconsidering Gallipoli* (Manchester, 2004).
Macpherson, William Grant,	*History of the Great War: medical services* (London, ii, 1922).
Martin, David, (ed.)	*The Fifth Scottish Rifles 1914 – 1919*, (Glasgow, 1936).
McCance, S.,	*The history of the Royal Munster Fusiliers* (Aldershot, ii, 1927).
McCarthy, John Paul, and O'Riordan, Tomás,	'Dublin 1913 – strike and lockout' in Ó Corráin and O'Riordan (eds), *Ireland 1870 – 1918*, pp 168-190.
McManus, Ruth,	'Blue collars, "red forts," and green fields: working-class housing in Ireland in the twentieth century' in *International labor and working-class history*, No. 64, Workers, suburbs, and labor geography (Fall, 2003) pp 38-54.
McQuilton, John,	*Rural Australia and the Great War: From Tarrawingee to Tangambalanga* (Melbourne, 2002).
Mitchell, B. R.,	*British historical statistics* (Cambridge, 1988).
Mitchell, T.J. & Smith, G.M.,	*Medical services: casualties and medical statistics of the Great War* (London, 1933).
Mitchinson, K.W.,	*Officers and gentlemen* (London, 1995).
Montmorency, Hervey, de	*Sword and Stirrup - memories of an adventurous life* (London, 1936).
Moorehead, Alan,	*Gallipoli* (London, 1956).
Moran, Charles M.W.	*The anatomy of courage* (1966).
Morgan, Prentice G.,	The forward observer, in *Military Affairs*, 23, 4 (Winter, 1959 -60), pp 209-212.
Moss, Michael and Hume, J. R.,	*Shipbuilders to the world: 125 years of Harland and Wolff, Belfast 1861-1986* (Belfast, 1986).
O'Brien, Joseph V.,	*'Dear Dirty Dublin' a city in distress, 1899-1916* (Berkeley, 1982).
Ó Corráin, Donnchadh, and O'Riordan, Tomás (eds),	*Ireland 1870 – 1918 Coercion and Conciliation* (Dublin, 2011).
Oldham, C. H.,	'The history of Belfast shipbuilding' in *Journal of the Statistical and Social Inquiry Society of Ireland*, xii, part 91 (Dec. 1911), pp 417-434.
Oldham, C.H.,	'The public finances of Ireland' in *Journal of the Institute of Bankers of Ireland*, xiii (1911).

Oman, Charles   *Wellington's Army 1809-1814* (London, 1913).

Oram, Gerald   *Worthless men: eugenics and the death penalty in the British army during the First World War* (London, 1998).

Orr, Philip,   *Field of bones: an Irish Division at Gallipoli* (Dublin, 2006).

'The road to Belgrade: the experiences of the 10th (Irish) Division in the Balkans 1915 – 1917' in Gregory & Pašeta (eds) in *Ireland and the Great War – 'A war to unite us all'*.

The Road to the Somme: men of the Ulster Division tell their story (Belfast, 1987).

Pedersen, P.A.,   *Monash as military commander* (Melbourne, 1985).

Perry, Nicholas,   'Maintaining regimental identity in the Great War' in *Stand To!* no. 52 (Apr. 1998), pp. 5-11.

'Nationality in the Irish infantry regiments in the First World War' in *War and Society*, xii, no. 1 (1994) pp 65-95.

Prior, Robin,   *Gallipoli, the end of the myth* (New Haven, 2009).

'The Suvla Bay tea-party, a reassessment' in *Journal of the Australian War Memorial*, no. 7 (1985) pp 25-34.

Prior, Robin and Wilson   *Command on the Western Front: the military career of Sir Henry Rawlinson* (paperback ed., Barnsley, 2004).

Rattray, Melville J.,   *Three years in the Balkans - further recollections of 107th Field Coy, R.E.* (Darlington, 1920)

Riordan, Edward J.,   *Modern Irish trade and industry* (London, 1920).

Robbins, Simon,   *British generalship on the Western Front 1914-18 defeat into victory* (London, 2005).

Roskill, Stephen,   *Hankey: man of secrets* (London, 1970), i.

Samuels, Martin,   *Command or control? Command, training and tactics in the British and German armies, 1888-1918* (London, 1995).

Scott, Sir Arthur B.,
and Brumwell,
P. Middleton,   *The history of the 12th (Eastern) Division in the Great War 1914-1918* (London, 1923).

Shaw, C.,   'The largest manufacturing employers of 1907' in *Business History*, 25, 1 (1983) pp 42-60.

Sheffield, Gary,   *Leadership in the trenches: officer-man relations, morale and discipline in the British army in the era of the First World War* (London, 2000).

Simkins, Peter,   *Kitchener's army: the raising of the New Armies, 1914-16* (Manchester, 1988).

'Soldiers and civilians: billeting in Britain and France' in Beckett and Simkins (eds), *A nation in arms*.

Simpson, Keith,   'The officers' in Beckett and Simpson (eds), *A nation in arms*, pp 63-97.

Spiers, Edward M.,   'The regular army in 1914' in Beckett and Simpson (eds), *A nation in arms*, pp 37-61.

Stanley, Jeremy,	*Ireland's forgotten 10th* (Ballycastle, 2003).
Steel, Nigel,	*Gallipoli* (Barnsley, 1999).
Steel, Nigel, and Hart, Peter,	*Defeat at Gallipoli* (London, 1994).
Stewart, A.T.Q.,	*The Ulster Crisis* (London 1967).
Strachan, Hew,	'The real war: Liddell Hart, Crutwell, and Falls' in Brian Bond (ed.) *The First World War and British history* pp 41-67..
Swift, Roger,	'Crime and the Irish in Nineteenth Century Britain', in Roger Swift and Sheridan Gilley (eds), *The Irish in Britain 1815-1916.*
Terraine, John,	*Mons: the retreat to victory* (paperback ed., Barnsley, 1991).
Thompson, William J.,	'The Census of Ireland, 1911' in *Journal of the Royal Statistical Society*, Vol. 76, No. 7 (June 1913), pp 635-671.
Travers, Tim,	'British army command and leadership styles in the British army: the 1915 Gallipoli model' in *Journal of Canadian History*, no. 29 (1994) pp 403-42.
	Gallipoli 1915 (Stroud, 2004).
	'Technology, tactics and morale: Jean de Bloch, the Boer War, and British military theory, 1900-1914' in *Journal of Modern History*, ci, no. 2 (June 1979) pp 264-86.
	The killing ground – the British army, the Western Front and the emergence of modern warfare 1900-1918 (Barnsley, 2003).
	'The offensive and the problem of innovation in British military thought 1870-1915' in the *Journal of Contemporary History*, xiii, no. 3 (1979) pp. 531-553.
Tredgold, C.H.,	'The prophylactic use of quinine in malaria: with special reference to experiences in Macedonia' in the *British Medical Journal*, i (1918), pp 525-9.
Trevor-Roper, Hugh,	'The invention of tradition: the highland tradition of Scotland' in Hobsbawn and Ranger (eds), *The invention of tradition* pp 25, 30 – 31.
Tucker, John F.,	*Johnny get your gun: a personal narrative of Somme, Ypres and Arras* (London, 1978).
Turner, W.,	'The record book of Mr Thomas Glover', in *Stand to!* Summer 1989, 26, pp 6-8.
Vaughan W.E., (ed.)	*A new history of Ireland – Ireland under the union, II 1870-1921* (Oxford, 1996).
Vaughan W.E. & Fitzpatrick A.J. (eds.)	*Irish historical statistics – population 1821 – 1971* (Dublin, 1978).
Wakefield, Alan, and Moody, Simon,	*Under the devil's eye - Britain's forgotten army in Salonika*

	1915–1918 (Stroud, 2004).
Walker, R.W.,	*To what end did they die? Officers died at Gallipoli* (Worcester, 1985).
Walker, Stephen,	*Forgotten Soldiers – the Irishmen shot at dawn* (Dublin, 2007).
Wauchope (ed.), A.G.	*A history of the Black Watch in the Great War* (London, i, 1925).
Wavell, Archibald P.,	*Generals and generalship* (New York, 1942).
	The Palestine campaigns (1941).
Whitaker, Joseph,	*Whitaker's almanack* (London, 1912).
Whitton, F.E.,	*The history of the Prince of Wales's Leinster Regiment* (Aldershot, ii, 1926).
Williams, Jeffery,	*Byng of Vimy: General and Governor General* (London, 1983).
Willoughby,	
G.M. & Cassidy, Louis,	*Anti-malaria work in Macedonia among British troops* (London, 1918).

Unpublished Theses

Callan, Patrick, 'Voluntary recruiting for the British army in Ireland during the First World War' (Ph.D. thesis, University College Dublin, 1984).

Grew, J. A., 'The Derry shirt making industry 1831-1913' (M.Phil. thesis, University of Ulster, 1987).

Otley, C.F. 'Origins and recruitment of the British Army elite' (Ph.D. thesis, University of Hull, 1965).

Staunton, Martin, 'The Royal Munster Fusiliers in the Great War, 1914-1919 (M.A. thesis, University College Dublin, 1986).

INDEX